H. L. MENCKEN

Critic of American Life

HENRY L. MENCKEN about 1927.
Courtesy Culver Pictures.

H. L. MENCKEN

Critic
of American Life

by

GEORGE H. DOUGLAS

ARCHON BOOKS • HAMDEN • CONNECTICUT • 1978

©George H. Douglas 1978
First published 1978 as an Archon Book,
an imprint of The Shoe String Press, Inc.
Hamden, Connecticut 06514
Printed in the United States of America

Library of Congress Cataloging in Publication Data

Douglas, George H., 1934-
    H. L. Mencken, critic of American life.

        Bibliography: p.
        Includes index.
        1. Mencken, Henry Louis, 1880-1956—Criticism
and interpretation.   2. United States—Civilization—
20th century.   I. Title.
PS3525.E43Z552   818'.5'209   78-854
ISBN 0-208-01693-7

To my father, H. M. Douglas

Contents

Acknowledgments

I owe a considerable debt of gratitude to a number of persons who were helpful to me at one time or another while I was writing this book. I would like to thank especially Professor Carl Bode of the University of Maryland, surely the foremost living Mencken scholar, for his generosity in discussing Mencken with me on a number of occasions.

I am grateful to the late Betty Adler of the Enoch Pratt Free Library of Baltimore, former editor of *Menckeniana* and curator of the library's Mencken collection, for her help at an earlier stage of this study. I would also like to thank Mr. Richard Hart, former Chairman of the Department of Humanities at the Enoch Pratt Free Library, and Miss Kathryn Dean of the same department for courtesies extended to me on visits to their library.

In addition to my indebtedness to staff members of the Enoch Pratt Free Library who are always more than generous when it comes to anything having to do with Mencken, I would like to thank staff members who have been helpful to me at the following libraries, and who have assisted me in obtaining books, letters, or other items related to Mencken: New York Public Library, Princeton University Library, the University of Pennsylvania Library, the Newberry Library of Chicago, and the University of Illinois Library.

9

I am grateful to Mr. Paul Poirot, editor of *The Freeman,* and Mr. Maclean Patterson, editor of *Menckeniana,* for allowing me to reprint material of mine that appeared earlier in a somewhat different form in their respective publications. Two colleagues of mine at the University of Illinois, Professor Arnold M. Tibbetts and Professor Robert W. Mayer, have shared my interest in Mencken and have read parts or all of the manuscript, always to my benefit. I am especially grateful to my editor, James Thorpe III, whose critical comments resulted in numerous changes in the text of this book and, I feel, considerable improvement in its substance. I would like to thank Mrs. Mary Kay Peer and Mrs. Louise Steele of the Department of English at the University of Illinois who typed the manuscript.

G.H.D.

Chronology

1880	Henry Louis Mencken born September 12 in Baltimore, Maryland, son of August and Anna Abhau Mencken.
1896	Graduated from Baltimore Polytechnic School with the highest average received up to that time.
1899	Started newspaper career as a general duty reporter for the *Baltimore Morning Herald*.
1901	Sunday Editor of the *Herald*.
1905	First book, *George Bernard Shaw*, published by Luce in Boston.
1906	Began his long-time association with the *Sunpapers* of Baltimore.
1908	The *Philosophy of Friedrich Nietzsche* published.
1908	Began writing literary criticism for *The Smart Set*.
1914	Became co-editor, with George Jean Nathan, of *The Smart Set*.
1918	Published *In Defense of Women*.
1919	*Prejudices First Series* appears. First book of Mencken's to be published by Alfred A. Knopf.
1919	First edition of *The American Language*.
1924	Inauguration in January of *The American Mercury*, with Mencken and Nathan as editors. Both men leave *The Smart Set*.

11

1925	Mencken becomes sole editor of *The American Mercury;* Nathan steps down to contributor.
1926	Hatrack affair in which Mencken is arrested in Boston for peddling smut in *The Mercury.* The case was later thrown out of court.
1926	*Notes on Democracy* published.
1927	The sixth and last series of *Prejudices* published.
1930	Marries Sara Powell Haardt in Baltimore on August 27.
1932	*Making a President,* 1932.
1933	Steps down as editor of *The American Mercury.*
1934	Started contributing to *The New Yorker,* some later contributions resulting in *The Days Books* of the next decade.
1935	Sara Haardt Mencken dies, May 30.
1936	The first major revision of *The American Language.*
1938	Again working full-time for the *Sunpapers.* Editor of *The Evening Sun* for three months.
1940	*Happy Days, 1880-1892,* first book of Mencken's reminiscences.
1941	*Newspaper Days, 1899-1906.*
1943	*Heathen Days, 1890-1936,* last of Mencken's reminiscences.
1948	After covering the last of many national political conventions, Mencken suffers stroke, severely limiting his further literary activities.
1956	Mencken dies at his home at 1524 Hollins Street, Baltimore, January 29 (age 75). *Minority Report* published posthumously.

Introduction

In spite of the ups and downs of his literary reputation, there is still a good deal of interest in the life and writings of Henry L. Mencken. Critics first pronounced Mencken dead in the 1930s, but he seems to have a way of coming back from his assigned places of rest. Indeed the number of articles and books written about him in the fifties and sixties exceed both in quality and quantity those written when he was at the height of his popularity. There is something solid and enduring about Mencken, a liveliness and force that are lacking in many of the popular writers of the twenties—Sinclair Lewis, for example.

Even the academic world, which once spurned Mencken for the shallowness of his thinking, has contributed to a kind of Mencken revival. The past decade has seen the appearance of Carl Bode's readable and well-researched biography (*Mencken*) in 1969, a massive scholarly study in French by G. J. Forgue (*H. L. Mencken, L'Homme, L' Oeuvre, L'Influence*) in 1967, and a solid biographical/critical study by Douglas C. Stenerson (*H. L. Mencken: Iconoclast From Baltimore*) in 1971, which makes a systematic attempt to trace the origins and morphology of Mencken's thought and intellectual style. Of course the old academic stereotypes are there for those who want them, but the renewed interest in the scholarly study of

Mencken, and the growing richness of the literature about him, suggest that Mencken will continue to be a living force in the years to come.

I assume in undertaking this book that Mencken's criticism of American life is still valuable; that beside the sparkling wit and polished literary style which keep him fresh and eminently readable, his achievement as a critic of the American scene is not solely of antiquarian or anecdotal interest. Mencken's ideas, then, are what this book is about. My project is to examine these ideas, to investigate in some detail the major ingredients in Mencken's thought, not so much from a biographical or developmental standpoint—since this has already been done well in the studies mentioned above—but from a determinedly critical standpoint. In short, I shall be trying to present Mencken's ideas about American life in a coherent framework.

Many may think that no side of Mencken is less susceptible to revival than his intellectual side. A satirist, a humorist, a writer, yes. A thinker, no. His ideas, some have said, haven't stood the test of time.

In one sense, of course, Mencken was not a thinker. He was certainly not a philosopher, especially if the role of philosopher is identified with sustained linear argument or with a complicated architectonic of thought. Mencken, of course, never applied the word philosopher to himself, and preferred to think of himself as a critic of ideas. It might be still better to think of him as a dramatist of ideas, since it is not the systematic quality of his ideas that is important but their ingenious and highly stylized development. Nevertheless, his huge gifts of historical imagination could not have been possible without a strong intellectual framework to contain this imagination, to give it shape. While Mencken never used ideas in the manner of the philosopher, never wanted to be tied down to the hardness of intellectual formality and exactitude, his ideas are of no small importance as artistic vision.

This last point was made quite well in 1926 by Edmund Wilson, in a review of Mencken's *Notes on Democracy*. Remarking upon Mencken's inability to conduct a thoroughgoing, rational inquiry, upon the fewness and frequent

rigidity of his ideas, Wilson nevertheless came to the conclusion that *Notes on Democracy* was a remarkable achievement
when considered in its own uniqueness and artistic sin-
gularity:

> It is Mencken's same old melodrama, with the gentleman,
> the man of honor, pitted against the peasant and the boob.
> We are not told what makes people gentlemen or what
> makes them boobs, or how it is that both these species
> happen to the same human race, or how it is that we often
> find them merging or becoming transformed into one
> another. With his fierce inflexibility of mind, Mr. Men-
> cken is capable neither of the sympathy of the historian,
> of the detachment of the scientist, nor of the subtlety of
> the philosopher. And his new book is not to be taken as a
> contribution to political science: it is simply another of
> his "Prejudices" treated on a larger scale than the rest. Yet
> although these *Notes on Democracy* are not precisely
> politics, they are quite remarkable as literature. Poe said
> of his treatise *Eureka* that it was to be taken as neither
> science nor philosophy, but what he called a "prose
> poem," which was, nevertheless, in its own way, true.
> The same thing may be said of Mencken's *Notes*.[1]

Not exactly the whole truth, then, are these *Notes* of Mencken's—not science, not philosophy—but they have about
them a truth of their own. As the philosopher must always be
reminded, the artist has his own realm of truth. The most
arresting thing about the truths of the writer is that they
cannot be put down, they cannot be laid aside or ignored.
Conceptualizations, the truths that belong to the specialized
departments of learning, can be conveniently ignored by all
who choose to ignore them, but one cannot ignore the artist,
the dramatist of ideas, who, by means of his craft, isolates and
intensifies. Obviously the enduring power of Mencken's vision is due to his wizardry with words and his large gift for
simplifying and vivifying ideas, for chopping off little blocks
from the vast and inert morass of human knowledge and
holding these blocks up to the glare of light, featuring them in

their full dramatic intensity. Mencken's greatest genius was not only that he could do this, and do it better than any of his contemporaries, but that he happened to hit upon, with fine and exact precision, most of the great verities of life in America, upon our most persistent and troublesome social conditions and disorders. The continuing interest of Americans in Mencken is due not merely to the fact that he was a vivid though now somewhat remote and alien figure of the twenties, that he captivated a generation of intellectuals who were struggling against small-town smugness and complacency, or against an impoverished cultural and social life, but that he continues to address himself to our problems today.

Those who continue to read Mencken often remark that we are living in an age in which Mencken's services as a national sage are more needed than ever. "Oh for Henry Mencken Now," was the title of a 1957 article by Gerald W. Johnson in the *New Republic.* Where are you now, Henry, now that we need you?—this is the response of Mencken's many admirers. On collecting a number of Mencken's papers for a *Vintage Mencken* in the 1950s, Alistair Cooke expressed this feeling to perfection when he wrote in his introduction:

> This book was put together in a period which, in spite of the anxious humility forced on us by the atom and hydrogen bombs, has much in common with the 1920s that Mencken came to immortalize and deflate. Since his day there are slicker types of demagogues in politics and new schools of necromancy in advertising, show business, industry, psychiatry, and public relations, to go no further. Following their antics in these later days as a newspaper reporter, I have often thought that Mencken should be living and writing at this hour.[2]

In catching hold of the major patterns and directions of American life, Mencken filled a role, a seat of authority, in our culture that is vacant today. We have slicker types of demagogues, Alistair Cooke says—in politics, in show business, industry, psychiatry, public relations, and so on—but the implication is that these are only variants, in modern dress, of types that Mencken had gotten directly within his sights years ago.

This work assumes that the continuing interest in Mencken is due to the fact that the ideas Mencken popularized in the 1920s deal with enduring phenomena of American life. It is true enough that we have lost the flora and fauna of Mencken's landscape. We do not have on the American political scene the likes of William Jennings Bryan, Warren G. Harding, Billy Sunday, or Anthony Comstock, but we still have the forces that produced them, and it is doubtful that the forces are giving us anything very much better. Anthony Comstock, the Bible Belt, the small-town Rotary, the cow college may all seem little more than historical relics now; our society has reached a level of sophistication that has left these phenomena far behind. Yet, somehow, they haven't been left behind. Somehow the puritan, the pedant, the Rotarian have merely changed their outward form. Somehow, too, we instinctively feel that if Mencken were alive he would catch them up on every trick.

As I said earlier, Mencken has been treated richly and thoroughly in a biographical framework. Similarly, his career as a literary critic has been dealt with by literary historians (see, for example, the excellent study, *H.L. Mencken: Literary Critic*, by William H. Nolte). There is no intellectual study that deals exclusively with Mencken as a critic of American life, which attempts to make some kind of coherent whole out of Mencken's vision of the American experience. This is strange. When Mencken gave up the editorship of the *Smart Set* in 1923 and founded *the American Mercury*, it was because he felt he had exhausted himself as a literary critic. He had fought many a literary battle, he had defended many younger writers in their battles for recognition; now he was ready to devote himself to what he considered his true vocation.

The *American Mercury* years, then, were ones in which he could bring his earlier journalistic talents into full play. As George Jean Nathan observed upon leaving the *Mercury* a year after its founding, Mencken was abandoning *belles lettres* for something bigger and more elusive. He was trying to capture America on the run. He was trying to figure out who we are and what makes us tick. No easy enterprise this, and when, in later years, Nathan reflected on the abandonment of the *Smart Set*, he concluded that Mencken was happier with the narrower and more modest goals of the *Smart Set* format. Whether or not Mencken was happier, more tranquil, before 1923, his greatest and most ambitious efforts as a writer were then only starting.

This book, then, is mainly concerned with Mencken's creative work of the middle and late twenties as revealed in his later volumes of *The Prejudices*, in his *Notes on Democracy*, and in his editorship of the *American Mercury*. It was in these years and not in the *Smart Set* years that Mencken's full talents were realized. Here he brought together in a period of great productivity and fertility his brilliant literary style, his journalistic talents, his awesome encyclopedic knowledge of American culture both high and low. Some will say, and undoubtedly this is what troubled Nathan about the editorial design of the *Mercury*, that Mencken was casting his net too broadly, that he was trying to do too much. The truth is, in spite of the short life of the *Mercury* and the short time-span of this period in Mencken's literary life, the period was just right for Mencken's combination of gifts and brought all of his best talents into climax and fruition.

Robert Frost once remarked that Mencken was America's greatest essayist. If this is true it is not simply because he amused a generation of college students and city intellectuals anxious to scoff at the Bible Belt or the ladies' literary tea, or because he bloodied the noses of an occasional pedant or schoolmarm. No, Mencken deserves praise because he was a major literary talent who made a Herculean effort to comprehend his countrymen. He was not an expatriate like those who came to the fore around this time; instead he stayed home and dug in hard. He gave us what is perhaps the most successful critique of American life that we have had, and if it is more often harsh and implacable than it is pleasing and attractive, it is also one that cannot be ignored or put down.

I

H. L. Mencken
The Man and His Work

When Henry L. Mencken was growing up in the 1880s and 1890s, his father was the proprietor of a successful cigar manufacturing business in Baltimore, Maryland. The elder Mencken, a substantial and portly German-American burgher, maintained only scant ties with the very large German-American community in Baltimore; yet, in a way, he was not exactly an assimilated American either. Through a mask of old-world values he viewed the American scene with an amused and sometimes cynical detachment.

For American politics, the elder Mencken had little but contempt; more precisely, he saw in American politics something shadowy, something half-real and illusory. Politics and political heroes were not things that should be taken seriously, let alone offered the kind of reverence Americans feel is needed to obtain their salvation in this earthly vale. Many years later, in the first volume of his autobiography, *Happy Days*, Henry Mencken recalled a skirmish his father had with local politicians, which seemed to reinforce an already long-standing distrust. In 1885, when August Mencken had built himself a new cigar factory, he paid the neighborhood councilman $20, "in full settlement forevermore, of all permit and privilege fees, easement taxes and other such costs and imposts" on a large sign that hung out front. The councilman pocketed the money and then managed to keep away police, building inspectors, and the like for his term of office. The councilman, being an honorable man, according to his lights, kept his bargain, and for ten years "the sign flapped and squeaked in the breeze."

But then, in 1895, Baltimore had a reform wave, the councilman was voted out of office, and the idealists in the city hall sent word that a license to maintain the sign would cost $67.76 a year. It came down the next day. This was proof to my father that reform was mainly only a conspiracy of prehensile charlatans to mulct taxpayers. I picked up this idea from him and entertain it to the present day.[1]

For Mencken, father and son, the average American's faith in politicos was misplaced to the point of being grotesque and pathetic. There is something of a naive belief running in the veins of most Americans that politicans here and there, now and then, are corrupt, but that the game they play—the system, as we sometimes call it—is a good one. It is universally believed that if only the citizenry will go to the ballot box and turn out the bad rogues and put in their place a group of "honest" politicans all will be well. August Mencken, and Henry Mencken, when in later years he became a prominent observer of American life and a critic of American mores, could hardly avoid being struck by the comic side of this naive faith that there are two classes of politicians, one of them good and the other bad. The more obvious and realistic truth is that if some politicians in a given milieu act venially another group will act likewise, with only slight variations. The trouble with Americans is that they keep their faith in ideals they have been taught from infancy even when it means rejecting the evidence of their own senses.

There was another conviction of August Mencken's that seems to have strongly influenced his son, namely the conviction that the American spends too much of his time poking into the affairs of his neighbors, that the American is not the great individualist or lover of liberty that native historical writers have cracked him up to be, but that he is a kind of moral busybody, always looking over his shoulder, always looking for demons and transgressors. In the matter of polygamy among the Mormons, for example, which was the all-encompassing moral question in the years before 1890, August Mencken was a champion of the Mormon cause, arguing "that it was nobody's business how many wives they had, so long as they paid their bills, which seemed to be the case."[2] For both Menckens, a very distasteful trait in the American was a tendency to try to encroach on the sovereignty of his neighbors, to rob the other fellow of his delights.

The Baltimore cigar manufacturer's son, bred on a whimsical and detached distrust of American social life and the curious political order known as democracy, grew up to be one of America's most celebrated writers, and not surprisingly, one of her most skillful and indefatigable social critics. Henry Mencken never entered the family cigar business as in those days it was ordained that he should; instead he took up a career in journalism, first as a local newspaperman in Baltimore. As he developed his personal style and habit of thought, he came to see that asking questions about the distinctively American style was his true vocation, his commanding passion. He wrote much startlingly effective literary criticism in his youth; as the years passed, Mencken became increasingly absorbed in his chosen vocation as a critic of American life. With greater and greater frequency and force he returned to the same basic questions he had been tossing around since his youth—Who are we? What makes us tick? What kind of animal is *homo Americanis*, and how does he differ from other human creatures around the world? Henry Mencken came as close as any in our century to being a comprehensive national man of letters; in the several decades of his greatest productivity he attacked the entire American experience with passionate intensity and unrestrained creative energy.

One of the reasons that the more serious and substantial side of Mencken has been overlooked—or simply denied to exist—is that Mencken's brand of social criticism was out of tune with the mainsteam of social and moral criticism in his time. Mencken did not, as has often been asserted, get out of touch when the depression years of the 1930s came along. His ideas, in a sense, were always out of tune: it was a historical fluke that they seemed to beat in tune with the drums of the twenties. Mencken's most important ideas are more in accord with criticisms of America made in the nineteenth century; they recall in tone, mood, and substance the writings of Henry Adams, Charles A. Dana, and James Fenimore Cooper rather than the writers of his own generation—whether those who stayed home to closely observe the passing American scene, like Sinclair Lewis or Sherwood Anderson, or those who sought aesthetic distance in expatriation, like Hemingway and Fitzgerald. Above, all, Mencken's ideas were never in alignment with the main currents of social thought in the twentieth century.

Consider Mencken's attitude toward the muckrakers, and the Progressive movement generally. To Mencken the muckrakers merely muddied the shoal waters; they took haphazard, scattered reforms and do-goodism for serious social thought. As early as 1908, for example, he was writing to complain that Upton Sinclair's reforming zeal had become simplistic. In a *Smart Set* review of Sinclair's *The Moneychangers* he wrote that year: "Hordes of the *bacillus platitudae* have entered Sinclair's system and are preying on his vitals. They have already consumed his sense of humor and are now devouring his elemental horse sense."[3]

There was much hustle and bustle among the journalistic reformers, much piecemeal patching up of this problem area or that. In Mencken's eyes, it was all carried on in a simplistic way. The trouble with the muckrakers was that they never really asked any important questions; they were good at snooping out individual abuses, at pointing out inequities in the system, but they never got down to the basics. Fundamentally, from Mencken's viewpoint, the muckrakers were not really social thinkers at all. They were armchair do-gooders and Pollyannas. They arose, after all, during one of the most self-confident and prosperous eras in American history, and quite instinctively they felt that the American way was the only way, that it was good, that the system works, that all it needed was to have a few wrinkles ironed out. This was true of nearly all the writings on reform of the first two decades of the twentieth century, whether in the milder works of superficial distaste by David Graham Phillips, or in the more violent fulminations of Upton Sinclair. The first premise of all these writers was that the conditions they deplored were transitory ones, that they could be overcome by a return to the amenities of an agricultural or small owner's way of life, by return to some more traditional individualism, or perhaps simply by the government's taking in hand the indiscretions and abuses of the "malefactors of great wealth," as Theodore Roosevelt liked to call them.

To Mencken, however useful these genteel reformers may have been in excoriating this or that transgression, they refused to take a long and objective look at the prevailing American institutions. They refused to inquire whether popular democracy is a tolerable form of government, whether it is conducive to the maintenance of civilization, whether it presents abuses that no amount of picking ourselves up from the side of the road and brushing the dirt off the trousers will manage to help. Do we Americans ever do any more than get ourselves out of individual scrapes when we go through one of our many paroxysms of reform, or do we simply delude ourselves that we do?

Mencken was a skeptic of democracy, a more thick-skinned realist. He doubted that reform would stick, that all the rogues could be washed away in a few trips to the ballot box. Of course, this did not mean he wanted to promote some kind of return to European absolutism. Nor was he a propagandist for the propertied classes; he despised the same abuses as did the leaders of reform. Always and persistently he asked what good is *ad hoc* problem solving in 1910 if you are going to be encountering another set of rogues and troublemakers down the same road in 1930 and 1970, wearing only a slightly different set of clothes?

Mencken was a critic of democracy—not a denouncer of it. He reminds one of the great nineteenth-century critics of democracy: of Macaulay and Carlyle in England, Henry Adams, perhaps, in the United States. Indeed the comparison with Henry Adams is a particularly apt one, not so much because Mencken resembles Adams either in temperament or in style of thought, but because Adams, try as hard as he might to accept American life and to affirm the values of the industrial and commerical revolutions, could not avoid becoming a doubter. Adams started out by trying to make his peace with the scandals of the Grant administration, and with the general knavery of the commercial classes in the 1870s. For a time he tried his hand at being a reformer in the manner that was soon to become popular. With his brother, Charles Francis Adams, he took a stab at exposing Jay Gould and Cornelius Vanderbilt, the railroad buccaneers of the 1860s and 1870s. He soon came to see that patching up the system here and there, was not enough. By the time he came to write *Mont-Saint Michel and Chartres* and *The Education of Henry Adams*, his pessimism about the usefulness of simple nostrums was almost complete. He tried to fathom our national depths only to turn away and absorb himself in the past, in medieval history where there were no dynamos, no railroad boards of directors, no stock market exchanges. He did not despise the dynamo or the force of American industry, but he could not see where they were leading us; he cried out for a transvaluation of American standards, but he could not find the way to accomplish this transvaluation himself.

Mencken, like Henry Adams, was a critic of democracy, a skeptic, a realistic reappraiser of American values, but he was not similarly given to retreat. He did not share the temperament of the scholar or historian; he could not take refuge in some dark recess of the past. If in the end he had no road of salvation to offer, he could nevertheless stay with his subject, in hopes of carving some meaning, some pattern out of it. By training and disposition Mencken was a journalist, a close observer of the American scene. Combining his journalistic temperament with his Germanic love of collecting he became a great encyclopedist of American life. His instinct was not to escape the complexity and diversity of American life, either in the manner of the scholar/historian or in the manner of the youthful expatriates of the 1920; rather it was to luxuriate in the American landscape, to enjoy it as a kind of phantasmagoria. Mencken's life work was thus a harmonious blending of the talents of writer and social thinker. Mencken as a blend of intellectual forces must be studied as a blend. We must look at him simultaneously as a writer and thinker, satirist and social critic.

In the face of the traditional placement of Mencken in American literary history this is not easy to do. Mencken has been, and is, respected for his style, his literary daring and virtuosity, but the standardized view has always made of him a half man. Mencken preferred to think of himself as a critic of ideas; he believed that he wrote from a vantage of ideological coherence and philosophical solidity. If this is true, his satire must always remain thin and superficial to those who reject or misunderstand his ideas. Mencken is certainly not thin and superficial. His essays are still readable—charming, witty and intelligent today because the truth still rings in them. Far from being intellectually anemic, they mask a hard and relentless struggle to understand and make sense out of American life. They are only intellectually thin when the philosophical matrix from which they spring is rejected out of hand.

In short, if we are to understand Mencken as a critic of American life, as an essayist who took the American scene as his all-engaging subject matter, we must rethink the traditional portrait that we have of him. We must begin by establishing with some care the kind of writer Mencken was. We must see him in the context of his time, but we must also try to transcend the vicissitudes of his literary reputation. This book is preeminently a book about Mencken's ideas because it is Mencken's ideas that have been most neglected, but a writer's ideas can never exist in isolation from the total style of the man. So our starting place must of necessity be the whole man, H.L. Mencken in the round. He was, as we know, the sage of Baltimore to those who were young in the 1920s. He is also one of our great national resources; one of our few home-bred giants with the power to make us think and laugh at ourselves.

The Dual Paths of a Literary Vocation

Mencken was first, a journalist, drawn always to the living present, to the great diversity and multifariousness of the common life. The second volume of Mencken's autobiography, *Newspaper Days*, begins: "My father died on January 13, 1899, and was buried on the ensuing Sunday. On the Monday evening immediately following, having shaved with care and put on my best suit of clothes, I presented myself in the city room of the old *Baltimore Morning Herald*, and applied to Max Ways, the city editor, for a job on his staff."[4]

As things turned out, Mencken didn't get a reporting job right away, but he was invited to hang around the city room in the evening on the chance that something might turn up. For a good many weeks, nothing did turn up, and Mencken continued working at his family's cigar business which in time fell entirely into the hands of August Mencken's younger brother. Eventually, though, those evenings of sitting around the city room paid off and Max Ways gave Mencken a job as a general duty reporter. The job became much more than a job; it became a lifetime vocation. Mencken kept his association with newspaper work throughout his life, even when a national reputation and affluence would have permitted him to give up all associations with the copy desk and the daily deadline. As late as 1948, and only shortly before a crippling stroke brought his creative life to an effective end, Mencken was writing newspaper copy; he covered the Progressive Party campaign for the *Baltimore Sun*, just as he had covered every national presidential campaign since 1904. Mencken considered himself a newspaperman by profession, and to a very great extent, by spiritual disposition. If occasionally he made fun of the weak moral sense and imperfect educational equipment of the average working newspaperman, he always delighted in the opportunities newspaper work afforded the close student of American life. He firmly believed that there is no better way for a serious writer or thinker to have a firm hold on his subject matter than to have regular and intimate involvement in it.

Mencken's journalistic scope soon outgrew the central city beats of Baltimore: the jail, the morgue, the city hall. After joining the *Sunpapers* of Baltimore in 1906 (the *Herald* having folded), he found himself filling diverse roles, sometimes in editorial management, but also, from the earliest times, as a writer of editorials, of serious drama criticism, and, of course, of his own brand of pungent comment, as in the very lively "Free Lance" column which he wrote for the *Sunpapers* for many years. Mencken's journalistic career expanded still further after 1908 when he joined the *Smart Set* and reached a climax in the 1920s when he founded and edited the *American Mercury*. It is only natural that Mencken held his journalistic background in high esteem and insisted that nobody could understand his work who failed to see it as having grown out of a journalistic environment.

It is also a mistake to be misled by Mencken's brisk literary style, and to think of him merely as a slightly more elevated columnist. If Mencken became the sage of Baltimore, it was not because of superior newspaper savvy, but because he was, from young manhood, a very erudite and tough-minded critic of ideas. When Mencken thought of himself as a journalist, this was so that he could forcefully affirm his interest and grounding in the rich particularities of the world around him; his unique value as a newspaperman is that he was a serious writer.

One of the things that Mencken told Max Ways when he applied for a job on the *Herald* was that he had been bursting with literary ardors for four or five years. In the early years of his newspaper career he was also bristling with activity as a poet and short story writer, selling many of his things to national magazines. Many of his poems appeared on the editorial page of the *Herald* between 1900 and 1901, and these eventually made up the contents of a first little book, "Ventures Into Verse."

From an early age Mencken was also an independent and self-propelled reader and thinker. By the time he was nine years old, he had had a card in the Enoch Pratt Free Library in Baltimore and had begun "an almost daily harrying of the virgins at the delivery desk." In later years, Mencken looked back on his voracious appetite for reading in a way that will be understandable to all those who have at one time or another lost themselves in the world of books. "I acquired round shoulders, spindly shanks, and a despondent view of humanity. . . . I read everything I could find in English; . . . to this day I am what might be called a reader, and have a high regard for authors."[5] In his early years on the *Herald* his reading must have continued unabated; then it was that he must have read the writers who had the greatest influence on his style and thought—George Bernard Shaw, Thomas Henry Huxley, and James Huneker. Mencken's intellectual interests must have inspired the confidence of his superiors on the *Herald*, for as early as 1901 he was assigned duties as a drama critic. It was in this capacity rather than as a poet or short story writer that Mencken found the road to his true literary vocation. Mencken recalled in *Newspaper Days:*

> Through the theatre I became interested in George Bernard Shaw, and through Shaw I found my vocation at last. My first real book, begun in 1904, was a volume on his plays and the notions in them, critical in its approach. It was the first book about him ever published, and it led me to begin a longer volume on Nietzsche in 1907, and to undertake a book on socialism two years later, in a form of a debate with a Socialist named La Monte, now recusant and forgotten. After that I was a critic of ideas, and I have remained one ever since.[6]

A "critic of ideas"—this, then, was to be Mencken's chief literary calling for the rest of his days. He was, many years later, to turn his hand to something more nearly resembling formal philosophy (as in *Treatise on the Gods* and *Treatise on Right and Wrong*), and to a successful and highly admired work of scholarship—*The American Language*—but Mencken was first and foremost an essayist, a writer. He was by choice a writer who interested himself in ideas—a critic of ideas.

Insofar as Mencken has an enduring reputation as an American writer it is in two areas; he was, most prominently in the years before 1923, an astonishingly good and highly influential literary critic. After the First World War, and especially after the establishment of the *American Mercury*, his work moved on the broader stage of American social and political life. He became what Van Wyck Brooks called "a critic of things American." In a way, this second of Mencken's two literary arenas was more in harmony with his early experiences as a daily journalist. Literary criticism was something of a diversion, a *cul de sac*, albeit a vital one for the history of American letters. The Mencken of the *American Mercury* period, who unfolds in the essays of the *Prejudices* and in *Notes on Democracy*, represents a flowering of his talents as an encyclopedist, a great collector of Americana.

While it is to this second phase of Mencken's work that the present study is devoted, it is only fair to say a little about his devotion to both of these magazines, since both had a great deal to do with the formation of his individual style and contributed a great deal to the establishment of his literary reputation. Needless to say, Mencken's interest in the *Smart Set* waned as he felt more keenly his mission as a commentator on politics and the common life—for the *Smart Set* was a magazine for sophisticated urbanites, not ideally suited for penetrating analysis in the front sections. Nevertheless, both the *Smart Set* and the *American Mercury* fitted Mencken's talents like a glove, each in its own special way; each had something to contribute to his defining style as writer and thinker.

Mencken was not, of course, the founder and shaper of the *Smart Set*, but he had had his eye on it since he was a cub on the *Herald* in 1899. In *Newspaper Days* he recalls: "Between 1899 and 1902 I must have bombarded *The Smart Set* with at least forty pieces of verse, always in vain."[7] Mencken's association with the *Smart Set* began in 1908, when he started to write for it a monthly series of book reviews. After a number of years of experience as a drama reviewer in Baltimore, Mencken was offered the position of book reviewer by the magazine's editor, Fred Splint, probably on the recommendation of Splint's assistant editor, Norman Boyer, an ex-newspaperman from Baltimore who was acquainted with Mencken.[8]

The *Smart Set* had been founded in 1890 by Colonel William D'Alton Mann. 'A Magazine of Cleverness," it fancied itself, but at first it was little more than a shaky attempt to cash in on the scandalous juices of New York society. Somehow, though, in straining after sophistication and trying to associate itself with the avant garde, it managed to attract a capable group of younger writers. Naturally it was not so much the stated editorial policy of the magazine that attracted Mencken to it; what made Mencken suitable for the staff and the magazine a suitable vehicle for his writing was the flexibility and modernity of its format. Here was a magazine whose style was fluid, unfixed, and which could conceivably be moulded in a number of different ways—in fact, like a chameleon, it did manage to change its image several times during its short life. The Smart Set never had to brush off the maudlin sentimentality of the average mass-circulation magazine of the day, nor the stodgy and stultifying conventionality of Harper's or the Atlantic Monthly. In short, it was a magazine made to order for a talent like Mencken's.

Mencken was associated with the Smart Set for fifteen years, and wrote for it copious amounts of material. As literary critic alone his output is staggering; while on the Smart Set staff he reviewed some two thousand books. In later years, especially after 1914 when he became, with George Jean Nathan, coeditor of the magazine, he continued to contribute such a large portion of the magazine's content that he frequently had to resort to pseudonyms like "Owen Hatteras" to disguise the fact.

The Smart Set had its ups and downs even before Mencken and Nathan took the helm, and it was never a great money maker, but by the early 1920s it made something of a literary celebrity of Henry L. Mencken. In this same period, Mencken was contributing to other national journals and was involving himself in a number of literary feuds. He was beginning to collect his Smart Set pieces in book form (e.g. A Book of Burlesques, in 1917; Damn! A Book of Calumny, in 1918, and finally the first volume of his Prejudices in 1919). By the twenties there could be little doubt in the mind of literary America that Mencken was one of the coming leaders, one from whom much could be expected in the postwar years.

If Mencken's national reputation was firmly cast before 1920, it was mainly in the American Mercury that he found his voice as a critic of American life. His association with the

Smart Set came to an end in 1923, and, with the financial backing of Alfred A. Knopf and the continuing editorial assistance of George Jean Nathan, Mencken inaugurated a new monthly, this time a magazine wholly of his own design, a magazine with no strings to the past, no commitments to this or that region or strata of society, a magazine of truly national scope and importance. The *American Mercury* was to become distinctly Mencken's magazine. (Nathan remained co-editor for only one year, after which, following a dispute with Mencken over the basic style of the magazine, he stepped down to the role of "Contributing Editor," leaving Mencken in sole charge.) So closely allied to the *Mercury* was Mencken that it would be fair to say that the two rose to fame and glory at the same time, and, more or less, faded from the national scene at the same time. (The *Mercury* is still alive in the 1970s but in such a different style and format that it bears no relationship to its forebearer.)

The birth of the *Mercury* had been some time in the offing. For a number of years before 1923 Mencken had been unhappy with the *Smart Set,* and that year wrote to his future wife, Sara Haardt: "I am sick of *The Smart Set* after nine years of it, and eager to get rid of its title, history, advertising, bad paper, worse printing, etc."[9] When approached by Knopf with the idea of starting a new magazine, Mencken had a pretty good idea of what he would like to do. He had been greatly impressed by the hero of H. G. Wells's novel *The New Machiavelli,* who created a "Blue Weekly," a magazine for enlightened Tories, and, when the *Mercury* was being planned, he toyed with the idea of calling it "The Blue Review."[10] In general, Mencken knew what kind of product he wanted. He wanted a general magazine for the civilized minority that would avoid the dullness of traditional magazines like the *Atlantic,* and yet offer a kind of substantiality, an intellectual responsibility that was lacking in the *Smart Set.* At the same time he wanted a publication that would not be harnessed to some intellectual doctrine or coterie—the kind of thing he saw plaguing *The Freeman* or *The Nation.* The aim of the *Mercury* was explained in a press release which appeared in the *New York Times* on August 18, 1923:

The aim of *The American Mercury* will be to offer a comprehensive picture, critically presented, of the entire American scene. It will not confine itself to the fine arts; . . . there will be constant consideration of American politics . . . , American industrial and social relations, and American science. . . .

It will strive at all times to avoid succumbing to the current platitudes, and one of its fundamental purposes will be to develop writers in all fields competent to attack those platitudes. . . .

It will cover a larger ground than other magazines, and it will diligently avoid the formal thinking that characterizes most of them. No cult or tendency will dominate its pages.[11]

Whether it is true that any magazine can be free of any intellectual habit or settled outlook is doubtful—and the *Mercury's* detractors would soon point out that the magazine's irreverence and iconoclasm were a kind of cult of its own. Naturally the magazine did develop a coherent style and character. The *Mercury* also became a very fine American periodical; beautiful in typography and printing, beautiful in appearance, well edited, exciting in content. It caught on quickly. By 1925 it reached an average monthly circulation of fifty thousand copies; early in 1928, at the peak of its circulation, it reached nearly eighty-four thousand copies per month. College students carried it with them, and its familiar green cover became a commonplace sight on the nation's campuses.

The important thing about the *Mercury* however, was not its popularity but its uniqueness and stature. No magazine of such consistently high standards had been produced before in America; no American magazine had dared to develop a character so completely its own; no magazine produced before in America had been so completely American in its style and outlook. Herbert Read, who conducted the "Foreign Reviews" section of T. S. Eliot's *Criterion* in the 1920s observed that only four of the 361 authors of the *Mercury* were living in England, and that the magazine was distinctly and consistently American. In June 1927 he wrote of the *Mercury*: "Nowhere does the American nation wear the aspect of a cohering and decisive unity as in the pages of this magazine, and this despite its denunciation of national shams." Later that same year, in what is surely one of the most trenchant observations ever made about the *Mercury*, Read elaborated on this theme:

> Mr. Mencken is creating a new kind of literary interest, even a new kind of culture. He studiously avoids the normal components of a magazine—taste, learning, romance, politeness, all the conventions—and concentrates instead upon what can only be rather lamely called human interests. . . . *The American Mercury* has the effect of making the *Dial* look like an exotic bird and most of the other magazines like bazaar goods. The mystifying quality about Mr. Mencken's achievement is a certain unity, consistency and character which is maintained month after month. It is this quality which suggests a new type of culture . . . an indigenous culture, and there is no parallel in England . . . no possibility of parallel. To appreciate and understand the *American Mercury* implies an *a priori* interest in the American scene.[12]

The *American Mercury* was intimately and inextricably tied to the American scene, an indigenous product of the American soil. No more vital observation can be made about it than this. Since so much of the *Mercury* was given over to railing against American sham and humbug, our own writers have often tended to think of it as somehow standing outside the stream of life in America, as taking a stance of aloof indifference to the passing show. Of course this was only the outward garb of the magazine, the public façade. As Read pointed out, Mencken conceived the magazine not only as a window on American life, but also as an actual expression of it. It stands to reason that no magazine could hope to provide a valid critique of the culture it served unless it had roots in that culture, was a genuine product of it. The greatness of the *American Mercury* was not that it laughed at America, or that it exposed the Babbitts or the Billy Sundays, but that it developed within itself a uniquely American style and way of perceiving the world. The *American Mercury* offered itself as a higher expression of American life, an extrapolation from the very stuff of American life, not some gratuitous addition standing off at the periphery, although of course this was always the most obvious and superficial view of it.

The same may naturally be said of the man Mencken, of Mencken the writer, for clearly the *Mercury* was a mirroring of Mencken's art. Mencken guided and edited the *Mercury* so that it would fill the same role on a larger scale that he himself was filling as an individual writer. The *Mercury* was Mencken writ large, Mencken expanded and assisted by a multitude of other writers who shared his sympathies and, by virute of their own expertise, extended his range. A frequent criticism of the *Mercury* was that it was too strongly dominated by Mencken, that Mencken had the bad habit of meddling with the prose of other writers, often inserting in their articles his own highly characteristic phraseology, his own outlook, his own style of humor and invective. This criticism is of trivial importance, even if not altogether untrue. Most of the time Mencken let his writers be themselves; his strongest influence was felt in the total vision of the magazine. What he wanted was a national magazine that expressed the best that was being thought and done in America, but which eluded the traps that had snared the average serial publication—the tendency to be pitched too low so as to reach only the lowest common denominator; the tendency to become a stodgy relic of some former time or already hardened culture; the tendency to retreat into an arcane specialty that must sacrifice the excellences of literary merit and common humanity. For Mencken, the ideal of the magazine, as the ideal of the essayist, is to push to their furthest limits the excellences of both thought and expression, calling a halt only at the point where each starts cutting into the virtues of the other.

As Herbert Read pointed out, the aim of the *Mercury* was to avoid the conventional components of a magazine—slickness, taste, specialized learning—and to focus instead on large contemporary human issues. If Mencken selected an article on medicine or science, it was not merely to fill a slot, or to satisfy a belief that a magazine should have this or that section (as in *Time*, for example, where there are the requisite number of conventional sections—education, science, medicine, books, theatre), but because the article filled some kind of void in contemporary American intelligence or culture. The goal Mencken set for himself was to bring into his magazine both the best and most useful thinking that was springing from native American culture.

The *American Mercury* was undoubtedly among the most distinctive and distinguished magazines to appear on American soil; certainly it was the pinnacle of Mencken's achievement as a public man of letters. The greatness of the *Mercury* was in its style and its largeness of vision, its unity and coherence, the high seriousness of purpose which always showed through its sprightly and seemingly frivolous exterior. Naturally it is now hard to think back to the *Mercury* in these terms. Nothing is more dead than a dead magazine, and it was the *Mercury's* fate to be short lived as a force in natural letters. The reasons for its short life have been debated at some length, and probably will never be explained. A most obvious reason for its demise was its very greatness. Insofar as the *Mercury* was highly stylized and developed a close existential relationship to the age in which it was conceived, it was not easily able to endure the trauma of a sudden change in the exterior surface of the national life. The start of the great depression at the end of the 1920s was just such a trauma. The failure of the *Mercury*, far from being a sign of its weakness, was probably a sign of its strength, as a work of art, if not as a business venture.

The student of Mencken, the Mencken of the twenties, must take the *American Mercury* as a starting point. The magazine mirrors and is a full flowering of his work both in style and substance. Those who preferred to identify with the earlier, more belletristic Mencken, saw The *Mercury* as a kind of falling off. George Jean Nathan, who came over to the *Mercury* from the *Smart Set*, was one of the dissenters who believed that the *Mercury* was a turning away from the paths of the true and the beautiful. Remembering many years later the arguments during the first year of the *Mercury's* life, Nathan noted a new, more serious Mencken. "His relative sobriety took the alarming form of a consuming interest in editorial politics and a dismissal of his previous interest in *belles lettres,* which had been so great a factor in our former periodical." As Nathan and many others saw it, this must be a kind of slumming, a debasement of talent. "The newspaperman in Mencken superseded the literary man and he favored filling the *Mercury* with pieces written by assorted jailbirds, hobos, politicians and riff-raff of all species."

Naturally there is a certain amount of justice to this, especially when seen from Nathan's perspective as an aesthete who looked on the *Smart Set* as mainly a literary magazine. It is true that the *Mercury* adventure represented for Mencken a new ascendancy of his original journalistic moods and directions. What Nathan didn't realize or didn't admit, was that these original tendencies called forth Mencken's highest talents. Not only did they provide him with an outlet for his tremendous erudition as an Americanist, as a sage of American life (Nathan, after all, was never an Americanist), it gave free play to his literary talent as a satirist—a talent always underutilized by Mencken in the *Smart Set* years. The *American Mercury* meant so much to Mencken (just as it meant something debased to Nathan) because the force bursting in him was the joint force of satire and historicism. This force was "cabin'd, cribb'd, confin'd" in the *Smart Set,* but when it was finally released it was the real making of the sage of Baltimore. It was the making of the Mencken who is still alive today.

The Serious Art of Satire

In 1927, in what is decidedly one of the best essays about Mencken ever written, Walter Lippmann, a young but already well-seasoned prophet of his age, came close to pinning down Mencken's value as a critic of American life. In a review of Mencken's *Notes on Democracy,* Lippmann pointed out that here was a treatise of a philosophical nature, but a very curious one indeed. We cannot really discuss it in quite the same way that we might discuss the treatises of professional philosophers—those of Russell, Dewey, Whitehead, or Santayana, let us say. Lippmann nevertheless found a unique personal force and style in the work, and also a highly individual kind of intellectual strength. The book, he said, is "subrational," in the best sense of the word; it is addressed to "those vital peferences which lie deeper than coherent thinking," which transcend the pedestrian business of rational argument. Mencken is effective "just because his appeal is not from mind to mind, but from viscera to viscera. If you analyze his arguments you destroy the effect. You cannot take them in detail and examine their implications. You have to judge them totally, roughly, approximately, without definition, as you would a barrage of artillery, for the general destruction rather than for the accuracy of the individual shots."13

The most fascinating thing about the scattering of the shots along the horizon, about the incessant raillery, the fires, the rhetorical effusions, is that they are manifestations of a tremendous personal effort and of a scrupulous intellectual honesty. Mencken's satire, if such it must be called, his warcries against the boobsie, may sometimes be harsh, but they are never cruel or dishonest. Mencken the man is admirable, says Lippmann, and when he is unfair he is not unfair in a personal and intimate way. He is painless. "His wounds are clean and they do not fester." One cannot help being caught up by the exuberance and infectious quality of the man, even when one is being wounded by his barbs. "I lay it to the subtle but none the less sure sense of those who read him that here is nothing sinister that smells of decay, but on the contrary the holy terror from Baltimore is splendidly and contagiously alive. He calls you a swine and an imbecile and he increases your will to live."14

This passage gives a good idea of what the Mencken spirit did to its age. Mencken was infectiously and joyfully alive and his contemporaries drew in and admired this liveliness and motion. What was he alive to? What was it about Mencken that inspired a generation of intellectuals? Here, again, Lippmann succeeds in locating the heart of Mencken's contribution to American history. It was a curiosity, a tremendous will to learn and to experience the whole range of

American life—the whole of our national creation, or of our national folly, if you will—that accounted for Mencken's genius. Mencken was a gourmand of American culture. As such he stood in sharp contrast not only to the masses of men, but to the educated elite of his time.

> Most educated men are so preoccupied with what they conceive to be the best thought in the field of their interest, that they ignore the follies of uneducated men. A Jacques Loeb would spend very little of his time on biology as taught in an Oklahoma high school. Even William James, who was more interested in the common man than any great philosophers of our time, was looking always for grains of wisdom in the heaps of folly. But Mr. Mencken is overwhelmingly preoccupied with popular culture. He collects examples of it. He goes into a rage about it. He cares so much about it that he cannot detach himself from it.[15]

Perhaps Lippmann needs to be slightly rephrased here. It was not popular culture alone that fascinated Mencken, or at least not popular culture thought of as a special department of learning, rather it was the whole range of American culture from top to bottom—the whole range insofar as any human being could encounter it. Mencken never limited himself to the culture of *hoi polloi*, to the doings of the man in the crowd; he was as interested in what Paul Elmer More was teaching at Princeton as he was in what was being taught in the Oklahoma high school. Both would have been treated in much the same way, of course, for they appear equally as objects of an immediate encounter in the vast pageant of American life. For Mencken, neither phenomenon is more important than the other, neither must be given priority; there is amusement and edification at both ends of the ladder; something to be learned from the high and the low.

The clue to Mencken's genius was his boundless capacity for gathering raw materials, to the skill with which he could drag forth every little tidbit of American life, with which, like some overeager puppy dog, he could pick up every scrap of information that came his way and give it a few tosses. He was a great American encyclopedist with a Teutonic love for masses of facts and raw material; indeed it is fair to say that his many years of work on the *American Language* did not really represent a departure from the rest of his work, for he was always collecting, cataloging, and amassing his materials. Still, this collecting was nothing other than a starting point for Mencken; his aim was always to take these raw materials and pump life into them, to render them meaningful, intelligible, and exciting. Mencken was the American journalist *par excellence*, a newspaperman who took the whole nation as his beat. He was never content with dull reportage, and insisted on infusing everything he touched with the power of his own personality.

This is what good writing always is—the combination of keen powers of observation and strong personal judgment and vision. Neither can survive without the other, and Mencken had both in a high degree. He combined a vast store of knowledge about America with an ability to filter and articulate that knowledge into meaningful form. Of this meaningful form a little more needs to be said. If Mencken was an encyclopedist of American life—if this was the stuff or substance of his art—we must remember that the form of his art was humor, satire. Mencken was a man who used satire to bring life and verve to reportage and history, so that if we are to understand his writing and to get it in proper perspective, we have to view all of his work simultaneously in both its dimensions as form and content; it has to be seen from its intellectual perspective as historical analysis and its artistic perspective as humor and satire. Always these two dimensions form a single coherent whole; style and substance cannot be wrenched apart and assigned separate compartments; they are simply two sides of the same coin.

It could be that one of the principle reasons Mencken has had his detractors over the years is that he attempted to combine a serious approach to historical analysis with high humor and satirical power. Perhaps it is one of our national weaknesses that we find it hard to tolerate an intellectual who laughs. We except very grave and sober deportment in our intellectuals; perhaps we believe that humor and satire disqualify a person as a penetrating thinker.

A careful reading of Mencken's work always reveals that his principal genius is his ability to combine a superb comic gift with a very serious penchant for social criticism. He plays with ideas, but he is not a trifler. He makes fun of American life, but it would be hard to find a writer who took it more seriously. One must never come to the mistaken conclusion that his ideas are thin or lacking in gravity—the most common error in all the criticism of Mencken since the twenties.

What I am suggesting, then, is that a full understanding of Mencken's genius comes about only after an effort is made to read his essays on two levels simultaneously. He must be read for his brilliant satiric style without sacrificing attention to his gift for critical penetration, for his historical substantiality. Mencken is something of a hybrid in the *globus intellectualis*—neither wholly artistic visionary nor critical historian, but a unique blend of the two. He is a serious and deep-thinking Americanist who makes his ideas felt and heard through satire. This partly explains Walter Lippmann's instinctual feeling that Mencken's satire makes clean wounds, that it doesn't hurt. He never intended to hurt the objects of his satire because he was in fact passionately devoted to the things he was writing about, took them with the utmost seriousness.

Select any of Mencken's essays, then, and read it not only for its immediate impression, its cleverness, surface glitter, and dramatic punch, and you will invariably be rewarded by a solid and coherent piece of thinking about some aspect of the American scene. As a convenient illustration, we might look at a short piece entitled "Want Ad," from the *Prejudices, Fifth Series*. Any number of others would do just as well, but I take this essay as quite representative of Mencken's writing and quality of thought. It is exceptional as Mencken's writings usually are in economy and precision of language, but at the same time it is full of his usual richness of detail. In fact it is little short of startling how much of American life Mencken can cram into a mere thirteen hundred words, from how many different angles he can simultaneously attack his subject and still bring the essay to a solid and revealing unity. The subject is, shall we say, the present state of letters in American life. It begins with a comment on the death of Howells and a few words about the significance of his passing.

The death of William Dean Howells in 1920 brought to an end a decorous and orderly era in American letters, and issued in a sort of anarchy. One may best describe the change, perhaps, by throwing it into a dramatic form. Suppose Joseph Conrad and Anatole France were still alive and on their way to the United States on a lecture tour, or to study Prohibition or sex hygiene, or to pay their respects to Henry Ford. Suppose they were to arrive in New York at 2 p.m. today. Who would go down the bay on a revenue-cutter to meet them—that is, who in addition to the newspaper reporters and baggage searchers— who to represent American literature? I can't think of a single fit candidate. So long as Howells kept to his legs he was chosen almost automatically for all such jobs, for he was the dean of the national letters, and acknowledged to be such by everyone. Moreover, he had experience at work and a natural gift for it. He looked well in funeral garments. He had a noble and ancient head. He made a neat and caressing speech. He understood etiquette. And before he came to his growth, stretching back into the past, there was a long line precisely like him—Mark Twain, General Lew Wallace, James Russell Lowell, Edmund Clarence Stedman, Richard Watson Gilder, Bryant, Irving, Cooper, and so on back to the dark abysm of time.[16]

In an essay which expresses much of the disillusionment of the twenties, Mencken nevertheless manages, in very few words, to paint an accurate picture of the place of literature in contemporary life. By the simple illustration of the arriving vessel and the revenue-cutter which formerly carried Howells to greet the foreign literary dignitaries, an illustration which might occur to a journalist, but probably not to the scholarly critic of American literature, Mencken is able to pin down the mood, the feel, of a transitional period which might otherwise take twenty thousand words—probably twenty thousand less powerful words.

Who is to perform this function now that Howells is dead? inquires Mencken. What if Thomas Hardy or Gabriel D'Annunzio were to arrive on our shore, who do we have who could jump into a frock coat (and look appropriate in it) to make the windy trip through the Narrows, prepared with a sonorous speech, ready to see that "American literature had been represented in a tasteful and resounding manner?" Nobody, says Mencken. The strain of gentility has died out— well, not died out exactly, but somehow faded away.

Where might one look for a successor to Howells? Who is available to carry on as grand old man of letters? How about the "mystic nobles" of the American Academy of Arts and Letters? How about William C. Brownell, Augustus Thomas, Hamlin Garland, Owen Wister, and Henry Van Dyke? Well, these men have the homely virtues. "They spell correctly, write neatly, and print nothing that is not constructive. In the five of them there is not enough sin to raise a congressman's temperature one-hundredth of a degree." The trouble with them is that they are all without literary distinction, nobody has ever heard of them, they have no stage presence. To be welcomed by such figures would appear to a Thomas Hardy or a Gabriel D'Annunzio "as equal to being welcomed by representatives of the St. Joe Missouri Rotary Club."

Well, says Mencken, we do have some important writers in America at the present moment. We have Dreiser, Lewis, Cabell, Hergesheimer, Upton Sinclair, Sinclair Lewis, Sherwood Anderson. How differently they function in our life.

> Try to imagine any of these gentlemen togged out in a long-tailed coat, shivering on the deck of a revenue-cutter while Gerhart Hauptmann got a grip on himself aboard the *Majestic!* Try to imagine Cabell presiding at a banquet to Knut Hamsun, with Dr. A. Lawrence Lowell to one side of him and Otto Kahn to the other! Try to picture Sinclair Lewis handing James Joyce a wreath to put on the grave of James Whitcomb Riley! The vision indeed is more

dismal than ludicrous. Howells, the last of his lordly line, is missed tremendously; there is something grievously lacking in the official hospitality of the country.[17]

Howells died in 1920, and, says Mencken, he was missed almost immediately. Several weeks after his death, Nicholas Murray Butler, President of Columbia University, gave a soiree in honor of the centenary of Lowell. Although himself a member of the American Academy of Arts and Letters, Butler must have been keenly aware of the deficiencies of his colleagues. "To conceal the flabbiness of the evening he shoved them into the back seats—and invited John D. Rockefeller, Jr., Tex Rickard, General Pershing, and the Board of Governors of the New York Stock Exchange to the platform!"

What is most striking about this piece of writing, and so many like it, is not the jeering, iconoclastic tone, the satirist's animus to expose and destroy, or the cynical and sardonic shadows that fall over the world of American letters as Mencken viewed it in the twenties, but simply Mencken's ability to cast around for just the right imagery, just the right examples from a vast store of knowledge that enable him to paint the picture he wants. As always there is a great economy of language. Out of the flux of his subject matter he selects a very few points of dramatic emphasis, but these are just the ones he needs to pin down his main idea.

It is the main point that needs to be grasped—the totality and not the parts. Mencken is trying in this essay to portray the state of the world of letters in the mid-1920s, to capture the flavor of the period, and although the details at first blush may seem extravagant, the whole portrait is really a rather dispassionate and objective one. Why, we may ask, the ship-news reports, the revenue-cutters, the attendance and seating arrangements of The Lowell Centenary at Columbia University? Why the thrusting out this way and that? Why not a straightforward naming of names and cataloging of literary virtues that one expects of the average literary evaluation? The answer, again, of course, is that Mencken is a writer, a writer possessed of historical imagination, and wants the power of words to do some of his work for him. He believes that you cannot deal with any fragment of reality unless you have free and open access to every other aspect of reality that impinges upon it; that reality itself consists not of a series of static problems or entities each sealed away in its own compartment, but of a huge panorama of experience needing the creativity of the artist to make it come to life. The man of specialized learning thinks of the world as a cluster of problem areas, all somewhat distinct. The general critic, the man of historical imagination, has to be able to wander around freely in a large number of interrelated ideas before he can capture and elevate in dramatic relief the idea he is trying to place before the reader. Thus it isn't at all irrelevant to the state of American letters in 1926 to ask why it might be unseemly to send Upton Sinclair out in a frock coat on the revenue-cutter to meet a foreign dignitary, or to ask why we can't imagine Sinclair Lewis handing James Joyce a wreath to put on the grave of James Whitcomb Riley.

What then is the real content, the real intention of this essay? The answer isn't very hard to find, but the conventional treatment of Mencken leads us away from it. Because of Mencken's penchant for satire and ridicule, because of his frequent tendency to cartoon and burlesque, because we have a standardized portrait of him as a debunker of Americana, it is very easy to take as the point of the essay something that is not there at all. For example, give a copy of "Want Ad" to a contemporary student of American literature and ask him what the purpose of the essay was, and you will get an answer something like this: "Mencken is using the genteel tradition as a foil for the kind of modern writers he approves of. Howells is rendered the fool in funeral garments, a mere notch above the other effete men of letters who came after."

Mencken said nothing of the sort. What he said is written clearly on the page, namely, that the American tradition in men of letters had suffered greatly with the loss of figures like Howells and Lowell, and that for all their greater gifts, the Dreisers and Lewises don't really fill the breach any more than do the professors or the spinsters who review books for daily newspapers. In a standardized view of Mencken that is widespread today, Howells is being dressed up to play the fool to allow Mencken to parade his own literary tastes before the public. There is no truth to this view. To be sure, Mencken believed Mark Twain to be a more important writer than Howells. He believed Dreiser to be a greater writer than Lowell. But this did not mean that Mencken saw no important distinction between Howells, on the one hand, and Owen Wister, William C. Brownell, and Herman Hagedorn and that he lumped them all together in the same category. A careful reading of Mencken on Howells from the *Smart Set* period onward reveals that Mencken was quite aware of Howells' literary virtues, and could make a fair and impartial judgment of them. Indeed there is no indication that Mencken's placement of Howells is very much different than that presently accorded him by most respectable literary historians. There is no indication, either, that Mencken would regard James Branch Cabell as a more important writer than Howells simply because he felt a closer personal sympathy to him, or because Cabell belonged more securely to the twentieth century, and shared more of Mencken's own comic disposition than did Howells.

"Want Ad" means precisely what it says, namely that we lost something valuable with the passing of Howells, and with the passing of the culture of New England, with its highly intellectual and literate traditions, something that we haven't quite replaced, even though we now have Dreiser who happens to be a greater artist than William Dean Howells—or, one might add, just because we have a Mencken who happens to be a more important critic than James Russell Lowell. "Want Ad" is not primarily, or even importantly, a piece of literary evaluation, rather a very incisive and carefully executed mood piece which tries to give an accurate rendering of a shifting about of the statuary in the American pantheon. If read in a straightforward manner, most Americanists will find in it very little of the bias and historical distortion usually attributed to Mencken. There is a stretching, exaggerating, in artistic expression, but not in the underlying thought.

"Want Ad" illustrates Mencken's main strength as historical critic and writer, his skill and facility in moving over the whole American landscape in search of his ideas and literary materials. Such uninhibited exploration has always been permitted the novelist, but the critic or essayist who deals with living history, with real people, is always open to suspicion and accorded little thanks for his efforts. He is open always to the charge of bad taste—the naming of actual people in imaginative writing is a sign of bad taste—or to the charge that his work is superficial, unintellectual; that the wide spread of his net never catches anything important.

Against these charges Mencken can be convincingly defended. Mencken's writings are rich, but again it is the richness of the imaginative phenomenologist, not the logician, that is in evidence. Ultimately the observations of the phenomenologist provide raw material for the logician that he would not otherwise be able to get for himself. As Walter Lippmann pointed out in his review of Notes on Democracy, the specialist is so preoccupied with his subject matter that he has no time to see it from any other angle, let alone a multitude of angles. Jacques Loeb would indeed be so busy and preoccupied in his laboratory that he would not care how biology was taught in an Oklahoma high school, or, if he cared, his caring would probably extend only to the mechanics of pedagogy, not to the actual ambience of the classroom.

Mencken, of course, was interested in the ambience, the feel of the Oklahoma classroom. He would also be interested in the ambience of learning at the higher levels as well, and would not, when turning his critical glare on the scientist in his laboratory, consider that here is where human folly ended and critical intelligence began—he would accept this as true only if it were true. In short, Mencken would be as careful to scrutinize the activity of a Jacques Loeb as he would the high school biology teacher.

Consider, for example, Mencken's long well-known battle with the New Humanists in the years between 1915 and 1930. Consider how Mencken carried on his side of the battle. Obviously he did not carry it on the way the genteel intellectual would do, taking up, one by one, the ideas of Paul Elmer More, or Stuart Pratt Sherman, or Irving Babbitt, examining each of them under intellectually antiseptic conditions, taking each idea apart and dissecting it according to the usual rules of scholarship. Rather, he often struck below the belt, landed his punches in the places where they would do some good. What is striking below the belt? In this case it was a matter of forcibly drawing the New Humanists away from the safe haven of educated discourse by virtue of which they expected preferential treatment. More and Sherman were stripped of the robes of their profession; they were revealed instead in terms of the baser human emotions and drives, just as one might, more routinely see the high school biology teacher in Oklahoma. More and Sherman—unlike the man on the street—were protected by the authority of their own intellectual establishment, and sought to hide their foibles and poverty of imagination under the cloak of that authority. The genius of comedy is that it does not allow self-conferred authority to stand unchallenged. The mask must be torn away, and the elemental human being exposed.

Accordingly, Mencken did not evaluate what Paul Elmer More wrote in a field of safe abstraction; he continually asked questions that revealed to his readers who Paul Elmer More was. In Mencken's mind, you couldn't get a grip on a writer or thinker without knowing who he was, how he lived, what he looked like, perhaps we might say, what he smelled like. If you limit yourself to what he wrote, you would be accepting very stringent limitations indeed. To Mencken, Paul Elmer More's study was not one jot more sacrosanct than the high school teacher's classroom. Mencken was continually trying to break into More's life, to peep into his window at Princeton to see if the sophomores were throwing spitballs at him, or if he was being nagged by his wife or his department head—all matters of no professed interest to his colleagues or even to the average professional adversary. Mencken was never content merely to pass judgment on More's latest treatise on Jonathan Edwards; he had to know why he wrote the treatise and what it revealed about More himself, and about our intellectual life in general.

Consider the very language and imagery of Mencken's essay on More in his *Prejudices, Third Series* (only one of the many references to More in his writings). More is revealed as someone who would prefer not to fight, would prefer to put only his ideas, not his personality, on the line. Mencken, on the other hand, sees the matter wholly in terms of getting More into the fray, of getting him to expose his flank. The essay is couched almost wholly in terms of battle. The Goths and Huns are at the gate, says Mencken, but where is More?

> High above the blood-bathed battlements there is a tower, of ivory within and ferro-concrete without, and in its austere upper chamber he sits undaunted, solemnly composing an elegy upon Jonathan Edwards, "the greatest theologian and philosopher yet produced in this country."[18]

Some of More's followers enter the fray, says Mencken; they will come out and get their noses bloodied. There is Stuart Pratt Sherman in Iowa (Iowa was Mencken's generic term for the midwest; actually Sherman lived in Illinois). Consider how Mencken goes about bloodying his nose:

> Even Prof. Dr. Stuart P. Sherman is no antagonist to delight a hard-boiled heretic. Sherman is at least honestly American, of course, but the trouble with him is that he is *too* American. The Iowa hayseed remains in his hair; he can't get rid of the smell of the chautauqua; one inevitably sees in him a sort of *reductio ad absurdum* of his fundamental theory—to wit, the theory that the test of an artist is whether he hated the Kaiser in 1917, and plays his honorable part in Christian Endeavor, and prefers Coca-Cola to Scharlachberger 1911, and has taken to heart the great lessons of sex hygiene. Sherman is game, but he doesn't offer sport in the grand manner.[19]

Here Mencken is doing the thing he does best, nailing his prey to the wall with a few deadly words. We do not know, of course, how true the individual words may be. Nor does it matter. The detail, as always, is at the service of the total effect. The final picture we get of Stuart Pratt Sherman in these few sentences is probably more useful and accurate than would be a long tract dealing with his philosophy of literature. So, too, do we know more about Paul Elmer More after a few jabs from Mencken than we do from all those symposia of the early thirties which ever so gently raked the New Humanists over the coals. Of all the Humanists it was More who was the most interesting to pursue.

> The really tempting quarry is More. To rout him out of his armored tower, to get him out upon the glacis for a duel before both armies, to bring him finally to the wager of battle—this would be an enterprise to bemuse the most audacious and give pause to the most talented. More has a solid stock of learning in his lockers; he is armed and outfitted as none of the pollyannas who trail after him is armed and outfitted; he is, perhaps, the nearest approach to the genuine scholar that we have in America, God save us all! But there is no truculence in him, no flair for debate, no lust to do execution upon his foes. His method is wholly ex *parte*. Year after year he simply iterates and reiterates his misty protests, seldom changing so much as a word. Between his first volume and his last there is not the difference between Gog and Magog. Steadily, ploddingly, vaguely, he continues to preach the gloomy gospel of tightness and restraint.[20]

Behind the bad boy language and stridency of Mencken we learn almost everything we need to know about the style and mind of Paul Elmer More—Mencken's longtime adversary, and, if there could be such a thing, his polar opposite. More's gifts as a scholar are undeniable, but the trouble with him is that there is no zip in his thinking, no imagination; he is the specialized scholar *par excellence*; he is a pigeonholer, an assembler of neat piles of learning. Mencken's ideas of what an intelligent man should be doing are quite the reverse. For him the world already has all the tightness and restraint it needs. Instead he prefers to go his merry way stepping on feet, lifting up skirts, overturning neatly set tables in the hope of prodding sluggish minds to action. "A brawling vulgarian," More once called Mencken in way of rebuttal, and so Mencken must have seemed when he figured at all in More's orderly universe. But Mencken always had the advantage over More in that his writing was spun out of the imagination rather than out of plodding intelligence, because the imagination is a rarer faculty than intelligence, and especially because of the energy, the wild and free-ranging playfulness with which it roamed over the American landscape.

This brings us again to the relationship between Mencken's subject matter—American experience—and his art, to the relationship between historical criticism and satire. Mencken was a writer who sought to understand American society thoroughly and rigorously, but he did this not by the usual anemic means open to scholarship, not by cool detachment, but by engagement—by wrestling with his subject, punching it, knocking it down. This might not be so strange were it not for the fact that we so seldom think of the writer engagé as a humorist or satirist. Mencken thus appears puzzling and enigmatic to the student of literature; his motives seem obscure or ambiguous. Consider the conventional picture of Mencken. It is that he is first and foremost a satirist of American life. In turn, this suggests that Mencken thought of himself as standing at some remove from the American scene—the intellectual aristocrat standing outside the gates of the circus and taking amusement at the follies within. Again it must be said that Mencken did not think of his relationship to American civilization in those terms at all. He did not believe that he himself was in the American world, but not of it; he believed that he was a *bona fide* American product, a participant, and never once did it occur to him to renounce his native land, however much he denounced it. Mencken was thus a satirist of a peculiar kind; he thought of himself always as undetachable from his subject matter. Satire for him was a way of getting involved, a form of intimacy; it did not have at its root revulsion, but intellectual passion.

In his recent study, *H. L. Mencken, Iconoclast From Baltimore*, Douglas C. Stenerson offers as one of his chapter headings Mencken's quality of "loving and loathing American life." Here there are two antithetical and conflicting forces at work in Mencken's psyche, two visions of America that cannot be easily reconciled. Perhaps the concept is apt, although it may be that it is better not to view Mencken in this light at all; it may be preferable to dissolve the dichotomy entirely. His loathing was part of his loving, wrapped up with it in dialectical harmony. While Mencken made much fun of American life this should not imply that he took his relationship with America as a subject-object relationship of a scoffer and, on the other side, the object of derision. Perhaps when we say that Mencken made fun of the tent evangelist, the Rotarian, the chiropractor, we mean that he had fun with them, for he actually savored their doings and took some pleasure in holding them up as objects of fascination. This need not suggest loathing; loathing appears to require some kind of fixed hostility.

The analogy of Mencken as a lover and loather of American life is misleading for two reasons. First of all, Mencken did not regard himself as detached from the American scene, rather he interacted with it on all its levels; he was as much drawn to William Jennings Bryan whom he made a show of despising as he was to Mark Twain whom he keenly admired. Secondly, the analogy is not a good one because Mencken held a view of American life which suggested that the good and the bad come from the same root, that there is as much to learn from the bad fruit as from the good. Mark Twain and William Jennings Bryan are similarly products of the freer, more flexible, more buoyant social life that exists in America. When considering Mencken's perspective, it is always important to remember that first and foremost he was a phenomenologist, a topologist, a collector of American life, not at bottom a moral opponent. His dominant desire was not to attack but to relish American life, to take delight in it. Satire for Mencken was not the center of gravity, as it may well have been for a writer like Sinclair Lewis; rather it was a dramatic technique, a way of serving up his subject matter. He adopted satire not as a world view, but as a way of lending force to his portrait of American life.

Most importantly, perhaps, we must always keep in mind the personality of Mencken, the man himself. He was not, as was Sinclair Lewis, a lonely saturnine individual, his cup running over with bile; if he had victims we can only say that he toyed with them, not that he tracked them down systematically and relentlessly. (T. K. Whipple once likened Lewis to a red Indian stalking his victims, and the analogy is a good one.) Mencken could be cruel and unfair, but it must be remembered that he was a man of ideas, of abstractions, and if he picked on a Bryan or a Harding it is because he could not have gotten across his ideas unless he wrapped all his abstractions in a concrete garb. But Mencken the German burgher's son was every inch a gentleman. He was by disposition no dyspeptic, ungenerous and ill-mannered fellow tuning his ear to the foibles and indiscretions of those who entered his orbit. Indeed, the rather courtly, warm-hearted, beer-drinking Mencken seems a strange candidate for national satirist (or, as some would have it, misanthrope), for it is impossible to imagine him taking anything but enjoyment from his contact with individuals. It is hard to imagine that he would have given the slightest personal offense to an evangelist, an Iowa farmer, or a chiropractor had he met one on the street. Mencken relished the company of all sorts and classes of men, and if it can be said that there were any he loathed it must have been only in a very special sense. Mencken may have cataloged and classified a great many specimens of boobhomerie in his books, but one doubts that he ever talked to a boob or met a man in whom he took no delight whatsoever. Mencken always dealt in ideas, never in personalities for their own sake; but he could not have made his ideas stick had he not been a namer of names. The genuine weaknesses and foibles of people seem to have offended him not at all.

Mencken's ambivalence toward the American scene can be resolved, and a further appreciation of the stuff of his art can be gained from a careful examination of his essay "On Being an American." Read superficially, the essay, one of the longest in the *Prejudices*, seems to be little more than a vast cataloging of Mencken's grievances against his countrymen. The main argument of the essay is purportedly that "the United States is essentially a commonwealth of third-rate men." Every country, he assures us, is well populated with third-rate men, but here alone the Methodist, the Odd Fellow, the Ku Kluxer, the Know Nothing is put at the head of the pack— "here alone he rules, here alone his anthropoid fears and rages are accepted gravely as logical ideas, and dissent from them is punished as a sort of public offense."[21]

Interestingly enough the essay begins with an attempt to answer the question so often asked of Mencken by the antagonistic readers of the *Saturday Evening Post* and by the apostles of sweetness and light: if this country is so bad, why don't you leave it? A good question says Mencken, and one that demands an answer. "Here I stand," he says, "unshaken and undespairing, a loyal and devoted Americano, even a chauvinist, paying taxes without complaint, obeying all laws that are physiologically obeyable, accepting all the searching duties and responsibilities of citizenship unprotestingly." All this at a time when younger Americans are on the high seas, "Why did I answer with only a few academic 'Hear, Hears' when Henry James, Ezra Pound, Harold Stearns and the *emigres* of Greenwich Village issued their successive calls to the corn-fed *intelligensia* to flee the shambles, escape to fairer lands, throw off the curse forever?" The first answer is put in Mencken's usual tongue-in-cheek tone. I live here, he says, because the United States is an easy country to be happy in. To be happy, he says, he must be three things:

(a) Well-fed, unhounded by sordid cares, at ease in Zion.

(b) Full of a comfortable feeling of superiority to the masses of my fellow-men.

(c) Delicately and unceasingly amused according to my taste.

In explaining how the United States satisfies these needs, some paradoxical, perhaps contradictory, but still very revealing views emerge. In explaining, for example, how it is that he finds himself well-fed, untroubled, at ease in Zion, Mencken first tells us that the United States is a country which seems to have no place in it for men of culture and refinement—for philosophers, oboe players, water colorists, epic poets. Such people are nowhere in demand. On the other hand, he tells us, "the Republic has never got half enough bond salesmen, quack doctors, ward leaders, phrenologists, Methodist evangelists, circus clowns, magicians, soldiers, farmers, popular song writers, moonshine distillers, forgers of gin labels, mine guards, detectives, spies, snoopers, and *agents provocateurs*."[22] While the Unites States seems not to put out the call for metaphysicians or oboe players and is likely to pay a composer of string quartets no better than a railway conductor, the belief also seems to emerge that the United States is not such a bad place for a man of talent to live after all. It is a land of plenty, of splendid materiality, and—contrary to romantic superstition—the best work of the artist, the philosopher, or the scientist is done when he is not plagued by unsatisfied wants (an idea, by the way, stressed in ancient times by Aristotle). Thus our society is actually a rather good place for a man of talent to work. "In the older countries, where competence is far more general and competion is much more sharp, the thing is almost cruelly difficult, and sometimes almost impossible. But in the United States it is absurdly easy, given ordinary luck."[23] In short, while believing the United States to be a place where talent is not in high demand, Mencken still believes that the country is a good place for an artist to live.

Even in observing that the older European cultures seem to be oversupplied with talent, Mencken is posing those ideas for a special kind of dramatic emphasis, or so we must assume after reading other parts of the essay. In places Mencken writes as if Europe were well stocked with savants, men of culture and refinement, artists, philosophers, while America produces stock brokers, salesmen, and church deacons. The average American is "a member of a Chamber of Commerce, an admirer of Charles M. Schwab, a reader of *The Saturday Evening Post*, a golfer—in brief, a vegetable." All this gives Mencken what he claims to be the second reason for being content on American soil—"a feeling of comfortable superiority to the masses of my fellow men." Another glance immediately shows that in no way does Mencken really hold the view that there is something manifestly superior about the culture of European nations, and that America is less well supplied with talent than they.

True enough, Mencken sometimes says that an American is just a pale imitation of an Englishman (for example), or that all our main ideas are borrowed from England. "I often wonder, indeed, if there would be any intellectual life at all in the United States if it were not for the steady importation in bulk of ideas from abroad, and particularly in late years, from England." Where would the average American scholar in almost any field of endeavor be if he could not borrow wholesale from English scholars? "Who would show our statesmen the dotted lines for their signatures if there were no Balfours and Lloyd Georges? . . . By what process, finally, would the true style of a visiting card be determined, and the *hoflich* manner of eating artichokes, if there were no reports from Mayfair?"[24]

One must not thereby conclude that Mencken himself believed English culture, taken altogether, is any more inspiring than American culture. In all of Mencken's writings there is no indication that he believed in the inherent superiority of things English. What he does is point out the pathetic faith Americans have in that superiority. His own view turns out to be something altogether different. For Mencken, modern England was in a cultural decline, it was no longer the England of Shakespeare and Milton or Burke or Nelson, any more than America was the land of Jefferson and Madison. Earlier, in a "Free Lance" column, of September 29, 1914, he made it clear that the middle class England of today suffers all the woes of middle class America.

> The England of Drake and Nelson, of Shakespeare and Marlow, of Darwin and Huxley, of Clive and Rhodes is not the England of Churchill and Lloyd-George, of Asquith and McKenna, of mongrel allies and bawling suffragettes, of "limehousing" and "mafficking," of press-censors and platitudinarians, of puerile moralizing and silly pettifogging. The England that the world yet admires and respects was a country ruled by proud and forthright men. The England that today poses as the uplifter of Europe is a country ruled by cheap demagogues and professional pharisees. The slimy "morality"

of the unleashed rabble has conquered the clean and masculine ideals of the old ruling caste. A great nation has succumbed to mobocracy, and to the intellectual dishonesty that goes with it.[25]

Pretty much the American story over again. Nor is there any indication that Mencken believed any other European nation to be presently at the pinnacle of its achievement or at some historical high point. America may be a nation of third-rate men, but so apparently are England, Russia, and yes, even France and Germany—two countries Mencken considered to have coherent cultures and social solidarity. Mencken may say of the leading American musical director that "if he went to Leipzig he would be put to polishing trombones and copying drum parts," but this does not imply that the mass of Germans are more civilized than the mass of Americans. Indeed, in "On Being an American" Mencken says of the Germans that they are "taking one with another, on the level of green-grocers." While proud of his own German heritage, Mencken did not find a great deal to be proud of in the vast horde of Germans, especially those he observed in the United States. In the many Germans he met since the 1914 war he found in the whole lot of them only "a score or two who could name offhand the principal works of Thomas Mann, Otto Julius Bierbaum, Ludwig Thoma or Hugo von Hofmannstahl. They know much more about Mutt and Jeff than they do about Goethe."[26]

The second of Mencken's reasons for remaining in America is a window that opens upon a larger side of Mencken's ideology, namely, his belief that most modern nations are staggering under the weight of middle-class morality; that the strong, salty, and forthright men who brought forth the style and essence of most European countries have given way to uplifters, do-gooders, and professional pharisees. The American boob, the Babbitt, may be a distinctly American product, but his counterpart exists and is taking the reigns in England and Germany as well. The standardization of manners and morals is international in the twentieth century; in America it can be seen in its most advanced and dramatic form.

Mencken's second reason telescopes into the third, namely that America is the place to live because one may more easily enjoy here a feeling of superiority to the mass of men. In America the masses pass before you in a glorious and colorful parade—one has more time to enjoy the parade. Mencken gives several reasons for this. First, "getting a living here has always been easier than anywhere else in Christendom; getting a secure foothold has been possible to whole classes of men who would have remained submerged in Europe."[27] This suggests that in spite of all his attacks on the American system and on democracy, Mencken is also convinced that in America there is a certain value to the fluidity of the social structure that makes life and art possible. He believes that economic prosperity and freedom from the rigidity of the class structure are good for the creative man—especially, of course, good for a man of Mencken's own talents.

Secondly, the passing show is harmless and innocuous enough to remain purely and totally impersonal. "Here one may howl over the show without any uneasy reminder that it is serious, and that someone may be hurt." Take politics, for example. "Here politics is purged of all menace, all sinister quality, all genuine significance, and stuffed with such gorgeous humors, such inordinate farce that one comes to the end of a campaign with one's ribs hanging loose, and ready for 'King Lear' or a hanging, or a course of medical journals."[28]

America is thus the place where one can laugh freely, where one can laugh with impunity. "'Ridi si sapi', said Martial. Mirth is necessary to wisdom, to comfort, above all, to happiness. Well, here is the land of mirth, as Germany is the land of metaphysics and France is the land of fornication. Here the buffoonery never stops." In England the passing show may be dull, productive mostly of sleep; in Germany it may be "harsh and implacable"—only in America can one be ceaselessly amused without having to feel guilty about it; only in America, perhaps we might say, can one be a Mencken.

To be sure, there is a great deal in the essay "On Being an American" that is outwardly and ingeniously tongue-in-cheek. Under the guise of elaborating the reasons why he has remained in America, Mencken restates and reinforces his own views about his homeland, and about the social life of the modern Western world in general. What is especially important is that the mocking tone does not reveal the substance of the essay. The substance of the essay is a highly complex and sometimes obscure revelation of Mencken's philosophical ideas about democracy and the decline of Western civilization; to be fully understood, it has to be read in the context of Mencken's work as a whole. It is not mainly (and perhaps not even peripherally) an attack on America or a humorous exposure of American foibles. It is a kind of personal testimony, an explanation of how Mencken himself fits into the American world; how he and his work have a dialectical relationship with America; how the writer and his subject merge.

Even if one were to take an essay of this kind and extract from it all the negative comment on American life and set this aside as Mencken's view of America, Mencken's work considered *in toto* does not support the idea that he is at base a detached or hostile critic. The mood of too large a proportion of his work is one of enjoyment and relish, and even in "On Being an American" it ought to be noted that Mencken gives as one of his main reasons for remaining in America his belief that life is more bearable here than in most countries, that it gives freer range to the imagination.

And to reinforce this, we need only stress again that throughout Mencken's writings there are instances where praises of the American way are sung long and loud, where the advantages and virtues of being an American are forcefully and unequivocally stated. Consider Mencken's lavish and continual praise of the American language. In the theoretical chapters of *The American Language*, Mencken takes pains to prove the point that Americans—not just American intellectuals, or writers, but Americans generally—are much more inventive with language than the peoples of other contemporary civilizations, that they have a lively and often astonishing sense of words and word play. If we can take our Western philosophical traditions seriously, this is identical with saying that they are more lively thinkers than those encountered elsewhere.

Mencken attributes this to the fluidity of the social structure, to Americans' early (although now often stifled) tendency to be nonconformists. The English, for example, have lived "under a relatively stable social order and it has impressed upon their souls their characteristic respect for what is customary and of good report." The English have a stern and high regard for precedent, for correctness and decorum—in fact, too high a regard. The English are shackled on all sides to convention and habit. Americans, on the contrary

> have plunged to the other extreme, for the conditions of life in their country have put a high value upon the precisely opposite qualities of curiosity and daring, and so they have acquired that character of restlessness, that impatience of forms, that disdain of the dead hand, which now broadly marks them. From the first, says a literary historian, they have been "less phlegmatic, less conservative than the English. . . ." Thus, in the arts, and thus in business, in politics, in daily intercourse, in habits of mind and speech. The American is not, of course, lacking in a capacity for discipline; he has it highly developed; he submits to leadership readily, and even to tyranny. But by a curious twist, it is not the leadership that is old and decorous that commonly fetches him, but the leadership that is new and extravagant.[29]

Mencken quotes with agreement Otto Jesperson's statement that "the essence of language is activity," and believes that the American language more richly displays that essence than English. English has been "arrested in its growth by its purists and grammarians, and burdened by irrational affectations, by fashionable pretension." Not only is English weighted down by the grist of its purists and pedants (Mencken does not deny that our own pedagogues and schoolmarms have made gallant efforts to mummify American also) but the rigid class structure of England is not favorable to the development of lively and vigorous language. The greatest enemy of English, George Orwell once said, is "standard English"—the dreary dialect of "leading articles, and B.B.C. news bulletins." The trouble with standard English, or "educated English" as

Orwell called it, is that it suffers from a social anemia. The language is not reinvigorated from below, since the educated classes lose touch with the manual workers who are likely to use simple concrete language that calls up vivid visual images. American, according to Orwell, has gained a foothold in England, because of "the vivid, almost poetic quality of its slang . . . and most of all because one can adopt an American word without crossing a class barrier."[30]

While American has done much in recent years to infect English, the opposite is not true. The dreary B.B.C. dialect, the stuffiness of "educated English" have not taken hold in America. Even the most determined and self-conscious Anglophiles on our shores, said Mencken, even our most devoted pedagogues tend to slip and slide, and give way to the freer spirit of American. "I glance through the speeches of the late Dr. Woodrow Wilson, surely a conscientious purist and Anglomaniac if we have ever had one, and find, in a few moments, half a dozen locutions that an Englishman in like position would certainly hesitate to use, among them *we must get a move on, to gum-shoe, to-hog, ornery* in place of *ordinary*, and *that is going some.* I turn to the letters of that most passionate of Anglomaniacs, Walter Hines Page, and find, *to eat out of my hand, to lick to a frazzle, to cut no figure, to go gunning for, nothin' doin', for keeps,* and so on."[31] Thus even on the higher levels of American speech, where one might expect there to "still linger some eighteenth century tightness," there is plenty of rebellion. American is a freedom-giving and a freedom-loving language, even to those most determined to resist the call of freedom where language and learning are concerned.

What is important in all this is what we learn about the American people. The American language is expressive of the American psyche, and, in Mencken's eyes, a people who are inventive and imaginative in their language will be inventive and imaginative in their social being. Mencken quotes with strong approval the judgment of another Englishman, Basil de Selincourt, a product of the stuffy and inhibited public school system of England, who nevertheless brilliantly perceived the vital connection between the American language and American life:

The English of the United States is not merely different from ours; it has a restless inventiveness which may well be founded in a sense of racial discomfort, a lack of full accord between the temperament of the people and the constitution of their speech. The English are uncommunicative; the Americans are not. In its coolness and quiet withdrawal, in its prevailing sobriety, our language reflects the cautious economies and leisurely assurance of the average speaker. We say so little that we do not need to enliven our vocabulary and underline our sentences, or cry "Wolf!" when we wish to be heard. The more stimulating climate of the United States has produced a more eager, a more expansive, a more decisive people. The Americans apprehend their world in sharper outlines and aspire after a more salient rendering of it.[32]

De Selincourt, in drawing a distinction between the English and American language and the English and American people, does a great deal more. He gives us the clue to why Mencken valued the American language so highly, why he spent so many of his years studying it, why he considered the language so suitable to himself as a writer, and why he preferred to think of himself as a strictly American writer. Americans are more communicative than Englishmen (they may not necessarily be more articulate, for this is another matter). They have a habit of speaking to one another. They prefer contact to serene withdrawal. They are, as de Selincourt put it "a more eager, a more expansive, a more decisive people." They like to view the world in bolder and sharper outline. No better description of Mencken himself as thinker and writer can be imagined. Rather than sink into the cautious economies and leisurely assurance that mark the cultivated Englishman, he preferred head-on encounters. Everything is fair game in this world of Mencken's, everything is questioned, nothing is held in reserve, nothing is sacrosanct.

In spite of occasional lapses into foolish idealisms or inert passions of the mind, this is the American way. Mencken was a man who wanted to push this way, this style, to its limits, to wring out of it everything that he could. The American is the one who looks into everything, talks about everything, lets nothing get past him—at least if he's paying attention. *Rubberneck* was one of Mencken's favorite American neologisms. It reveals, he said, "the national habit of mind more clearly than any labored inquiry could ever reveal it. It has in it precisely the boldness and contempt for ordered forms that are so characteristically American, and it has too the grotesque humor of the country, and the delight in devastating opprobriums, and the acute feeling for the succinct and savory."[33] This in a nutshell is Mencken's faith in Americans— their national genius stems from their desire and willingness to look around and laugh at everything, even, when necessary, America itself. The English may need the Irish to do their laughing for them, but Americans can perform this function for themselves. To be able to look at ourselves, to criticize and laugh at ourselves is precisely our most valuable and enduring national trait.

Just as language is somehow the clue to the American character, to whatever national genius we may possess, it is also the clue to the art and thought of Henry L. Mencken. Imaginative play with the language was always at the center of his creative activity, and it was his own unique way of encountering the American environment. In Mencken, comic use of language was a bold and imaginative way of dealing with the social life, a way that had already borne fruit in some of our greatest writers—Mark Twain being perhaps the best example.

A long essay might well be devoted to Mencken's genius for word play and the relationship of this genius to his social criticism. Briefly, one might mention several characteristics of the Menckenian style which he perceived as indigenous virtues of the American language. Mencken often spoke of the American habit of mind (at its best) as revealing "boldness and contempt for ordered forms," "the grotesque humor of the country, and the delight in devastating opprobriums, and the acute feeling for the succinct and the savory." What better description could we have of Mencken's own writing.

Outright challenge of stale and ordered forms—that is the American way. In Mencken's writing we find a constant battering away at settled forms, a spit-balling of all kinds of pretentiousness and social rigidity. Consider some of the best-known and oft-recurring idiosyncracies of Mencken's style—for example his habit of mockingly bestowing titles on those whose reputations he was trying to deflate—Prof. Dr. Woodrow Wilson, or at other times "the Archangel Woodrow."

Or consider Mencken's high genius for deflating the sort of language which disguises most social mischief; the euphemisms and phony politenesses with which people constantly deceive themselves, especially in matters of morals and politics. Mencken's method is to undercut an opponent's whole intellectual superstructure, to reveal the simpler, more direct, more brutal impulses lying underneath, which actually determine the course of history. Consider, for example, his way of dealing with the Mann Act, which forbade the transporting of women across state lines for immoral purposes:

> The aim of this amazing law, of course, is not to put down adultery; it is simply to put down that variety of adultery which is most agreeable. What got it upon the books was simply the constant gabble in the rural newspapers about the byzantine debaucheries of urban Antinomians—rich stockbrokers who frequented Atlantic City from Friday to Monday, vaudeville actors who travelled about the country with beautiful mistresses, and so on. Such aphrodisiacal tales, read beside the kitchen-stove by hinds condemned to monogamous misery with stupid, unclean, and ill-natured wives, naturally aroused in them a vast detestation of errant cockneys, and this detestation eventually rolled up enough force to attract the attention of the quacks who make the laws at Washington. The result was the Mann Act. Since then a number of the cow states have passed Mann Acts of their own, usually forbidding the use of automobiles "for immoral purposes." But there is nowhere a law forbidding the use of barns, cow-stables, hay-ricks and other such familiar rustic ateliers of sin. That is to say, there is nowhere a law forbidding yokels to drag virgins into infamy by the technic practiced since

tertiary times on the farms; there are only laws forbidding city youths to do it according to the technic of the great municipalities.[34]

How different this is from the standard approach to questions of this kind. Mencken simply does not allow the matter to be solidified in the high moralistic terms with which the law was probably formulated and on which polite persons would insist that it be discussed. He simply disallows and dismantles the language of polite discourse whereby simplistic and stereotyped thinking is reinforced; he sees the matter wholly in terms of simpler and more primitive human emotions. To be sure, the brilliant effect of the language is due to witty turns of speech, picturesque metaphors and to the richness and suppleness of Mencken's vocabulary, but the important thing to notice is Mencken's great talent for stripping the mask away from the habitual ways of talking about problems of this kind. He does not allow it to settle down into a comfortable, benign and mediocre reasonableness, but rather deals the topic a devastating blow in its most vulnerable spot. Some will say, of course, that this method is lacking in dignity, that it is unworthy of the man of intellect. Truthfully, Mencken does not discuss, he does not reason; the method is essentially the method of the comic, even the clown. He gets his opponents in the face with a custard pie; he kicks them in the seat of the pantaloons.

One of the most remarkable features of Mencken's language is the variety and range of the diction, the startling contrast in levels of usage. Most of us are locked into some particular linguistic level and we never struggle to escape from it; we may be coarse or we may be refined, but we chain ourselves to one kind of linguistic pattern or habit without putting up a fight, without trying to give vent to our more primitive emotions. Not so with Mencken. He selects his language with care to achieve the effect he wants to achieve, but he does not take every word out of the same bin. He playfully shoves the educated (and sometimes even arcane) word up against a common everyday word, or even a barroom word. He is always taking delight in words, playing with them, finding out what kinds of tricks can be done with them. Words are there to enflame, to excite, to disturb, not merely to convey meaning.

This is a radical departure for the essayist, to whom we customarily look for gentility and politeness. One must in fact look long and hard to find another essayist who so skillfully and energetically mixes and plays with the various levels of the language. It might be said that Carlyle had a great facility for jumbling different levels of discourse with remarkable rhetorical effect, that he had a gift for spinning out wild clashes of tone, structure, and diction. On closer analysis it will be seen that Carlyle's ultimate intention was not to grapple with the world of immediate reality, but to establish a self-contained historical vision. He was frightened by the world of immediate reality; he could make fun of it from afar but he chose not to encounter it in direct collision. In the end Carlyle, for all his verbal genius, was shackled to his strange historical vision.

In Mencken's mind the freedom to play with language, to mingle the talk of a streetcar conductor or an ice wagon driver with that of a professor of classics is a distinctly American prerogative and distinctly American achievement. He would have agreed with George Orwell that one of the best features of the American language is that it can be used freely without crossing any class barriers. Of course we Americans have built our own kind of lethargy into the language, and Mencken's art was one which constantly strove to shake off this lethargy. It was always his wish that his countrymen would follow him in this as in the past they so often showed signs of doing. Language can shackle us or it can set us free; but if we play with it, if we romp with it in full abandon, if we allow it to challenge everything that passes us by, we will be freed from the heavy burdens that have tormented mankind since the beginning of history.

Beyond Mencken's innate comic gift and his remarkable facility with the language, lies another of his great resources, one which, above all else, produces his unique force and individual style. Mencken devoted himself ceaselessly to American problems, to the American way of life. It would be unjust to be endlessly distracted by Mencken's wordplay, his relish of the lampoon. His strongest drive, at least in the years of his greatest creativity, was his drive to explore, to catalog, to fathom the American psyche in all of its blendings and ramifications. To do justice to the whole Mencken—which is the purpose of the present study—we must fasten on his all-consuming passion. He lived with this passion day and night, he sweated over it in every word he wrote. He was endlessly fascinated by Americans and what makes them tick. His conclusions were more often than not gloomy, but this never dampened his enthusiasm to know, to understand, and to construct an exuberant and high-spirited vision of the American experience. Because of his deep seriousness of purpose and his solid commitment to this singular subject, Mencken must be regarded not only as one of our great comic writers, but as one of our national sages—not the sage of Baltimore, as popular legend would have it, but of all America. His ideas about his native land are still persuasive, there is a permanence and universality about them, and it is impossible to deny that most of them still have their original force and truth.

II

The Soul of Man
under Democracy

By disposition Mencken was a hearty and genial man who thoroughly savored the color and diversity of American life. He enjoyed living in his native land and relished the passing show; he believed that the artist or writer can thrive pretty well in America if he manages to dwell in the interstices of the social fabric. He also had a deep underlying faith in the imagination, flexibility, and resourcefulness of the American people. Still, his work was predominately a devastating critique of life in America. The question that arises is, why? What's wrong with us? Why haven't we fulfilled our great promise?

There is something stale or flat at the heart of our social life, says Mencken. The hope and possibility of a vivid and audacious national experience still exist, the door remains open to a full flowering of the idea of freedom, but in its actual historical development America has not realized its greatest potentials. There is something wrong with the way that democracy has actually developed, and this leads us away from the kind of America envisioned by the founding fathers—a land of freedom where people may live in peace and harmony with one another.

Freedom for a large segment of any nation's population was never experienced in any period of the world's history. For the tired and careworn nations of Europe there was never the land or the space to permit any kind of freedom of movement, or flexibility in life style. The social structure was harsh and unyielding; everywhere there was restraint without expectation of mobility and personal development.

In America this harsh destiny was obliterated—at least on paper. But built into the very idea of freedom was a defect that would be a source of trouble as soon as people crowded in on one another and the new world became as populous and as frantic as the old. The rigidity of the class structure in the older sense was gone, but it was replaced by other kinds of social lethargy and hostility. Even in the early days of close-knit communities in New England, said Mencken, and certainly since the heavy industrialization of the nineteenth century, Americans never developed a warm and genial sense of community. Americans never learned to tolerate their neighbors, to live with them in harmony. Rather than a society built on trust, we have a society built on suspicion, distrust, and self-aggravation. We pay lip service to the idea that our neighbor ought to be allowed freedom of expression and lifestyle but ceaselessly we are moving in on him, trying to cut down on his own freedom of action and the free play of his ideas. The end result is a deadening, a stultification of the national manners and morals.

Part of the trouble stems from a defect in democratic theory, or a misinterpretation of it. We want people to be free and equal to one another, but we soon forget that freedom must be struggled for, and we mistakenly shift from the concept of equality under the law to another, but false, ideal, namely that men actually are equal in achievement, ability, and natural endowment. Not content with the idea that men should be allowed to realize themselves equally, we move illogically to the notion that men are by personal endowment equal. The denial of a belief in human inequality eventually leads to a hostility toward all kinds of excellence and meritorious achievement. We are a people suspicious of the first-rate; we prefer the spirit of leveling, of egalitarianism.

For Mencken, the citizens of a democratic state deny the harsh but obvious truth that men differ in their mental and

spiritual endowment as they differ in their physical endowment, that there are some men who start out life with superior
mental equipment and are cut out for arduous or heroic deeds,
while there are other men whose minds "never get any further
than a sort of insensate sweating, like that of a kidney." Many
intelligent people acknowledge in a hushed or muted way that
there are degrees of excellence in the human condition, that a
Matthew Arnold is somehow superior to a chiropractor or
taxi driver, but we live in a society which commands alle-
giance to another and quite different proposition, that "all
men are created equal." The framers of our constitution did
not intend that the kind of abstract equality under the law
that they were writing about should progress into a meta-
physical and psychological doctrine about the uniform value
and import of human achievement. The first trouble with this
later distortion of our working national philosophy is that it is
an obvious untruth. There is "no more evidence for the
wisdom of the inferior man, nor for his virtue, than there is for
the notion that Friday is an unlucky day."[1]

A striking fallacy is bound up with the primitive assumptions and beliefs of people in a democracy, and most Americans either refuse to recognize it or are cowed into disguising
it from themselves. Because we live in a democratic society
where everyone's vote is said to be worth as much as everyone
else's, we progress illogically to the belief that everyone's
ideas on any given subject are worth as much as anyone else's
ideas on the same subject. On a practical level we are occasionally forced to admit, let us say, that the doctor knows
more about illness than we do, but we refuse to raise this into
the more general proposition that some people either by
endowment, personal effort, or ultimate achievement, are
superior to other people. Graduations in human excellence are
denied, and products of excellence are objects of suspicion.

Mencken's critique of American civilization is founded on
the assumption that democracy, which appears so harmless
as a naked ideology or legal doctrine, is actually the root of a
kind of infectious disease which spreads throughout our
social and political life. This disease, which proceeds from a
belief that is noble and in every way morally appealing,

manifests itself in a kind of suspicion and distrust of the possibility of levels of human excellence, in a denial of a scale of human value, and eventually in a distrust of other people. Democracy, which is almost universally thought to result in better interpersonal relationships, actually ends in suspicion and hostility; it ultimately undermines the virtues of neighborliness, altruism, and most of the other blessings it is supposed to confer.

Before describing how this disease expresses itself and how it spreads, it may be worth while to say how it arose in America. To Mencken, democratic theory was not part of the intellectual baggage of the founding fathers or the framers of the constitution, but a later accretion—one that has gradually compounded until we have developed a system of democratic beliefs and ideals that would have been unintelligible and frightening to the citizenry at the time of the founding of the republic. The founding fathers were struggling for what they believed to be freedom and independence, not democracy. They wanted to free themselves from the English king, or at any rate from his tax collector, and they wanted to govern themselves. They did not start with a faith in egalitarian democracy; liberty, not democracy, was what motivated them.

The two words are not identical. Liberty is not the same as equality; in fact it is a higher ideal, far more difficult to attain, which is a fact the modern American seems incapable of grasping.

> Liberty means self-reliance, it means enterprise, it means the capacity for doing without. The free man is one who has won a small and precarious territory from the great mob of his inferiors, and is prepared and ready to defend it and make it support him.[2]

Love of liberty requires courage, enterprise, and self-reliance, and these are precisely the qualities democratic man lacks and would like to stamp out. Democratic man does not want to be left alone, he wants to rely on the collective; he wants certainty, sure and simple truth. "Liberty is unfathomable to him. He can no more comprehend it than he can comprehend honor. What he mistakes for it, nine times out of ten, is simply the banal right to empty hallelujahs upon his oppressors."

Libertarianism and egalitarianism are not only dissimilar, they are polar opposites. The democrat, as we observe him today, is scarcely interested in liberty at all and most Americans tend to blur the distinction between freedom and democracy and pretend that they are the same thing. William Graham Sumner, the political economist from Yale who strongly influenced Mencken's thinking, put the distinction clearly and forcefully in one of his numerous essays on the nature of liberty. A democracy, he said, is a belief in the efficacy of the popular vote, in the value of universal suffrage.

> A republic is quite another thing. It is a form of self-government, and its first aim is not equality but civil liberty. It keeps the people active in public functions and public duties; it requires their activity at stated periods when the power of the state has to be re-conferred on new agents. It breaks the continuity of power to guard against its abuse, and it abhors as much the irresponsible power of the many as of the one. . . . Democracy teaches dogmas of absolute and sweeping application, while, in truth, there are no absolute doctrines in politics. Its spirit is fierce, intolerant and despotic. It frets and chafes at constitutional restraints which seem to balk the people of its will and it threatens all institutions, precedents and traditions which, for the moment, stand in the way.[3]

The mob has little or no interest in liberty, at least no interest in the liberty of others. When it fights, says Mencken, it fights not for liberty but for ham and cabbage. When it wins it seeks to destroy every form of freedom that is not directed toward the satisfaction of its immediate desires. Our own founding fathers would today be objects of grave suspicion. A professional libertarian like Thomas Jefferson, says Mencken, had he been living in Paris in 1793, "would have made an even narrower escape from the guillotine than Thomas Paine."

The Washingtons, and Jeffersons, Madisons, Hamiltons, and Adamses seem to us an entirely different breed of men from the present-day American. They had no belief in the wisdom of the mob. They thought that whatever truths or goods there are in the world had to be struggled for by men working alone and independently. Above all, the founding fathers had no illusion that all men are created equal. Equality in their vocabulary referred to abstract rights under the law, not a psychological or anthropological doctrine about the equality of the human mind. Generally they put their faith in a quasi-aristocratic society, a social order much like that of the England from which they broke loose. An aristocratic society, according to Mencken, is one in which the function of govern-ment is left to those who are relatively high on the scale of human merit and achievement, having gotten there "either by their own prowess or by starting from the shoulders of their fathers—which is to say, either by God's grace, or by God's grace." If the early American men of state were suspicious of the rule of the masses it is because they shared Mencken's belief that human excellence is not equally distributed among human kind, and were suspicious of the idea that one man's notion of how the state should be governed is as good as another's.

The democratic ideal according to which political sagacity and intellectual excellence are equally distributed among the human race is a late arrival on the American scene. It must be left to historians to say just when and how it wormed its way in, whether it was the influence of the French Revolution, of the coonskin democracy of Andrew Jackson, or of a number of gradually increasing forces; but by stages we worked our-selves into the belief that one man's views, values, and achievements are as good as another's. However it developed, historically, the democratic weed came into full flower in the nineteenth century, and now touches most advanced nations, although perhaps ours more than others.

By 1828 in America and by 1848 in Europe the doctrine had arisen that all moral excellence, and with it all pure and unfettered sagacity resided in the inferior four-fifths of mankind. In 1867 a philosopher out of the gutter pushed that doctrine to its logical conclusion. He taught that the superior minority had no virutes at all, and hence no rights at all—that the world belonged exclusively and absolutely to those who hewed its wood and drew its water.[4]

Even though we Americans have not in fact accepted the Marxist ideology and the Marxist view of history, we seem to have accepted more of the spirit of Marxism than some other societies which have accepted Marxism in principle but hold to an elitist social structure in fact. Doubtless the clever Frenchman of our own day is right in saying that social revolution is taking place in America, "without Marx and without Jesus." We tend more than any other people on earth to believe in the destinies of egalitarian socialism. More and more, although somewhat slowly, we move toward the belief that the efforts and achievements of all citizens should be rewarded uniformly. Mencken had no sympathy with these views, and believed that all sane and rational societies in the past were guided by men of superior judgment, superior background, superior intelligence—men who were recognized as such. We Americans have pushed our democratic ideals too far, and accordingly we have to suffer all the indignities and inanities of mob rule.

Later we shall consider in more specific detail the effects of democracy on the political process in America. First, however, let us consider Mencken's more general point about the effect of democracy on American life. His objection to the excessive democratization of American life is not solely a political belief; it is a more general spiritual idea with psychological and anthropological underpinnings. Democracy is not just a political disease, but rather a complicated syndrome effecting all kinds of social units, and, of course, the roots of the syndrome can be traced back to the individual himself.

To understand how the collective will operates in a democracy, we must see it as the result of the workings of the ordinary human mind. Democracy is a form of government that presupposes the high intelligence, reasonableness, and good will of the vast majority of people. It was Mencken's contention that high intelligence, reasonableness, and good will are qualities found only in a small portion of the population. A democracy is a government that must respond to the majority of the people, but the majority never rise above the level of adolescence in their mental processes. Their bodies mature and age, and we think of them as adults, but "in the overwhelming main" the populace of any given society is composed "of men and women who have not got beyond the ideas and emotions of childhood. Some few individuals eventually rise to an estate of mental maturity, but the mental age of the majority hovers around the time of puberty, chiefly below it."

The psychologists who have studied the developing child claim that the earliest and most powerful human emotion is fear, and we are going to have to fully understand how this elemental emotion works if we are to grasp the nature of democracy. "Man comes into the world weak, naked, and almost as devoid of intelligence as an oyster," but he brings with him a complex sensitivity which makes him immediately susceptible to the emotion of fear. He can tremble and cry out in the first few minutes of life, said Dr. John B. Watson, the leader of the behaviorist school of psychology. Watson attributed this to a phylogenetic trait, inherited racially from the dark recesses of time—traceable perhaps to the hazards of the arboreal life of early ape-man, to the fear of falling, for example. Whatever the origin of this emotion of fear, says Mencken, it is obviously deep-seated—it is instinctive if anything in man is instinctive. "And all the evidence indicates that every other emotion is subordinate to it." As the infant grows into the child, the fears do not disappear, but continue to grow. The child in time begins to fear ideas as well as things, strange men as well as natural events and happenings. At the age of three, the mental baggage of the child is often little more than a vast storehouse of dreads, trepidations, superstitions, anxieties. As the child grows older it increases its stock of fears and superstitions in this storehouse.

It is the proclaimed business of education and enculturation to rid the child of these fears, but Mencken is dubious of the efficacy of education in genuinely reaching the masses:

The process of education is largely a process of getting rid of . . . fears. It rehearses, after a fashion, the upward struggle of man. The ideal educated man is simply one who has put away as foolish the immemorial fears of the race—of strange men and strange ideas, of the powers and principalities of the air. He is sure of himself in the world; no dread of the dark rides him; he is serene. To produce such men is the central aim of every rational system of education; even under democracy it is one of the aims, though perhaps only a subordinate one. What brings it to futility is simply the fact that the vast majority of men are congenitally incapable of any such intellectual progress. They cannot take in new ideas, and they cannot get rid of old fears. They lack the logical sense; they are unable to reason from a set of facts before them, free from emotional distraction.[5]

In Mencken's eyes the vast majority of individuals in any human society are uneducable in any important sense. Because all men speak and use symbols, we hastily conclude that all are responsive to ideas, to concepts, to abstractions, but this responsiveness is on an exceedingly low plane. The conceptual thinking of most men is done under the influence of a few primitive emotions and appetites, and at a level of low response. "It is thus a sheer impossibility to educate them. . . . The schoolmarm who has at them wastes her time shouting up a rainspout. They are imitative, as many of the lower animals are imitative, and so they sometimes deceive her into believing that her expositions and exhortations have gone home, but a scientific examination quickly reveals that they have taken in almost nothing."[6] The great masses of men are responsive only to emotions or to simple collections of facts.

Naturally it is one of the superstitions of American society that civilization is largely a forward-moving phenomenon, that education and all kinds of social betterment can somehow lift the general level of humanity. Mencken did not share these beliefs. He believed that the number of first-rate men remains constant, that human folly remains constant, and that no amount of breeding or social uplift will change the proportion of human blank cartridges to men of genuine intelligence. He did not base this conviction on any of the Darwinian theories he toyed with over the years, or on principles of eugenics, but on empirical observation. A casual glance at the world around us, he believed, will show us that what passes for progress in modern democratic societies like America is nothing other than a larger number of people having better homes, or a larger number of people decked out in the trappings of education—the educational system simply being cut to measure to fit them. Fifty million college graduates does not mean fifty million educated men, it means only fifty million college graduates. Our society produces outward symbols of progress, of betterment, but there is no evidence that it has produced any more first-rate men than any civilization back to the Neanderthal era. There has always been and probably always will be only a small number of first-rate men, because the vast majority of men in the world are simply not intellignet, not capable of thinking rationally and imaginatively.

The world we live in is a complex one, and afloat in it are many abstract and abstruse ideas and networks of ideas. The average man, of course, is in no way equipped to deal with these high levels of abstraction; he lacks the intellectual apparatus to pass judgment upon them. Since fear is the strongest and most primitive human emotion, his instinct is to cower before these complexities as the jungle simian cowers in the bush when some of his stronger brethren are struggling amongst themselves. Ideas, thoughts, logic are things to be feared, and, on the few occasions that it is necessary to deal with them, the ordinary man does the only thing that comes natural: he reduces them to simpler and more tangible ideas—easy formulas, platitudes, slogans, black and white truisms. These he erects into lofty principles which may be brandished like weapons and used to intimidate the foe who would seek to introduce something new, startling, or complex. Here, then, is the beginning of the road which leads to the development of the mechanism Mencken refers to as the Puritan instinct—fear, no longer the infant's simple fear of noises or of insecure placement on the dressing table, but fear of ideas, of that which challenges habit and which shakes one out of one's lethargy.

There are other emotions which Mencken sees as equally fundamental, even if not quite as primitive as fear. These are emotions which unfold in the development of interpersonal relationships—love and rage or frustration. Mencken shares Freud's belief in the dominance of the sexual instinct in human life. A need for intimacy and warmth is apparent in the early months of life, and the satisfaction or rejection of the need is one of the dominant forces in the development of the human personality. This emotion, in the years of adolescence when it becomes an exaggerated physiological response, runs away with the human personality. Thus far Mencken adds little to Dr. Freud, but Mencken was always concerned with the effect of emotional drives on the whole range of human behavior. Freud, and, in fact, poets and philosophers from time immemorial, have shown how the higher expressions of sages and troubadours are outpourings of the basic sexual drives. Mencken reminds us once again that the world is not populated with sages and troubadors. The average man, on reaching adolescence, is, truthfully, a vast geyser of hormones, but there is no chance that this great outpouring of hormones will result in any supreme work of imagination or ponderous treatise in philosophy. No, the average man will possess the drive, will be overpowered with the emotion, but can do nothing with it. What use is the passion of the farmer, the ice wagon driver, the street car conductor? What happens to the hormones not just in the select few, but in the vast run of humanity? It develops into a capacity for illusions, says Mencken, into "a powerful thirst for the not true." It may well spawn realms of fancy, frenzy, and even a kind of poetry, but these realms are chaotic, formless, incoherent, and irrational. "If you want to discover the content of that poetry go look at any movie, or listen to any popular song. At its loftiest, it is never far from the poetry of the rooster in a barnyard."[7]

Not only do the drives and passions of the average man lead to a low and tawdry kind of poetry, to systems of illusions, delusions and untruths, they lead always to a kind of self-centeredness. The world outside is too large and complex for the average man to deal with, so his thinking always returns to the one thing he can understand—his own immediate wants and desires. "He simply cannot formulate the concept of a good that is not his own good." Any kind of altruism, any noblisse oblige is completely beyond him.

Still, however small in intellectual stature a man may be, he secretly knows that in the world there are degrees of excellence in things. He knows that there are beauties that he cannot appreciate, ideas that he cannot comprehend, science, philosophy, and higher truths and values—but they are all beyond the reach of this average man who lives his days in a world of uninspired truths, lowly facts, simple comings and goings. He has the desire to reach out to this higher world but he cannot do it; his brain is inadequate to the task. He is condemned to frustration, to a feeling of alienation from the higher productions of the human spirit.

Naturally this frustration is kin to another emotion which Mencken also insists is primitive and fundamental in man—rage. Perhaps here again the emotion has a kind of inherited racial component to it. We know that younger or inferior primates of a troop often express rage when they see a superior or dominant male devouring a catch, refusing to share it with the rest. We know in any case that rage is one of the dominant shared emotions of anthropoidia. Again, the root of the emotion is not important, the point is that rage, controlled or uncontrolled, is one of the most important and basic emotions in the human environment.

We can see why it is especially important in Mencken's thinking. In our democratic society, frustration or rage at any sign of inequality or unfair distribution of goods and rewards is naturally going to be a dominant social phenomenon, perhaps the dominant social phenomenon. Once we accept publicly the idea that all people are equal, once we deny (or at any rate attempt to hide from ourselves) the truth of gradation in human merit, we fan the flames of social frustration and build a national social neurosis on it. We become a nation of hostile demanders, always finding someone who has a larger bunch of bananas than we do. Since our democratic ideology has told us that nobody should have a larger bunch of bananas than anyone else, we are enraged by anyone who actually does.

This was not a problem in earlier human societies, or at least the problem was kept in check. In societies where the social structure was more firmly fixed and where the farmer was kept on the farm, the worker in the shop, and neither was exposed to the daily blandishments of politicians, the inequalities and injustices of the world were peacefully taken for granted. Americans have paid dearly for a positive advance over the rigid social systems of the past, with their unequal distributions of the fruits of the economy. In Mencken's thought we have opened the door to other problems that are just as bad, if not worse. In a democratic society the citizen knows no contentment. He is always struggling for something. He gets more, but he wants still more. He is constantly whipping himself into a frenzy of rage whenever he finds someone who has something he doesn't have himself. This does not refer to money or material goods alone. What troubles democratic man the most is that he cannot abide excellence in ideas or respect superiority of achievement in any department of learning. He may sluggishly respect the achievement of a Henry Ford (although he would also miss no opportunity to dip into his wallet in the name of reform or progress), or perhaps the fame of some noted surgeron, but the respect is grudging, sluggish, ungenerous—and it is not likely to extend to the poet or violin player at all.

The perpetual mental state of democratic man is thus one of envy of his fellowmen. Envy is really a kind of devious refinement, a subtilization of the emotion of rage. Envy is a condition of smoldering hatred of someone who has something better or who enjoys life more. "The peasant hates; ergo, he envies." Enraged whenever he sees someone enjoying something he himself does not enjoy, the ordinary man works himself into a passionate state of envy. Envy, of course, always involves inner recognition of superiority and excellence—otherwise there would be nothing to envy—but it is accompanied by outward denial of such. The ordinary man knows instinctively and uneasily that Beethoven can write string quartets that are beautiful, although he himself cannot; he knows, if somebody takes the trouble to put it to him, that Professor Einstein has a greater gift for mathematics than he.

He would be a Beethoven or Einstein if he could, but alas, he cannot; his mind lacks the capacity. All he can do is envy, which means he can inwardly wish that he were a Beethoven or an Einstein, or, for that matter, a Ford or Rockefeller, but publicly he must deny that these people are intrinsically more important or valuable than he. The democratic man's first instinct is always to bring the other fellow down to his own level.

Envy, rage against one's betters, has always been a part of the psyche of the masses. In a democracy this emotion is stirred up in the people; the politicians take delight in it and pander to it whenever possible. A large percentage of the laws enacted in Washington or in the state legislatures have little impetus behind them but to cater to the primitive urgings of envy and the desire of the man in the street to thrive and prosper at the expense of someone else.

This attitude of Mencken's is clearly displayed in his essay "The Husbandman," perhaps the best known and the most brilliant of his "prejudices." What are we told about the husbandman, the humble farmer, in our civics books, what do we read about him in the *Congressional Record?* We read that he is the "Ur-burgher, the citizen *par excellence*, the foundation stone of the state." We are told that this mundane laborer scratching for the dollar, smelling heavily of sweat and dung (let us be realistic—the follower of the plow is not Thomas Jefferson dreaming his agrarian dream at Monticello) is the backbone, indeed the heart of our republic. The farmer is praised by all who mention him from congressmen to archbishops, "for his industry, his frugality, his patriotism, his altruistic passion. He is praised for staying on the farm, for laboriously wringing our bread and meat from the reluctant soil, for renouncing Babylon to guard the horned cattle on the hills. . . . He takes on, in political speeches and newspaper editorials, a sort of mystical character." He is inflated to lyrical and heroic proportions. "To murmur against him becomes a sort of sacrilege, like murmuring against the Constitution, Human Freedom, the cause of Democracy."[8]

The truth is that to see heroic proportions in the farmer, or any run-of-the-mill distribution of human protoplasm for that matter, is to make once again the democratic fallacy which Mencken sought to lay bare. There is no evidence to suport the assumption that the farmer is a good citizen, nay, the citizen *par excellence*. Only one issue ever interests or fetches him, and that is the issue of his own profit. He must be promised something definite and valuable, to be paid to him alone, or he is off after some other mountebank. He simply cannot imagine himself as a citizen of a commonwealth, in duty bound to give as well as take; he can imagine himself only as getting all and giving nothing."[9] The farmer—the average man—is not, as the myth would have it, a solid citizen or a man of altruism, but a grabber and a self-seeker.

In our society with its political mountebanks always promising, always offering some reward out of the public till, the farmer is a man who constantly feeds and replenishes his own fires of envy, so that he not only spends his days thinking of ways to get more for himself, he is perpetually working himself into a fury over what other people are getting that he is not. Thus it is not quite true that the only idea he can grasp is one which promises him a direct and immediate profit. He can also grasp an idea which has as its chief effect the annoying and hurting of other citizens—most often his enemy the city man.

After the politicians get to Washington and fulfill their promise to augment the farmer's gains and make good his losses, they "devote whatever time is left over to saddling the rest of us with oppressive and idiotic laws, all hatched on the farm." What is Prohibition, for example, but "the voodooism of country Methodists, nine-tenths of them actual followers of the plow." What is at the bottom of Prohibition? Not, says Mencken, any altruistic yearning to put down the evils of drink. Most of the state enforcement acts, even the Volstead Act, permit the farmer to make cider as in the past. No, he is not against the use of alcohol *per se*, but simply the use of alcohol in its more charming and romantic forms." His Prohibition statutes have only the effect of forcing the city man "to drink such dreadful stuff as the farmer has always drunk." Their ultimate aim is to bring someone else down to his own level.

So it is with the innumerable other moral statutes, "all ardently supported by the peasantry." Their intent is to injure, to damage the fellow who is enjoying something they are not. There was the Mann Act, the intent of which was to put a damper on sexual practices by city folk while leaving those of the farms untouched. There are laws in some of the middle western states "forbidding the smoking of cigarettes, for cigarette smoking to the louts of those wastes, bears the aspect of a citified and levantine vice." There are no laws forbidding the chewing of tobacco, and farmers frequently chew—and spit—at divine service. Chewing "not only lies within their tastes; it also lies within their means, and hence within their mores."[10] So it is with the Comstock enforcements against writing and works of literature. Comstockery is seldom employed against newspapers, for the printed matter of newspapers usually lies within the comprehension of the peasantry, and therefore is in their sphere of enjoyment.

> Nor is it often invoked against cheap books of a frankly pornographic character—such things as "Night Life in Chicago," "Adventures on a Pullman Sleeper" and "The Confessions of an ex-Nun"—for when the yokels read at all, it is commonly such garbage that they prefer. But they are hot against the infinitely less gross naughtiness of serious books, including the so-called classics, for these books they simply cannot read. In consequence the force of comstockery is chiefly directed against such literature.[11]

The specific context here, Mencken's diatribe against the farmer, seen in the ambience of the 1920s, with Comstockery, Prohibition, and the Methodist preacher still on the stage, is not what is at issue. The issue is democratic man—farmer or otherwise. The democratic man suffers from pangs of envy; envy disrupts his thinking and distorts his every rational process. Democratic man is always troubling to find out what others are getting, not only so he can have some for himself, but so he can spoil what others may have. The dominant mood of democratic man is puritanism. Indeed, as Mencken was inclined to observe, puritanism is the twin of democracy—the other side of the coin.

The notion of puritanism is central to Mencken's critique of American life. Puritanism is the very name and essence of the democratic disease, and if we are to grasp the main drift of his social philosophy we must clearly understand how he conceives and uses this term. Puritanism is a recurring malady which takes on a number of different manifestations: it is recognized chiefly by its form, not its content.

In Mencken's writings the term "puritanism" functions rhetorically. While it has a fairly circumscribed meaning, it is not intended to be an historical term in the usual sense. One repeatedly finds Mencken being chastized for failing to prove that the Puritanism of early New England has something to do with the puritanism of our own time. Mencken was not a tracer of doctrines; his conception of puritanism was never offered as an exercise in the history of ideas, and to search for such in his work is to chase after a chimera. The specific doctrines or ideologies of this or that puritanism may or may not be related in detail; on this question Mencken never bothered to expound. He merely insisted that the style of social life in a democracy remains constant.

Part of the difficulty in explaining Mencken's notion of puritanism is that the word has, since the 1920s, gone out of fashion as a term of social criticism. In the first three decades of the twentieth century the term was in continual use by American intellectuals; as early as 1903 George Santayana had been trying to show, from the perspective of a detached newcomer, the persistence of puritan tendencies in American life, and Van Wyck Brooks (in his *Wine of the Puritans* of 1908) shortly followed suit. By the time Vernon L. Parrington's *Main Currents of American Thought* appeared in 1927, the use of the term to describe a complex network of American intellectual trends had been long established. Indeed it might have been the overuse of the term for historical analysis in writings like Parrington's that led to its disappearance.

For Mencken puritanism and democracy are the same thing, or, perhaps we could say, they have the same root. Democracy is a condition of life in which people are set to worrying whether somebody somewhere is enjoying things that they are not, and take action to see that they don't. This is what Puritanism is also.

> The two, indeed, are but different facets of the same gem. In the psyche they are one. For both get their primal essence out of the inferior man's fear and hatred of his betters, born of his observation that, for all his fine theories, they are stronger and of more courage than he is, and that as they go through this dreadful world they have a far better time. Thus envy comes in; if you overlook it you will never understand democracy and you will never understand Puritanism. It is not, of course, a specialty of democratic man. It is the common possession of all men of the ignoble and incompetent sort, at all times and everywhere. But it is only under democracy that it is liberated; it is only under a democracy that it becomes the philosophy of the state.[12]

Naturally puritanism, which we might call the hyperthyroidism of democracy, manifests itself in the workings of the state, but it also reaches into all areas of the common life — into morals, business, religion, the arts and so on. As the tendency toward egalitarian democracy is aggravated, the tendency toward puritanism is also aggravated. In Mencken's eyes, the conception of puritanism as an attitude and mood of early New England which lingers here and there in American life is mistaken; puritanism is on the rise wherever democracy is on the rise; in the twentieth century we have more puritanism than we had in the eighteenth. This seems paradoxical as long as we continue to think of puritanism as defined in terms of specific restraints on conduct, or an individual set of beliefs. Mencken gives a more universal scope and use to this concept. The old beliefs and the old ways of spoiling the neighbors' fun die off, but puritanism remains to work its evils in new ways and the new ways are more troublesome than the old. Mencken discovered many more effects of the puritan blight in the 1920s than he did in reading history books about the eighteenth century. In truth, he never spent much of his time poking fun at the founders of New England, although he makes occasional reference to them. In general he seems actually to have looked on the eighteenth century in a rather favorable light. He found our founding fathers to be straightforward thinkers, with few foolish or empty ideal- isms rattling around in their heads; strong masculine types, with little faith in the efficacy of the weak and the unin- telligent. George Washington, for example, spawned by the tobacco aristocracy of the Old Dominion, was a model early American man. Mencken wrote of him that he had

> a liking for all forthright and pugnacious men, and a contempt for all lawyers, platitudinarians and other such fact-dodgers. He was not pious. He drank red liquor whenever he felt chilly, and kept a jug of it handy. He knew far more profanity than Scripture, and used and enjoyed it more. He had no faith in the infallible wisdom of the common people, and did his best to save the country from it. He advocated no sure cure for all the sorrows of the world. He took no interest in the private morals of his neighbors.[13]

By 1915, conditions were much different and we find Men- cken writing in the *Smart Set* that poor Washington "would be ineligible for any public office of honor or profit." The uplift magazines would be after him as would the yellow journals. "The suffragettes would be on his trail threatening him with their black-list." The prohibitionists would be denouncing him because he kept a still at Mount Vernon, and so on. No, puritanism is generally on the rise in America, not on the decline. By the 1920s, the era of the flivver and the flapper, the years when most of the old restraints seemed to be blowing out to sea—or at least so the historians liked to tell us— Mencken, like most of his contemporary intellectuals, was finding "an encroaching shadow of gloom." All around he was finding new outcroppings of puritanism, new forms of rigidity in manners and morals. Writing in *The Nation* in 1922, Mencken was observing that regimentation in morals, in political theory, in every department of thought has brought with it a stiffening, almost a deadening in manners, so that the old goatishness of the free democrat ... has got itself exchanged for a timorous reserve, a curious psychical flabbiness, an almost complete incapacity for innocent joy. To be happy takes on the character of the illicit; it is jazz, spooning on the back seat, the follies, dancing without corsets, wood alcohol.[14]

Sinclair Lewis was one of those who shared Mencken's doubt that every day we are getting better and better—as Coué was teaching in the twenties—and he rendered his doubt in the form of the satirical novel. What, after all, is the point of *Main Street* or *Babbitt* but to show that American society has no breathing room in it, that Americans permit themselves to be constantly pressed back into some common and acceptable mold, and that only mediocrity is allowed to thrive and prosper, all other achievement having to justify and fight for itself? Always present in Lewis's work is the notion that the community is there not to further spiritual growth, but to insure uniformity and sameness. Here, for example, in a particularly outrageous but majestic lampoon, was part of Mr. George F. Babbitt's speech to the annual dinner of the Zenith Real Estate Board:

> "With all modesty, I want to stand up here as a representative businessman and gently whisper, 'Here's our kind of folks! Here's the specifications of the Standardized American Citizen! Here's the new generation of Americans: fellows with hair on their chests and smiles in their eyes and adding machines in their offices! . . .' So! In my clumsy way I have tried to sketch the Real He-man, the fellow with Zip and Bang. And its because Zenith has such a large proportion of such men that its the most stable, the greatest of our cities. New York also has its thousands of Real Folks, but New York is cursed with unnumbered foreigners. So are Chicago and San Francisco. Oh, we have a golden roster of cities—Detroit and

Cleveland with their renowned factories. Cincinnati with its great machine-tool and soap products. Pittsburgh and Birmingham with their steel, Kansas City and Minneapolis and Omaha that open their bountiful gates on the bosom of the ocean-like wheatlands, and countless other magnificent sister-cities, for, by the last census, there were no less than sixty-eight American burgs with a population of over one hundred thousand! And all these cities stand together for power and purity, and against foreign ideas and communism.... A good live wire from Baltimore, or Seattle or Duluth is the twin brother of every like fellow booster from Buffalo or Akron, Fort Worth or Oskaloosa!"[15]

Perhaps Babbitt as an individual animal never really existed, but the buzz of the same mentality could be heard at a somewhat lesser volume anywhere in America in 1925. At least this is what writers like Mencken and Lewis were finding—Lewis in his satirical novels, Mencken in his *Prejudices* and in the choice selections of "Americana" in the *American Mercury*. Both believed that save for a few enclaves of learning in cosmopolitan centers, this is what America was about. Americans were a people of truncated imagination, and standardized patterns of behavior, always ready to crush the unconventional in thinking, put down all products of the free-wheeling imagination—a people essentially mirthless and joyless, who could force themselves to a little artificial "fun" when called for by convention, but ever willing and anxious to stamp out the fun of other people when it doesn't fit into any of the accepted forms.

"Puritanism" was the generic term that Mencken gave to this social disease. Perhaps a more fitting term might have been found, or at least one without distracting historical connotations. Mencken wanted to stress the malicious animus of the disease, its outward flowing nature, and for this reason the term "puritanism" turned out to be a particularly fortunate addition to his vocabulary. His most often quoted definition of "puritanism" was that it is "the haunting fear that someone, somewhere may be happy." The mind of the puritan does not focus on the self and on the individual's own work and activities, rather it focuses on the doings of others.

The puritan, as we have already said, is hostile to excellence, most especially to any kind of intellectual excellence. He is against intellectuality "because it is complex, . . . because it puts an unbearable burden upon his meagre capacity for taking in ideas. . . . His search is always for short cuts, simple formulae, revelation." Furthermore, if someone is found who has knowledge of histology, or philology, or palentology, he seems to the puritan to be a ridiculous figure, with a touch of the sinister. Learning survives among us, concludes Mencken, largely because the mob has not yet got wind of it. "If the notions it turns loose descended to the lowest levels, there would be an uprising against them, and efforts would be made to put them down by law."[16] Knowledge is safe in the republic as long as it is well concealed. When the mob discovered that evolution was being taught in the schools, when it was stirred up by the mountebanks of the pulpit, all hell broke loose in the boondocks. Of course evolution has been an accepted fact among biologists for generations, and had long been taught in biology classes in the universities, but the intellectual community managed to keep it a secret. Knowledge is tolerated in America only as long as it is so arcane or specialized that the average man can't be troubled to acquire it, or otherwise so innocuous that the platitudes and simple formulas of the populace are not threatened.

The puritan has no love of beauty, and is hostile to anyone who creates it. This is because he lacks the talent and capacity to create it himself. He reads no works of literature and is suspicious of anyone who writes them. "No Puritan has ever painted a picture worth looking at, or written a symphony worth hearing, or a poem worth reading—and I am not forgetting John Milton, who was not a Puritan at all, but a libertarian, which is the exact opposite."[17] Works of art, like great contributions in science and philosophy, require a high level of intelligence, an active and fertile imagination, gusto, and bravura. Of all such qualities the man of average mind is suspicious, and, when confronted by them, angry and resentful.

The Puritan himself is not a producer. He cannot be, as the artist usually is, wrapped up in his work, so that his small quantum of human drive is turned outward. The puritan has a pathological preoccupation with the activities of other people. Doubtless it is this quality above all others that warrants the frequency of the word "Puritan" in Mencken's writing.

Connected with this is the puritan's desire to punish and harm those who in some way do not conform to expected habits of behavior. Of course the puritan always tries to convince himself (and the rest of us) that the aim of puritan legislation "is grounded on altruistic and evangelical motives. . . . Such is the theory behind Prohibition, comstockery, vice crusading, and all its other familiar devices of oppression. That theory, of course, is false. The Puritan's actual motives are (a) to punish the other fellow for having a better time in the world, and (b) to bring the other fellow down to his own unhappy level."[18]

The puritan is infatuated with politics and is a hopeless believer in political remedies. He is a democrat, which means that he has no interest in freedom and liberty, except of course his own or the few others he favors. Liberty is too painful, too much of a burden. He may "mouth the phrases, as he did in Jefferson's day, but he cannot take in the underlying realities." The pangs of liberty "make him uncomfortable; they alarm him; they fill him with a great loneliness. There is no high adventurousness in him, but only fear. He not only doesn't long for liberty; he is quite unable to stand it. What he longs for is something different, to wit, security."[19] If it is not liberty that the puritan longs for, what is he seeking in the political realm? He wants his own platitudes and prejudices upheld and his special interests catered to.

The main flaw in the puritan democracy of which we are so proud is that it does little to develop good citizenship. "The democrat, despite his strong opinion to the contrary, is seldom a good citizen. . . . His eagerness to bring all his fellow-citizens, and especially all those who are superior to him into accord with his own dull and docile way of thinking, and to force it upon them when they resist, leads him inevitably into acts of unfairness, oppression and dishonor which, if all men alike were guilty of them, would quickly break down that mutual trust and confidence upon which the very structure of civilized society rests."[20] The basic fault in the puritan democrat is that his preoccupation with other people's habits and doings, other people's acquisitions, drain him of the milk of human kindness, of the generosity of the truly civilized man.

This irreconcilable antagonism between democratic Puritanism and common decency is probably responsible for the uneasiness and unhappiness that are so marked in American life, despite the great material prosperity of the United States. Theoretically, the American people should be happier than any other; actually, they are probably the least happy in Christendom. The trouble with them is that they do not trust one another—and without mutual trust there can be no ease, and no genuine happiness. What avails it for a man to have money in the bank and a Ford in his garage if he knows that his neighbors on both sides are watching him through knotholes, and that the pastor of the tabernacle down the road is planning to have him sent to jail? The thing that makes life charming is not money, but the society of our fellow men, and the thing that draws us toward our fellow men is not admiration for their inner virtues, their hard striving to live according to the light that is in them, but admiration for their outer graces and decencies—in brief, confidence that they will always act generously and understandingly in their intercourse with us. We must trust men before we may enjoy them. Manifestly, it is impossible to put any such trust in a Puritan. With the best intentions in the world he cannot rid himself of the delusion that his duty to save us from our sins—i.e., from the non-Puritanical acts that we delight in—is paramount to his duty to let us be happy in our own way. Thus he is unable to be tolerant, and with tolerance goes magnanimity. A Puritan cannot be magnanimous.[21] This is the very heart of Mencken's case against the puritan democrat.

One last characteristic of the puritan that is stressed repeatedly in Mencken's writing is joylessness. The puritan is largely humorless (he may of course laugh and tell jokes), by which is meant that he is incapable of perceiving the irony of his own views and patterns of behavior, incapable of bringing his own ideas and dogmas into question or laughing at these views. This tendency can be seen best in our thinking about our professions: for the doctor there may well be something worth scoffing at in the crookedness of lawyers, but medicine itself must be taken with complete reverence and deadly seriousness. One's personal and professional life is rigid and immovable; about these things we can never laugh. The puritan just doesn't seem to enjoy life. Happiness to the modern puritan comes from standardized and conventional forms of entertainment—"spooning on the back seat, wood alcohol," or, in our own time sitting before the TV watching a football game or private eye show, or joining in the chatter of a cocktail party. The "fun" of life in America has to be pre-packaged, commercially imported from outside the self, which is the same thing as saying that it is not really fun at all. It takes imagination to have fun, and the ordinary man is not possessed of imagination in any substantial degree. Even if a modicum of it were to be found in him, his preoccupation with the habits and doings of his neighbors and his struggle to live up to the conventions and standards of the mob would take up so much of his time that he would have little opportunity to exercise it.

The Origins of Mencken's Social Philosophy

Mencken liked to think of himself as a critic of ideas; philosophy in the narrow sense held little interest for him, and he generally expressed disdain for the fruits of highly abstract thought. "A horselaugh is worth a thousand syllogisms," he once said, clearly cutting himself off from any firm connections with formal philosophy and the history of ideas. Still, his critique of democracy, his notions of the puritan, do seem to have antecedents; they can be located in the intellectual milieu in which he grew to maturity in the first quarter of the twentieth century.

First, and most importantly for our purposes, Mencken's world view was shaped by the intellectual cross-currents of the Darwinian revolution. His ideas about democracy and human society were aligned with professional philosophers who were at the center of the stage in these years—philosophers as diverse as Nietzsche, Dewey, James, Bergson, Whitehead, each of whom had a distinctly biological flavor to his thinking, and were, in one way or another, responding to the Darwinian intellectual revolution.

Before the Darwinian revolution there was no lack of debate over the nature of mind, intelligence, and society, but this debate was all within the traditional framework of Western philosophy which began with the assumption that man is a rational animal, standing apart from all other animals and from the world of nature. The Darwinian explosion, however, upset all the old theoretical applecarts, and forced a new look at man from a number of different perspectives. Since man now came to be seen as an integral part of the natural world, not as a creature set apart from it metaphysically, new sciences rapidly appeared which attempted to consider man as part of the natural order—sciences like psychology and sociology. From every direction came attacks on Aristotle's sublime *animale rationale.* There was a sudden shift to empirical and scientific studies which looked into primitive language, myth and ritual, into the taxonomic relations of man with the lower animals, into man's own psyche and unconscious mind, and into irrational and abnormal social behavior,

No modern philosopher devoted himself more assiduously to understanding man the social animal than Friedrich Nietzsche. While he was still a young man Mencken fell under the influence of Nietzsche and appropriated a number of his ideas. Mencken's second book—published in 1908 and entitled *The Philosophy of Friedrich Nietzsche*—became the seedbed of many of his own later ideas. The book has never been highly regarded as a treatment of Nietzsche, but it opens a window on Mencken. Carl Bode has observed that Mencken's youthful exposition of Nietzsche makes interesting reading for the student of Mencken because it was stocked with themes that he would later develop in his major works. "The section on Christianity would be the seed for *Treatise on the Gods*, the section on women the seed for *In Defense of Women*, and the section on government the seed for some of *Notes on Democracy*."[22]

Nietzsche, more than anyone else of his time, was a psycho-pathologist of human culture, and it was in this role that Mencken discovered Nietzsche and sought to follow in his footsteps. Mencken also thought of himself as a pathologist of American society, and since American society is an extension of European society with many of the major European institutions retained in essentially the same form it is not at all unusual that Mencken should have preserved many of his early mentor's ideas, although he always applied them more specifically and without Nietzsche's philosophical apparatus. Mencken lacked Nietzsche's gift for abstract thought, but he more than made up for this in his own brilliant gift for highly particularized observation. He brought a thoroughly American approach and style to the ideas of the wearied and sorrowful German.

Nietzsche would have had a strong appeal to Mencken by virtue of his eruptive, oracular style and his iconoclasm; in addition, the foundation of Nietzsche's philosophy was a critique of German life as it confronted him in the late nineteenth century. Nietzsche was from the beginning—here again like Mencken—a foe of middle class life and middle class morality; he saw the drift toward egalitarian democracy as nothing but a decay of classical European civilization. The fall from the great heights of Greco-Roman civilization Nietzsche believed to be the mischievous work of Christianity and other emasculated forms of morality; the decline from the glories of Greece and Rome had surely begun with the spread of Christianity, and later democracy and middle class values had doubly corrupted the common life of the people, preparing for the growth of weak and spineless values in art, morality, politics, indeed, in all departments of life.

Nietzsche began his career with a shocking and sensational book, *The Birth of Tragedy*. Its thesis ran counter to the current interpretation of classical Greek culture—promulgated by such figures as Goethe and Winklemann—which attributed to the Greeks a cool, statuesque serenity, a detached reasonableness. This picture Nietzsche attacked with fury; the greatness of the Greeks in his mind was not their serenity but their hard and stern sense of reality, their ability to encounter the world head-on, without the intermediacy of corrupting philosophies and institutions.

Nietzsche analyzed Greek civilization in terms of the art of tragedy and pagan religion. The Greeks—here Nietzsche meant the early Greeks—worshipped both the calm all-seeing, all-knowing Apollo, patron of the arts, God of Symmetry and orderliness; and also Dionysus, the God of intoxication, frenzy, orgy, ecstasy, a god who, unlike Apollo, suffered and died like man. The art of tragedy mirrored these two primal forces of Greek religion. Greek tragedy fused the raw stuff of life in all its striving and suffering with the beautiful form of art. It gave form, balance, harmony to that which is savage, disorderly, turbulant.

With the coming of the rationalistic philosophies of Socrates and Plato, there began a decline of Greek civilization. No longer were the Dionysian and Apollonian spirits fused as they were at the zenith of Greek culture; instead they came to stand in opposition to one another, and the Apollonian, instead of giving form, articulation, order and symmetry to the Dionysian spirit, supplanted and suppressed it. The philosophies of Socrates, Plato, and Aristotle were overintellectualized; logic and analysis developed at the expense of emotional, imaginative activities, with Plato going so far in his *Republic* as to suggest that poets and artists needed to be kept under scrutiny lest they interfere with the "truth-seeking" and the "good-doing" of the philosopher.

Nietzsche turned the tables by suggesting that it was the artist, not the philosopher, who stands above his fellowmen and who is the master of wisdom, beauty and truth. The artist does not need to deal with reality by subduing it; rather he accepts all the Dionysiac and daemonic urges and transforms them into some definite form. Art is yea-saying, it reacts positively to life; it glories in all the turbulence, terror, and grandeur of the world; it does not attempt to hide it or take possession of it. The aesthetic, then, as opposed to the purely intellectual, is the proper realm for the man of strength. The philosopher who builds systems of thought is building systems of defense whereby he may hide from the coldness and sternness of reality. His position is one of weakness, not of strength. The artist, on the other hand, faces the world as directly as possible; he is not afraid of things in the universe and is willing to speak of that which frightens or terrifies the ordinary person.

As Nietzsche's thought developed he saw that Western civilization had received an even more cruel blow than that dealt it by the overintellectualizing philosophers. Beside the Socratic search for logical reasons to explain the spontaneous, bizarre, and violent action found both in nature and human life, Christianity adds another unfortunate ingredient—a demand for moral justification. The dual workings of Socratic intellect and Christian conscience brought about an insufferable deadening, a flattening of Western civilization. Not only was the spirit of Dionysus mercilessly killed off, what remained of Apollo was completely assimilated to the effeminate, life-denying Judeo-Christian God.

The wrath of Nietzsche's later work was mostly directed against Christian ethics, the many forms of "slave morality" that have grown up in the wake of Christianty. Christian morality is the work of creatures too meek to face life as it is; they want protection against the world and their fellowmen. Slave morality is a way for the weak to assert themselves at the expense of the strong. They are too feeble, too flabby of intellect and will to work out their own salvation. Thus they preach—and attempt to enforce through the powers of the state and the social order—humility, meekness, docility; they oppose and persecute freedom of thought and action, pleasure, and art.

Slave morality is founded on resentment and jealousy. The weak are suspicious and distrustful of the man of strength and human powers they do not themselves possess. It is aimed at keeping the superior man in subjugation. Nietzsche traces the origin of this kind of slave morality in Western civilization to the ancient Jews who had to compensate for

their inability to stand up to their enemies by calling them
sinners and evil-doers, thereby trying to capture for themselves virutes that they did not have. Naturally this "morality
of weakness" was transferred to Christianity (through the
agency not of Jesus—a man after Nietzsche's own heart—but
the cowardly St. Paul) and, with the spread of Christianity, to
the whole of European civilization.

Nietzsche agreed with the Darwinists that life was largely a
matter of struggle for existence, but he strongly opposed the
notion that the struggle is a matter of a given organism
adapting itself to its environment, especially since by adapta-
tion many of the Darwinists implied submission. In Herbert
Spencer's thinking, for example, the doctrine of the survival
of the fittest meant that the individuals and the species most
likely to survive were those that most completely surrendered
to their environment. Nietzsche saw in this the tendency to
sneak Judeo-Christian moral concepts into the reading of
nature. In Nietzsche's version of evolution the fittest are not
those individuals and species which surrender to the environment, but those which struggle against the environment.
Nietzsche could see no hope for human advancement unless
man pits himself against the environment and forces it to
bend to his will. Most men do not want such a struggle; they
want easy assimilation, the shelters of protecting institutions, tender-hearted philosophies, and life in a world of
dreams. According to Nietzsche only the man who exercises
his will to power will have any hope of advancing the human
condition. Such a man Nietzsche called Übermensch—Superman.

This concept of a superman, as well as books with titles like
The Will to Power seem to foreshadow German nationalism,
storm troopers, and other such twentieth century horrors. But
the true Superman, the man who could take responsibility for
advancing the human condition, would not be an enforcer and
glorifier of the values of the state, but rather a human being
who stands apart from settled and stale institutions, a man
capable of living fully and deeply by himself, of living more
exuberantly, of enjoying and suffering more intensely, of
"transvaluating" more values, of breaking more icons, of

hurling more blasts at the shibboleths and platitudes of the day. Such a superman hardly needs to be a man of physical force; he might just as well be soft and contemplative in thought and action. His strength is strength of soul and character. The Superman is not the soldier or the enforcer of right, but, the artist, the strong independent thinker, the disturber of the intellectual peace—the iconoclast.

On these points a fundamental intellectual harmony between Mencken and Nietzsche ought to be evident. Like Nietzsche, Mencken believed that humanity is presently overburdened with the dead weight of a motionless, sluggish slave class—individuals who seek only to survive in comfort and who offer no strength, courage and invention in the world. Like Nietzsche, Mencken believed that for civilization to advance there needs to be an elite *creative* class. Both believed "that an ideal human society would be one in which these two classes of men were evenly balanced—in which a vast, inert, religious, moral slave class stood beneath a small, alert, iconoclastic, immoral, progressive master class."[23] In using the word class, neither Nietzsche nor Mencken was referring to class in any of the customary senses; neither had an abiding faith in aristocracies either of the landed or commercial variety. They referred to an aristocracy of the spirit.

Under ideal conditions, the human pack would be led by men of evident intellectual superiority to the masses. To this class of men (perhaps we should say group of men to avoid the usual social connotation) belongs the advancement of mankind.

> To this highest caste belongs the privilege of representing beauty, happiness and goodness on earth. . . . Its members accept the world as they find it and make the most of it. . . . They find their happiness in those things which, to lesser men, would spell ruin—in the labyrinth, in severity toward themselves and others, in effort. Their delight is self-governing: with them asceticism becomes naturalness, necessity, instinct. A difficult task is regarded by them as privilege; to play with burdens which would crush others to death is their recreation. They are the

most venerable species of men. They are the most cheer-
ful, the most amiable. They rule because they are what
they are. They are not at liberty to be second in rank.[24]

The difficulty in obtaining a favorable balance between the
aristocracy of the spirit and the inert classes is that the dead
weight of the latter is so overwhelming that the potential
aristocrat is pulled down, kept from the soaring heights he
might hope to attain. There are still those who can and will
succeed—and every advancement in the human condition
depends upon their succeeding—but always there is the
strong pull of inertness.

As a philosopher of human experience Mencken is to a
much greater extent then Nietzsche a student of these dead
weights of culture and society. Indeed this is what Mencken's
writing is all about. He is an historian of social inertness, a
phenomenologist of the multitudinous forms of social inhibi-
tion and lethargy. His field of study is more narrowly circumscribed than Nietzsche's since he is an Americanist, but,
within these confines, his writing is much more detailed and
penetrating. Mencken is a collector of the dead artifacts with
which the American cultural landscape is cluttered. To be
sure, he also devotes time and energy to pointing the road to
recovery, but in the main he is largely a critic of what there is.

When we inquire exactly what this deadness and inertness
is, how it happens to be present in the universe, we again find
the answer in the language of biology and in the traditions
which grew out of the Darwinian revolution. In his reading of
Nietzsche, Mencken came to see that much of this deadness
and inertness is the product of historical traditions of long
duration in Western civilization. Mencken was also convinced that these stultifying tendicies are partly due to the
nature of man as an animal, and that they can be explained by
reference to psychological and anthropological findings. Men
are not all alike; there is no standard normative rational
animal as Aristotle believed, and, above all, men are not equal
in their intellectual and spiritual equipment; they differ
among themselves as much as one species of animals differs
from another. Some men are naturally more intelligent than

others, made for creative and imaginative thought, whereas others are incapable of anything but the most lethargic and unadventuresome thinking.

> Of one mind we may say with some confidence that it shows an extraordinary capacity for function and development—that its possessor, exposed to a suitable process of training, may be trusted to acquire the largest body of knowledge and the highest skill at ratiocination to which *Homo sapiens* is adapted. Of another we may say with the same confidence that its abilities are sharply limited. . . .[25]

There are very definite gradations among humans, and only a very small number are capable of exerting any vital influence on the world. All humans grow to adulthood and give the deceptive appearance of intelligence. Perhaps because they have language, perhaps because they are "God's creatures," perhaps because history has it that they differ from all the other animals by virtue of the capacity to reason, we have come to believe in the universality of human rationality. But it was Mencken's belief that actual observations show that there is no such universal human rationality. "Some men can learn almost indefinitely; their capacity goes on increasing until their bodies begin to wear out. Others stop in childhood, even in infancy. They reach, say, the mental age of ten or twelve, and then they develop no more. Physically they become men and sprout beards, political delusions and the desire to propagate their kind. But mentally they remain on the level of schoolboys."[26]

If this is true, we can see that one of the obvious reasons for the lethargy and tameness of social and cultural institutions is the large number of unproductive, dispirited and dull-witted people. Weak and spineless institutions are the product of weak and spineless individuals, or, more precisely, the individual and society sustain each other's vices and weaknesses. For Mencken, the man of inferior intellect and spiritual equipment is vulnerable to all sorts of aberrations and untruths; he is receptive to all kinds of deceits and delusions;

he is easily tricked and cozened; his appetite for nonsense and foolishness is great, while his appetite for the complex and the true is small and weak.

> Man on the lower levels, though he quickly reaches the limit of his capacity for taking in actual knowledge, remains capable for a long time thereafter of absorbing delusions. What is true daunts him, but what is not true finds lodgment in his cranium with so little resistance that there is only a trifling emission of heat. . . . The thinking of what Charles Richet calls *Homo stultus* is almost entirely in terms of palpable nonsense. He has a dreadful capacity for embracing and cherishing impostures. His history since the first records is a history of successive victimizations—by priests, by politicians, by all sorts and conditions of quacks. His heroes are always frauds. In all ages he has hated bitterly the men who were laboring most honestly and effectively for the progress of the race. What such men teach is beyond his grasp. He believes in consequence that it is unsound, immoral and of the devil.[27]

Individual men, very much like the great fabrications of social life from which they spring, are inclined to fall back on fossilized ideas. If Nietzsche was right that through the centuries Western civilization has selected those strains of thought with the least life force in them, and that it maintains these in good health in order to crush adventurous, exuberant, image-shattering thought and action, it is certainly because the vast majority of men are afraid of strong new ideas. Most men want a soft bed of safe and comfortable truths and platitudes to lie upon. Some very few, remarked Mencken, scale the dizziest heights. "But the great majority never get very far from the ground. There they struggle for a while, and then give it up. The effort is too much for them; it doesn't seem to be worth its agonies. Golf is easier; so is joining Rotary; so is fundamentalism; so is osteopathy; so is Americanism."[28]

Like Nietzsche—perhaps even more than Nietzsche—Mencken came to believe that middle class democratic society, to a greater extent than earlier forms and styles of political and social life, tends to encourage conformity and uniformity of thought and action, and tends to suppress men of strong individuality and imagination, men of forthright and forceful personality. Middle class democratic society breeds a kind of man who is unsteady, unsure of himself, suspicious of others, afraid to laugh, ever anxious to discover what the community around him has said to be right and good, in short a man who is peevish and unhappy. This is man in modern America. Not of course that this was America's destiny, for it was Mencken's belief that America started out with quite another kind of potential, that the colonial and pioneering conditions of the early America might have been fertile soil for a different kind of human being and a different kind of society—and that for a time it was.

What happened in American history? Why did the noble experiment fail? What happened to the race of strong and forthright men that seems once to have been leading toward a more vital, more creative, more refreshing form of humanity? Mencken's answer is that in pushing democracy to its extreme limits we opened the door to standardized manners and morals and that these standardized manners and morals have crowded in upon the few lovers of freedom and unbridled imagination, thereby imparting a staleness and airlessness to the common life.

Democracy is thus the source of our greatest social ills. It was Mencken's belief that America had been founded as a republic, a form of government predicated on the notion of liberty, but that it soon dwindled into a democracy, a form of government in which the people want not liberty but power; where they want government for the people not government of the people. In a democracy people want comfort and rewards from their government; they want to turn the government over to somebody else to run, although they expect their leaders to cater to their whims and desires, to ratify their inherited beliefs and ideologies. In a democracy, elected officials must deal with the people as if they were soverign but not responsible, quite the opposite of a republic where there is no sovereignty and all are responsible.

What is most important, however, is that our political system has not been conducive to a higher and better civilization. The bacillus of democratic politics has nourished all our indigenous social diseases—puritanism, suspiciousness, distrust of one's neighbors, an impoverished sense of community, rigidity of the interpersonal life. Politics is the dramatic stage where we may see the mechanisms of democratic society at work. It does not tell us all that we need to know about life in America, but when we look at it cooly and dispassionately it provides us with the key to the understanding of why we are the way we are. It tells us how the great American experiment in freedom collapsed and how our vigorous young nation became infected by the decadence of European civilization that our founding fathers had hoped to avoid.

The Durability of Mencken's Critique of Democracy

How do Mencken's ideas stand the test of time? Can we find traces of his thinking in the intellectual life of the past several decades, or do we have to consider Menckenism a self-limiting phenomenon of the twenties? Many have wished, with Alistair Cooke, that Mencken were still alive to deal with the "slicker types of demagogues in politics and new schools of necromancy in advertising, show business, industry, psychiatry and public relations," that cross the stage today. Do Mencken's ideas continue to have merit, or do they lead to a *cul de sac*, an intellectual graveyard?

Looked at from a historical perspective, Mencken has not worn well. His influence sagged swiftly in the 1930s; it is often said that the depression and the New Deal did Menckenism in as a literary phenomenon. Certainly Mencken's public popularity dropped off precipitously as the depression deepened, and he never regained the large audience he once held.

Perhaps in the 1930s Mencken's high and buoyant humor, his mood of raillery, seemed inappropriate. It was only natural that his ideas would be sucked into the maelstrom with the rest of his reputation. In these darkening years Mencken's essays no longer seemed amusing, and perhaps some of the

specific objects of his attack—Comstockery, Babbitry, fundamentalism—suddenly seemed to be lost as objects of national
concern. As far as democracy is concerned, the nation could
no longer afford the luxury of being disturbed about its
quality; with Hitler and Mussolini snarling in the distance
democracy had all it could do to keep alive.

Mencken tried to weather the depression years and kept on
the job as a critic of Franklin D. Roosevelt and the New Deal,
but these were his lean years. As far as the New Deal was
concerned, Mencken believed it to be a further encouragement
of the democratic disease. "The cure for the evils of democracy
is more democracy," was Mencken's succinct summary of the
way all social problems are dealt with in America. Thus he
saw little hope in the New Deal, which was merely the
promise of further doses of democracy and egalitarian socialism. He saw it as one more step away from the old republican
America, with uplifters, crusaders, and professional pharisees invited into the government in larger and larger numbers. Nor did he see any promise in the even more extreme
form of communism which was beginning to have widespread
appeal among college-age youth. For Mencken, neither of
these tendencies toward collectivization could be regarded as
progress, although the New Deal succeeded in selling itself to
the liberal mind as a flowering of the great reform movement
of the early twentieth century, as realization of the dreams of
the Progressive era. Mencken saw America in the thirties, the
New Deal, and the presidency of Franklin D. Roosevelt not as
a fresh new breath of freedom, but as a further push toward
egalitarian or populist democracy that he attacked in *Notes
on Democracy* in 1926.

If Mencken were alive today and looking back on the 1930s,
he would probably say that the depression and the war years
merely masked America's social problems, held them in suspension, and created a false sense of community and brotherhood. Mencken had little sympathy for the victims of the
economic crisis. As Carl Bode put it: "Though he saw more
than one effect of the Depression with his own eyes he did not
credit them. He did not comprehend it intellectually. He did
not feel it emotionally."[29] He tried to continue as his old self

during those difficult years. He went after Roosevelt and the New Deal the way he went after Archangel Woodrow and Lord Hoover, and although in retrospect his criticisms appear to be keen and highly perceptive, they came on the market at the wrong time. Perhaps the change was too sudden and violent to allow Mencken to accommodate by a change in the style and tone of his rhetoric. Perhaps, too, things did not stand still long enough in the thirties for Mencken to get a bead on any good targets, or perhaps Mencken himself was slowing down at that time and facing his own adversities—the loss of the *Mercury* and the death of his wife. It may be that the foibles of democratic man are best seen in times of affluence and prosperity, that adversity and hardship cluttered the scene Mencken was trying to paint in the 1930s.

In any case, one cannot help but think that if Mencken had survived until the 1960s or 1970s he would probably have been able to take to his legs once again and have found full employment for his vast talent. Almost certainly he would have had no difficulty identifying latter-day manifestations of puritanism and of puritan democracy. He would have to admit that the puritan has undergone many changes since the 1920s. He would doubtless recognize that the small-town Rotarian or Methodist pastor have lost their old powers but would probably insist that their types have taken up residence elsewhere, that they come on the stage in somewhat different garbs. Since the puritan is known by the form of his actions, it is entirely understandable that the same types could be present in new kinds of drama. Certainly since World War II our main stage has not been the local rotary or grange, but big government, the universities, and (as John Kenneth Galbraith calls it) the technostructure of the large corporation. While it is by no means immediately evident how the germs of puritanism invade these enormous, seemingly prosperous, and usually highly esteemed institutions, it is likely—if Mencken's general thesis about American life is correct—that they do, and every bit as virulently as in the simpler days of the 1920s.

In the years since Mencken's death, we can see a number of his central ideas surfacing in recent social critics and historians. These later thinkers do not use Mencken's direct frontal attack, his comic invective, nor his art, and few would want to be considered his followers, but many of our most prestigious contemporary intellectuals have arrived—by entirely different paths—at the same conclusions as Mencken.

We might consider an example from the field of American sociology. Of the more ambitious and imaginative attempts to come to grips with American life in the years since World War II, David Riesman's *The Lonely Crowd* is still one of the best known and most enlightening. There are, as one might expect, few mentions of literary figures like Mencken in this book, and no reason to suspect that Riesman was influenced by Mencken in any way. Still, just what do we find in *The Lonely Crowd*—what is behind the central point of view? Naturally we find a great many ideas in this book that are not in Mencken at all, and a good many empirical studies that point along lines that would be unfamiliar to Mencken. However, the main thesis of *The Lonely Crowd*, subtitled "A Study in the Changing American Character," is really a rendering in sociological terms of a number of Mencken's ideas about what happens to the soul of man under an affluent democracy. Riesman's book is an analysis of the changing American character since the time of Tocqueville's explanation of the American character to European readers. A number of factors are shown to be involved in the development of the personality type in which Riesman is most interested—population, land, technology, politics—and Riesman reports on a large number of directions in American life that have become evident since the twenties and since World War II. His main thesis is that Americans have become what he calls "other-directed" types. The "other-directed" character type is contrasted with the "tradition directed" character, produced in periods of high growth potential and the "inner directed" character found in periods of "transitional growth."

> What is common to all other-directeds is that their contemporaries are the source of direction for the individual—either those known to him or those with whom he is indirectly acquainted, through friends and through the

mass media. This source is of course "internalized" in the sense that dependence on it for guidance in life is implanted early. The goals toward which the other-directed person strives shift with that guidance: it is only the process of striving itself and the process of paying close attention to the signals from others that remain unaltered throughout life.[30]

The other-directed American is said by Riesman to be emerging in the upper-middle-class urban and suburban environment. The style, he says, has been observed by a number of social scientists since World War II, and is identified with "highly industrialized and bureaucratic America." He cites Fromm's "marketer," Mills's "fixer" Arnold Green's "middle class male child," and the mentions still other works by Jurgen Ruesch and Martin B. Loeb.[31] "Other direction" is synonymous with social conformity, and social conformity is one of the most prominent features of Mencken's puritanism.

Most of Riesman's analysis concerns itself with American social types under conditions in the 1940s; he deals not with Babbitt living in a small-sized American city in Ohio, but with Babbitt in a gray flannel suit—perhaps on Wall Street or in Washington. We are likely to think that something new has been discovered when Babbitt changes his suit and goes to a different office, but in substance we find that Riesman is saying pretty much the same kind of thing about American society that writers like Lewis and Mencken were saying in the twenties. Everywhere in Riesman we seem to find a very familiar *dramatis personae*. Of the teacher, we hear that her role is largely "that of opinion leader. She is the spreader of the messages concerning taste that come from the progressive urban centers." As such the teacher is little more than a modern dress version of Mencken's schoolmarm, inculcating a slightly different set of unimportant truths and shallow rectitudes. Indeed, many of Riesman's descriptions of American types appear to be in substance very similar to Mencken's types.

Riesman probably did not understand the basis of the kind of critique of American social life that was current in the

1920s. In the only mention of Mencken in his entire book, he speaks of the sallies of Mencken as being aimed at groups in which extreme moralizing was still to be found: "the country people, the midwesterners, the small-town Protestants, the southern APA's, the corn-fed shouting sects, the small lodge-joining businessmen."[32] For Riesman, these groups have been "somewhat more concealed in recent years during which other-direction has spread," although they continue to exist. His point seems to be that Mencken's social criticism was aimed at these groups alone, which does an injustice to the scope and richness of Mencken's ideas. True, Mencken used contemporary types as dramatic vehicles in his essays, but the conceptual framework of other-directedness and conformity in American life is ubiquitous in his writing. Mencken's concept of the puritan is more universal and more broadly historical than Riesman's "other-directedness."

Variants of Mencken's social criticism can be seen in a number of specialized areas. Among historians, Richard Hofstadter has written a number of solid historical treatises which borrow heavily from Menckenian themes, although he, too, scarcely ever mentions Mencken by name. In *The Paranoid Style in American Politics* he borrows Mencken's notion that "politics under democracy consists almost wholly of the discovery, chase and scotching of bugaboos. The statesman becomes, in the last analysis, a mere witch-hunter, a glorified smeller and snooper, eternally shouting "Fe-Fi-Fo-Fum!" As for the people, "it was long ago observed that the plain people, under democracy, never vote *for* anything, but always *against* something."[33] America, says Hofstadter, "has rarely been touched by the most acute varieties of class conflict, but it has served again and again as an arena for uncommonly angry minds." (Rage and envy were for Mencken the salient emotions of democratic man.) American politics has provided a rich and fertile soil for the development of a "paranoid style" of political action, the dominant traits of which are "qualities of heated exaggeration, suspiciousness, and conspiratorial fantasy." The paranoid attitude in politics is not so much an attitude of fear as concern for aggressions which the individual sees being directed at society as a whole. A spokesman for the paranoid style finds aggressions of some social group as "directed against a nation, a culture, a way of life whose fate affects not himself alone but millions of others. . . . His sense that his political passions are unselfish and patriotic, in fact, goes far to intensify his feeling of righteousness and his moral indignation."[34] The paranoid style is a facsimile of Mencken's puritan democrat.

From the hand of the same author is an earlier book, *Anti-Intellectualism in American Life*, which emphasizes another trait that Mencken uncovered in the puritan. Hofstadter studied anti-intellectualism in earlier American history, that is to say, he is not concerned directly and immediately with present phenomena, although he cites a few examples of the latter at the beginning of his book. In spite of some discussion of a few eighteenth-century revivalists, nearly all of Hofstadter's examples come from the nineteenth and early twentieth centuries, during which time democracy had been in the ascendancy. Hofstadter is inclined to find the source of the difficulty in the American drive for practical success in all matters, whether educational, technological, or religious, and does not push his questioning a step further to see whether the democratic spirit itself could be at the bottom of the trouble.

Since World War II, Americans have been so firmly locked into a populist/progressive world view that we cannot allow ourselves to see our social ills as rooted in the psychopathology of democracy itself. C. Wright Mills, for example, in writing his well-known sociological treatise on the American middle class, *White Collar*, decided that "the liberal ethos . . . developed in the first few decades of this century by such men as Beard, Dewey, Holmes, is now often irrelevant," and that "we need to characterize American society of the mid-twentieth century in more psychological terms, for now the problems that concern us most border on the psychiatric,"[35] precisely the point Mencken was making in the twenties. While Mills sees American society as corrupting the souls of the people who live in it, which is also Mencken's point, his tonic is quite different from the one offered by Mencken. For Mills, the anxieties and psychological disturbances of middle-class life can be cured by even larger doses of democracy.

While Mills offers no concrete program for the making over of American society, we must conclude that his program would be a variant of Marxism, calling for some kind of collapsing of the existing social classes. Mencken, on the other hand, would reject this as blind idealism, for his belief was that the more democracy you pumped into the people, and the more you broke down all class distinctions, the more unhappy, agitated, and bitter, the more "psychiatric," they would become. Still, the outward phenomenology of American life in writers whose political ideologies are as different as Mills and Mencken are often astonishingly similar. Both see the social life as bringing about psychological disturbances in the individual, and both see society becoming more totalitarian in spirit.

Although the specifics of our life style have changed somewhat in the years since 1948, I think that Mencken's characterization of the puritan democrat continues to be among the most useful and enlightening concepts of American self-criticism. Wherever one looks one sees all the old objects of Mencken's scorn still alive and healthy, even if they now appear in younger and more modern forms.

Consider Mencken's favorite hunting ground—politics. No other area seems to have been richer in puritan pathology in the years since Mencken's passing from the intellectual scene. In the twilight of Mencken's life, the United States fell into the clutches of one of the greatest modern puritans of them all— the late Senator Joseph McCarthy—who, more than anyone else in recent times, displayed all the familiar puritan vices on a large scale, as well as a few new ones of his own. In fact, where McCarthy himself was concerned, the scale was almost too large, which in the end was his undoing. In providing the nation with a near caricature of all the puritan traits—intransigence, rigidity, humorlessness, the desire to purge and cleanse, the compulsion to point out evildoers, the appeal to an important sense of mission and high moral purpose—he became the paragon of the modern Puritan, and it was this exaggerated position which led to his downfall. If McCarthy had been only one jot more subtle in his methods, he might have brought about a national catastrophe of devastating proportions.

President Richard M. Nixon is another example of a classical American puritan, and interestingly enough, he, too, came to prominence during the communist witch hunts of the 1940s and 1950s. Nixon's presidential administration began on the somewhat hopeful note of a return to individual initiative in American life and a diminishing of the powers of government, but the truth is that Nixon was a politician in the modern vein, with an ability and desire to play upon all the puritan bugaboos. From the very beginning of his administration there were the rumblings and hysterical denunciations of student life styles, of crime in the streets, of obscene literature, any one of which might be a genuine source of concern, but which in the hands of Nixon became tools for stirring up mass hysteria. Present from the beginning was the desire to "cleanse" the Supreme Court and make way for "true-blue Americans." Finally, with the Watergate scandal, the puritanical Nixon—following the terminology of Richard Hofstadter we could say the paranoid Nixon—came out in full flower. There were, we are told, official lists of bad persons, enemies of the administration, who needed to be watched and plenty of spying and snooping went on to make sure that suspicious citizens and officials were behaving themselves. Anyone who lived through the Watergate period can understand the prophetic force of Mencken's statement of 1926 that in a democracy the statesman becomes "a mere witch hunter, a glorified smeller and snooper."

Naturally puritanism is never limited to the political arena alone, however well it may show up there in dramatic relief, and Nixon's defense of his tactics was that he was being hounded by a liberal press. Doubtless there was justification for his fear, for in a democracy one segment of society is usually feeding and reinforcing the fears and suspicions of another. During the Nixon administration it appeared to be true that the various media were guilty of political moralizing, of simple-minded sloganeering and witch-hunting. For Mencken puritanism is not a characteristic only of the political right or the political left—the phenomenon is as likely to be found at one end of the political spectrum as at the other. In the past decade we have seen—even while the right domi-

nated the White House—the emergence of a particularly tru-
culent from of liberal puritanism and paranoia—sometimes
amounting to what former Under Secretary of State George
Ball called McCarthysim of the left. Liberal puritanism has
largely emanated from the mass media and the intellectual
establishment.

As far as the colleges and universities are concerned, Mencken would be shocked but not surprised to see the kinds of
puritanism and stereotyped thinking that characterized both
the professors and the young in the sixties and seventies. The
final years of the Vietnam war were especially keen times of
puritan agitation, and in that generation of college students
we were able to observe all the major symptoms of the disease
in full eruption—the deadly seriousness, the righteousness,
the conformist ideology, the desire to set the world aright and
point out wrong thinking and evildoers.

Of late, a particularly deadly form of seriousness and
rigidity seems to have crept into the "youth culture." The
amount of energy of the present generation that is devoted to
purifying the world instead of enjoying it and confronting it
creatively and realistically is alarming. Anyone who has
attended a student rally for one of the favored causes will be
terror stricken at the humorlessness and unimaginativeness
of the current student morality. To look down on the faces of a
thousand hostile Torquemadas, all with the zeal to do good,
all shining with certainty that the knowledge of what is good
is near at hand and easily accessible—indeed their own closely guarded possession—is a very frightening experience, and
one which bodes little good for the future of our civilization.
On such occasions one yearns for a few of the college capers of
old—the water trick, the short-sheeted bed, the firecracker
thrown in at the dean's office. Anything to make life a little
merry would do. From complete and full-time seriousness and
moral gravity among adolescents little good can come.

A choice example of the crabbedness of the present generation of college students appeared several years ago in a wire
story about an attempt by an Ohio University Student Activities Board to fire the editor of the university's student
newspaper after he ran an article about the undergraduate life

of Miss Laurel Lee Schaefer, then Miss America, and a student at the university. It appeared that Miss Schaefer insisted on maintaining an unwavering moral code, claimed that she did not so much as own a single pair of blue jeans, believed that "women aren't discriminated against in America," that "marijuana leads to hard drugs," that premarital sex is "not for me," and so on. That the present generation of students would not consider Miss America a true representative of the youth culture is more than understandable; that they would seek to establish a censorship board to protect a newspaper's readers against corruption by her views is enough to send chills up the spine of even the most tolerant elders.

We cannot entirely blame today's college students for their puritan tendencies; it is something they inhale from the atmosphere of the campus, a pervasive quality of present-day academic life. Not only the college student, but quite often his professor, has lost much of the geniality, warmth, and flexibility that was the mark of the old-time college intellectual. In the post-Sputnik era of higher education, the traditional educational values became distorted—the new emphasis being on professionalism rather than culture or learning. Whereas in days gone by the professor was a mild sort of chap who sought out a career in teaching because he liked the opportunity it afforded him to think, to meditate, to relax, to breathe, and to laugh, since 1958 the educational world has been one of hustle and bustle, of frenetic nervous activity, in which each additional unit of horsepower is put into the pursuit of narrow professional ends. The nervous intensity of professional education can only end in harrassed, humorless and unhappy professors—conditioned and ready to lash out at the world.

Professors, of course, were among the prime victims of the McCarthy hysteria, and for years it was natural to believe that the liberalism of professors was a healthy antidote to the threat of right-wing puritanism. However, in the more intense academic environment of the past few years, professors have built up their own set of puritan defenses, some of which may be harmless, others of which may be quite dangerous indeed.

The most obvious symptom of this change can be seen in the

increased stereotyping of views in the intellectual community. This is related to exaggerated professionalism, for what is professionalism but a narrowing of focus—a mood in which one claims expertise in but one area. The trouble with high-pressure professionalism in education is that it can never be publicly admitted—the intellectual is looked up to and must have answers to all of the major problems of the world. If the English teacher has to make pronouncements about a certain complexity in international affairs or in monetary theory, he is only going to be on solid grounds by falling back on a convenient and readily available doctrine which provides easy answers to all the problems outside his own realm, and serves too as a form of spiritual self-protection.

One recent manifestation of the new puritanism at the universities is an all too frequent tendency to deny freedom of speech where certain crucial or sensitive issues are concerned. Not only are there political or economic reprisals against nonconformists, but in the last few years there have been numerous instances where the very right to give expression to controversial or sensitive issues has been abridged. There is the case of William Schockley, the Nobel prize-winning scientist, who gained notoriety because of his belief in the genetic inequality of the races and soon found himself a pariah on college campuses, even Harvard, where he was refused permission to speak by hostile students. That Schockley's views would be unpopular, that they would meet with firm opposition is understandable; that he would be run off the speaker's platform is a sorry comment on contemporary American history and on contemporary freedom of expression. It confirms Mencken's belief that the puritan democrat is not a lover of freedom, but rather a person who will brook no opposition, whose tolerance extends only to those who do not stand in his way—in short, an authoritarian.

The reason for mentioning these latter-day examples of puritanism is not to anticipate how Mencken might respond to them, since we cannot know with certainty, but merely to show that puritanism in the sense defined by Mencken did not die out with the influence of the backcountry town, the Bible Belt, or the Rotary of Zenith, Ohio. It is alive and well in our major social institutions, especially in fields like government, education, business, religion. In succeeding chapters we shall deal with Mencken's prophecies about some of these major institutions. But first it would be wise to summarize the position we have reached.

For Mencken, most of America's problems stem from its democratic social order, which in definition and basic formulation seems to promise great human blessings, but which in actual fact is psychologically damaging to its recipients and practitioners. Democracy does not appeal to the better part of man's nature, but to the worst. For Mencken the two human emotions in a democracy which are most readily cultivated are greed and envy. Recall what Mencken said in his famous essay about the farmer. There are only two things that ever fetch the farmer. One is his own interest and profit. "He must be promised something definite and valuable, to be paid to him alone, or he is off after some other mountebank. He simply cannot imagine himself as a citizen of a commonwealth, in duty bound to give as well as take; he can only imagine himself as getting all and giving nothing." The only other idea the farmer can grasp and tolerate is any plan or scheme for annoying and damaging other people—city folk, people whose ideas and truths clash with his own, or any object of personal jealousy.

The farmer is not a special case for Mencken; he is used for simplicity of exposition and for dramatic emphasis. The farmer may be particularly simple of mind, he may not bathe too often by city standards, he may look preposterous in faded overalls and hickory shirt, and so may be especially easy to make fun of, but basically he is just another variant of democratic man whose aim is to grab more for himself and deprive other people of as much fun and profit as possible. The same may be said of the larger social units in a democracy—we need not limit ourselves to individual types, for the same mentality may be found in the great social institutions. Indeed larger institutions are much more subtle and insidious in their workings, and it is easier for them to disguise the nature of their dynamism under the cloak of impersonality. Thus it is that many power groups—"black power" let us say, or "women's lib"—are able to forestall criticism because they spread the illusion that they are working to redress wrongs of long standing. Mencken would see in these groups nothing but the primitive urges of the farmer writ large and polished to a high lustre—the desire to profit oneself and the desire to punish the other fellow.

The great pressure groups in our social welfare state Mencken would take to be despotic, intolerant, and totalitarian in nature, even as they clamor and insist that their ideas are liberal and freedom loving. This brings us to the heart of Mencken's critique of democratic man. The democratic puritan is basically authoritarian and totalitarian in nature, and so are the chief institutions of the democratic state. Democratic man believes that he upholds institutions that are freedom loving and liberal. These institutions are at heart centers of power struggling for personal interest and domination. Democratic man is caught up in a whirlpool of agitation for this or that "good" cause—usually his own in disguise. He has no real time to consider the interests of others. He does not trust his fellow man; he lacks the common decencies of civility; he knows no magnanimity. The democratic man is small in spirit, and the idea of a commonwealth or commonweal is foreign to him.

III

The Leitmotiv
of American Politics

As a critic of American life it is natural that Mencken
should have concerned himself with politics. He became more
and more involved in political issues as his philosophy took
shape. In his writing for the *Smart Set* Mencken wrote some
occasional lighthearted pieces on political topics, but they
were only a small part of his output at the time and they
constitute no coherent unity. During the *Mercury* years he
was much more involved in political matters, having come to
believe that most of our social ills are due to our system of
government, and that the puritan democrat makes his appearance because he lives in a puritan political democracy.
This growth and development of Mencken's interests can be
seen quite well in the several series of *Prejudices*. In the first
series there is not a single essay on politics. By 1924, when the
fourth series appeared, there are a number of very substantial
and searching essays on political topics. By the time the
Mercury was at the height of its influence in the late 1920s,
and long before *Making a President* appeared in 1932, it is
quite fair to assume that Mencken was recognized by a great
many Americans as a political commentator.

In the twenties Mencken had come to believe that the
political stage is where the American drama may be seen to
best advantage. If you want to find out what's wrong with

America look at American politics, for there you'll find the root of the trouble. Not that politics is all, but it is at the eye of the storm. Never in the history of the world has there been a people so infatuated with politics. "Nowhere else in Christendom, save only in France, is government more extravagant, nonsensical, unintelligent and corrupt than here, and nowhere else is it so secure."[1]

Mencken's political sympathies lay with the ideals of the founding fathers, who in the Revolution sought deliverance from the English king and his tax collector and from all the other burdens of expensive and meddlesome government. The early American libertarians were determined to establish a society which could survive and prosper with a very minimum of governmental interference. Unfortunately, even though men like Washington and Jefferson tried their best to see that government did not swallow up the whole life, and, as late as Jefferson's presidency, cabinet meetings of the federal government consisted of a few men sitting around the fire deciding matters of state while cracking nuts and sipping Madeira, the government did proliferate and soon had the very characteristics of the one that had been banished, together with some bad ones of its own. The American colonists, when they got rid of the English king, "believed fondly that they were getting rid of oppressive taxes forever and setting up complete liberty. They found almost instantly that taxes were higher than ever, and before many years they were writhing under the Alien and Sedition Acts."[2]

Mencken was too much of a realist to believe that we could return to the liberty-loving days of the eighteenth century. He in no way pretended to offer an alternate course to the one we have followed. He was necessarily also a pessimist who believed that what we have gotten for ourselves is a fraud and a delusion. In his own mind he agreed completely and wholeheartedly with William Godwin's theory that "government can have no more than two legitimate purposes: the suppression of injustice against individuals within the community, and the common defense against external invasion." The trouble is, however, that none of the forms of government now known to the world performs these functions satisfactorily.

Even in democratic states like our own the government does very little to protect a citizen from other citizens "who aspire to exploit and injure him—for example, highwaymen, bankers, quack doctors, clergymen, sellers of oil stock and contaminated liquor, and so-called reformers of all sorts." What is even worse, not only does the government do little to secure the safety, ease, and liberty of the citizen, it is itself among the biggest exploiters and harmful agents preying upon him. The government becomes, year by year, a greater and greater intruder on human liberty.

All the extortions and tyrannies practiced on the people, all the proliferation of taxing power and bureaucratic functions, all the enlargement of police activity in its many forms, are gently slipped over on the populace on the theory that they are not only unavoidable but laudable, "that government oppresses its victims in order to confer on them the great boons mentioned by Godwin." All of the complex apparatus of government is necessary, so we are told, to suppress injustice and preserve the state.

Government extends itself far beyond these simple functions, and one wonders how it is able to grow to monstrous proportions and pass all kinds of moral enactments and quack reform statutes without the citizens noticing and complaining. In Mencken's eyes, government has been able to grab so much power because, even in our so-called democratic society, it has been able to foist on the public a concept which was hatched in "the black days of absolutism" and which rightly should have been tossed overboard with the notion of the divine right of kings, a concept, to wit,

> that government is something that is superior to and quite distinct from all other human institutions—that it is, in its essence, not a mere organization of ordinary men, like the Ku Klux Klan, the United States Steel Corporation or Columbia University, but a transcendental organism composed of aloof and impersonal powers, devoid wholly of self-interest and not to be measured by merely human standards. . . . This concept, I need not argue, is full of error. The government at Washington is no more

impersonal than the cloak and suit business is impersonal. It is operated by precisely the same sort of men, and
to almost the same ends. When we say that it has decided
to do this or that, that it proposes or aspires to do this or
that—usually to the great cost and inconvenience of nine-
tenths of us—we simply say that a definite man or group
of men has decided to do it, or proposes or aspires to do it;
and when we examine this group of men realistically we
almost invariably find that it is composed of individuals
who are not only not superior to the general, but plainly
and depressingly inferior, both in common sense and
common decency—that the act of government we are
called upon to ratify and submit to is, in its essence, no
more than act of self interest by men who, if no mythical
authority stood behind them, would have a hard time of it
surviving in the struggle for existence.[3]

We American's have not been able to rid ourselves of the
delusion that the government is a lofty, impersonal, transcendental organism and that it is run by individuals who have
cleansed themselves of all baser human wants and needs. We
cannot help but see that individual public servants are falli-
ble, that bad men regularly get into the government; but
whenever there is some kind of flagrant behavior that we
disapprove of we blame it not on the system of government
but on a few individuals who at a given moment seem to be in
the glare of the spotlight. We believe that all we need to do is
turn out the rascals who have misbehaved and the next batch
will give us good government. The most foolish assumption
we make about politicians, says Mencken—and all Americans seem to be subject to this particular delusion—is that
"politicians are divided into two classes, and that one of those
classes is made up of good ones." On the contrary, there is no
group of "good politicians" because government as we know
it, being a body of individuals whose only interest is self-
interest, does not permit them.

How we Americans, who started out only two centuries ago
as the first people in the history of the world determined to
enjoy liberty became, in a few short years, the most over-

governed people in the world is a historical question of great moment. Considering that our founding fathers were fully aware of the possibilities and dire consequences of overextending governmental powers, it is not at all easy to explain how our present system of government came about. Mencken was fond of pointing out that throughout a good deal of the nineteenth century Americans resisted this development, and were aware, as we in the twentieth century are not, that government is invariably a government of men—men after something for themselves.

In the nineteenth century, the American politician had not yet found a way to implant the delusion that the government was other than a concatenation of human wants, and the exploitation of some individuals by others. Mencken pointed out that for fifty years after the inauguration of the spoils system under Jackson (the spoils system, ironically, passed itself off as a reform) the people generally held officeseekers and officeholders in very low esteem. "The job holder, once theoretically a freeman discharging a lofty and necessary duty, was seen clearly to be no more than a rat devouring the communal corn."

The way out of this particular kind of governmental disrepute was through civil service reform. The civil servant was thereby whitewashed, and the public's distrust of him subsided. The only difficulty was that while civil service reform was able to placate the public, it was a sorry downfall for the politician. The jobholder became a mere bookkeeper. "His pay and emoluments were cut down and his labors were increased. Once the proudest and most envied citizen of the Republic, free to oppress all other citizens to the limit of their endurance, he became at one stroke a serf groaning in a pen, with a pistol pointed at his head."[4]

This dismal position couldn't be long endured, "else politics would have tumbled into chaos and government would have lost its basic character; nay, its very life." The public servant could no more remain a plodding bookkeeper or clerk than he could a leech or peculator. If politicians are not believed in, if the work has no status or dignity, then it obviously can't continue to exist for no one will be drawn to governmental work.

The twentieth century brought the relief the politicians were looking for. The officeholder no longer needed to be either a blatant absconder or a drone; he could become a reformer. Politics has survived in marvelous health in our time because it has managed to "suck reform into the governmental orbit." The main business of the government these days is reform, good works, uplift. Such activities are almost invincible, since their weaknesses are incapable of detection. The civil servant is not only secure in a well-paid government job, but he offers himself to the world as "a prophet of the new enlightenment, a priest at a glittering and immense shrine." How can anyone in good conscience take out after him as one could the old-time officeholder? In the days of the spoils system one could say of the officeholder that although he had done his share in electing the ticket that he was obviously a loafer and deserved no place at the public trough.

> But what answer is to be made to his heir and assign, the evangelist of Service, the prophet of Vision? He doesn't start off with a bald demand for a job; he starts off with a Message. He has discovered the long-sought sure cure for all the sorrows of the world; he has the infallible scheme for putting down injustice, misery, ignorance, suffering, sin; his appeal is not to the rules of a sinister and discreditable game, but to the bursting heart of humanity, the noblest and loftiest sentiments of man. His job is never in the foreground; it is concealed in his vision. To get at the former one must first dispose of the latter. Well, who is to do it? What true-born American will volunteer for the cynical office? Half are too idiotic and the rest are too cowardly. It takes courage to flaunt and make a mock of Vision—and where is courage?[5]

The twentieth-century bureaucrat thus has something important and valuable to sell. He is either an expert, a man with a vision, or both.

> He is the fellow who enforces the Volstead Act, the Mann Act, all the endless laws for putting down sin. He is the

bright evangelist who tours the country teaching mothers
how to have babies, spreading the latest inventions in
pedagogy, road-making, the export trade, hog-raising
and vegetable-canning, waging an eternal war upon illit-
eracy, hookworm, the white slave trade, patent medi-
cines, the foot-and-mouth disease, cholera infantum,
adultery, rum. He is, quite as often as not, female; he is a
lady Ph.D., cocksure, bellicose, very well paid.[6]

The government thus becomes little more than an organ of
convenient and stereotyped ideas. The lady Ph.D. who dispenses wisdom on infant care from some government office
dispenses not only with a sense of mission but from a position
of almost unassailable authority. The public naturally believes that the lady Ph.D. reformer is not only knowledgeable
in the extreme, but, because she is working for the government, disinterested as well. Government becomes a mother
lode of technological expertise and assumes oracular authority—the very kind of oracular authority a liberty-loving
people would choose to do without.

Mencken rejects both of these generous assumptions about
the modern civil servants—that they are knowledgeable and
that they are disinterested. Both are mistaken for the same
reason. Government bureaucracies are nothing other than
individual power and pressure groups, like similar power and
pressure groups in the private sector, each seeking to push
themselves above the others in importance and authority. If
you have a Bureau of Narcotics, let us say, the people who run
it are going to be subject to a struggle for power among
competing agencies and viewpoints, and will tend to develop
a missionary zeal, a pathological belief in the importance of
"narcotics work." They become intoxicated, so to speak, with
the value of this narcotics work, can in no way detach themselves from their zeal, and can thus exercise no independent
and objective judgment on their own activities. They pull for
more and more power and recognition but they are no more
capable of a search for truth and virtue than we could expect
from the advertising department of an automobile manufacturer.

What we get from a government bureaucracy is what we get from any other special interest group. Because of the mulitiude of reform or uplift factions in the government in its twentieth-century democratic form, what we get may actually be worse—since the various power groups cannot be easily reconciled; they tend to struggle and war against one another for hegemony. Let us consider an example from more recent years. Since the appearance in the 1960s and 1970s of the ecological reform movement it is only natural that certain factions of the government should crusade to clean up the environment. However, cleaning up the environment is expensive and is bound to come into conflict with other branches of the government committed to stemming the tide of inflation. What happens when two such factions meet in a collision course? How is it possible, for example, to reconcile the desire to conserve petroleum when the antipollution devices on automobiles bring about a tremendous increase in the consumption of gasoline? These various demands will result in conflict, a conflict that will be resolved not in intelligent discourse but in a shouting contest which will be carried on the way all such contests must be carried on in a democracy— with the weaponry of slogans, half-truths, and simplistic formulas—the winner being the side which for the moment can most easily and successfully enflame the passions of the multitudes and cater to their immediate desires.

Even if it were possible to keep all the power centers of a democracy in check, it becomes increasingly difficult to do so because in our time agencies of government have so proliferated that their very size prevents them from being held in check. There is no evidence that any sector of the government has decreased in size in the twentieth century, or at least no evidence that any bureau, department, or office has willingly given up its authority and prerogatives. Every year some new area of reform can be expected to arise, but none of the old ones die. We now have agencies to police the safety in automobile manufacture which didn't exist at all in 1925 and were not perceived to be necessary. Similarly, we continue to have an unwieldy Agricultural Extension Service with an army of county agents prepared to advise the struggling farmer at a time when the only farmers left are businessmen who operate large farm businesses for big profits and know more about farm business and operation than the government agent himself. Why, then, doesn't the county agricultural agent vanish into the mist of history? Because he has tenure; he is secure in his position and has no intention of giving it up without a a struggle.

So it is with every branch of government. Far from being impersonal and detached, every office and every officeholder has a very personal and private reason for being. We are therefore completely deluded when we believe that public servants are motivated by the common good. "These men, in point of fact, are seldom if ever moved by anything rationally describable as public spirit; there is actually no more public spirit among them than among so many burglars or street-walkers. Their purpose, first, last and all the time, is to promote their private advantage, and to that end, and that end alone, they exercise all the vast powers that are in their hands."[7] The government officeholder is just another variety of democratic man, on precisely the same level as the farmer, the doctor, the lawyer, save that he has gathered more power unto himself so that he may more easily rob us of our cash, our pleasure, and our ease.

Behind Mencken's skepticism about the effectiveness of our system of government there are several assumptions which need to be explored. Mencken did not believe that our system is corrupt because it has grown too large; he believed that there is a corrupting element at the very heart of democracy itself, a promise in the concept of democracy that cannot be fulfilled.

Democracy is deficient in that it does not strive for liberty, but for a kind of sovereignty. Mencken believed that liberty is the only proper aim of government. Indeed he once wrote to Ernest Boyd, one of his early biographers, that "so far as I can make out, I believe in only one thing: liberty."[8] Democracy, however, is not concerned with liberty at all, but with sovereignty; it is a theory about who ought to rule. Its primary dogma is that all men are equal. Its secondary dogma is that power belongs to the majority. Since it believes that the *demos*, the people, ought to rule, it is a theory of who ought to rule. The first principle of civil liberty, on the other hand, is that there is no one who, of right, ought to rule.

Mencken's belief in liberty is not what is important here. "I do not believe in even liberty enough to want to force it on anyone." The central question remains: what is wrong with our system of democracy? What is the weakness of democracy as a form of sovereignty? Let us first determine what is supposed to be good about it. It is that power is said to be dispersed. In a system of feudalism, which we might take as the polar opposite of democracy, "degrading acts and attitudes are imposed upon the vassal." In a democracy such is said to be impossible because the people are sovereign. However, in actual practice democracy has its own insidious form of degradation. In a democracy "degrading acts and attitudes are imposed upon the men responsible for the welfare and dignity of the state," and since the number of such men increases beyond reason in modern democracy, the cruelties of the limitations on freedom are really not very different from those found in feudalism.

The sovereignty which is vested in the people is really very weak. Mencken's point is not that the people are really not sovereign in a democracy, but only think that they are. They are indeed sovereign and may, if they choose, throw off the yoke of the rogues who presently hold office. The trouble is that in practice this power is of no real value. The power to turn out one group of officeholders and put in another is a very small and insignificant form of authority. The people who have faith in it lose sight of the way the political process really works. The truth is that the focus of power is not in the hands of the people but in the hands of elected representatives, usually divided into several factions "each seeking to enflame, delude and victimize" the people in some way. The power of the mob, on the other hand, is little more than the power to yell hallelujahs over highly selected issues that are tossed out by leaders of this or that faction or power group (the power group, incidentally, need not be a political party— it might be the press or the oil interests). Not that total power passes thereby to the leaders of society, far from it. The leaders must theoretically bend the knee to the public on a regular basis. Since in the end they remain courtiers, their rule is not through power itself but through manipulation. The statesman in a democracy must be something of an advertising man, a demagogue, a player with words.

There are those who have perceived these weaknesses in democracy, but who defend it on the grounds that our particular style of democracy is not pure enough, that the weaknesses could be eliminated if only we could make it more perfectly democratic. The people are simply too far removed from the seats of power it is said. If we had a direct democracy rather than a representative one, the ills of the present system would disappear. For Mencken this is just another version of the fallacy that "the cure for the evils of democracy is more democracy."

What then of the notion that democracy could survive and prosper if only the final determination of all important public questions were left in the hands of the voters themselves? It is based, like so many popular notions about democracy, on a weak foundation that cannot stand when exposed to the historical evidence. There is no evidence that democracy has ever been other than a system whereby politicians mold and manipulate the sovereign electorate, or that it ever could be otherwise. Consider the New England town meeting, long considered the archetype of democratic practice. The town meetings were really nothing but small-scale versions of the democratic system we know today. "Certainly no competent historian believes that the citizens assembled in a New England town-meeting actually formulated en masse the transcendental and immortal measures that they adopted, nor even that they contributed anything of value thereof." The truth is that the New England town meetings were "led and dominated by a few men of unusual initiative and determination, some of them genuinely superior, but most of them simply demagogues and fanatics."[9]

The difference between direct and representative democracy is less marked than idealists and political sentimentalists assume. Under both forms the people use agents to execute their will, and in both cases the agents are certain to have ideas of their own, special interests of their own, and techniques at their disposal for manipulating and exploiting the people. What is more important, however, "both forms of democracy encounter the difficulty that the generality of citizens, no matter how assiduously they may be instructed, remain congenitally unable to comprehend the problems before them, or to consider those they do comprehend in an unbiased and intelligent manner." The voters in the New England town meeting, for example, "were all ardent amateurs of theology, and hence quite competent, in theory, to decide the theological questions that principally engaged them; nevertheless, history shows that they were led facilely by professional theologians, most of them quacks with something to sell."[10] It must be true, *a fortiori*, that our modern government, with its involved questions of foreign affairs or economics, with its huge mass of administrative law and red tape bureaucracy, is even more incomprehensible to the mind of the average person.

This view rests on the foundation of another of Mencken's key ideas, that the general run of humanity is not capable of ruling, since in will or intellect they are congenitally too weak to assume the responsibility of leadership. The trouble with democratic theory is that it always rests on foolish and fanciful idealisms. It assumes that because it would be nice if the people had the ability to govern, that they do in fact have the ability. The evidence gives no warrant for this belief. The belief would have to be supported by evidence that there is an enlightened and forceful electorate that knows what it wants, can rationally and dispassionately examine the issues before it, and then proceed to act on this knowledge. Neither of these assumptions is true, and there is no evidence to suggest that they have ever been true or ever will be true. An enlightened electorate requires a mass of enlightened individuals, and in Mencken's mind, a mass of enlightened individuals does not exist and will not exist, no matter how much we stuff the populace with the indigestible truths and facts of education. Even when put through all of the tortures and drummings of the most advanced and widespread educational system in the world, the mass of men remain at the intellectual and emotional level of adolescence or lower; the average person, no matter what steps are taken in an enlightened democracy, is deficient in imagination, insight, and discursive reasoning; to expect him to pass judgment on matters of state is little more than a romantic dream.

Even if enough intelligence could be mustered amongst the electorate, the people lack the will to govern; they do not want the responsibility of it. Thus the ideal of a "popular will" is also nothing more than a dream. There is no such thing as popular will except in regard to individual wants and needs. Nine times out of ten the electorate has no wishes on any principal matter of public concern; it simply passes it over as "incomprehensible or unimportant." It has made no analysis of the issues and has no wish to do so. The populace may either vote wantonly and irrelevantly, or it may stay away from the polls altogether.

> Both actions might be defended plausibly by democratic theorists. The people, if they are actually sovereign, have a clear right to be wanton when the spirit moves them, and indifference to an issue is an expression of opinion about it. Thus there is little appositeness in the saying of . . . the philosopher Hegel, that the masses are that part of the state which doesn't know what it wants. They know what they want when they actually want it, and if they want it badly enough they get it. What they want principally are safety and security. They want to be delivered from the bugaboos that ride them. They want to be soothed with mellifluous words. They want heroes to worship. They want the rough entertainment suitable to their simple minds. All these things they want so badly that they are willing to sacrifice everything else in order to get them. The science of politics under democracy consists in trading with them, i.e., in hoodwinking and swindling them. In return for what they want, or for the mere appearance of what they want, they yield up what the politican wants, and what the enterprising minorities behind him want.[11]

Although the people under a democracy have neither the intelligence to rule nor the will to rule, they are sovereign and theoretically retain the power to rule. They can do anything they want. "They could enfranchise aliens if they so desired, or children not taxed, or idiots, or kine in the byres. . . . They could introduce burning at the stake, flogging, castration, ducking and tar and feathering into our system of legal punishment," and such remedies are presented from time to time in legislatures around the country by politicians hoping to find new ways to curry favor with the electorate. Naive idealists believe that the Constitution protects us from idiocies that might arise from the emotions of the masses, but actually it is not the Constitution that protects us from these idiocies, but the fact that the masses are too weak and lethargic to pursue them even if they could imagine them. Our civilization persists and endures in fair equilibrium, but neither because of nor in spite of the will of the people.

The people rule, but they rule in name only—much as the king may be said to rule in a modern constitutional monarchy. The sovereignty rests with them but they are bypassed in the actual political process. They are there, they must be listened to, bowed to, catered to, but that is the extent of their rule. Of course sometimes they become noisy and clamorous, and then the politicians must act quickly lest the party or faction in power be turned out of office. They may not be able to answer to the need that is being shouted up, but they must act as if they could, and act convincingly and firmly. A democracy is run by politicians who have mastered the art of manipulating the mob, of soothing it with mellifluous words while swindling it under the table. The politician, Mencken believed, is the "courtier of democracy." Just as in the days of rule by kings, when the courtier's art was to flatter his employer in order to victimize him, to yield to his wishes in order to rule him, so it is with the politician under democracy. "Ostensibly he is an altruist devoted whole-heartedly to the service of his fellow-men, and so abjectly public-spirited that his private interest is nothing to him. Actually he is a sturdy rouge whose principal, and often sole aim in life is to butter his parsnips. His technical equipment consists simply of an armamentarium of deceits."[12]

The Politician: Clown and Corruptor

This brings us to the core of the weakness in the democratic system of government—the politician himself. Democracies are weak because of the kind of politicians they breed. When the people are sovereign, they must also be flattered, cajoled, tricked, and catered to. This would not be so bad were it not for the fact that people who master the arts of public flattery and manipulation are invariably of a low and unenviable sort.

Apologists for democracy often try to answer Mencken's charges, and those similar to them, by agreeing that the mob is incapable of ruling by itself, while insisting that in a democratic society the man with strong leadership qualities will somehow emerge. The masses may be incapable of governing themselves, but they can select from their number those who are. For Mencken this is just another sentimental ideal of the sort with which we Americans love to delude ourselves; it simply is not in accord with observed reality. The facts are that in a democracy politicians are not taken from the very best and highest elements of society—its artists, philosophers, poets, or natural aristocrats—but from the mainstream, in short, from the very segment of society that is not ideally suited to governing.

This does not imply that the politician in a democracy does not stand above the mob. Of course he stands above the mob, probably in intelligence among other things, but mainly he is more suited to govern than someone selected at random for office in one important way. He stands above the mob mainly in force of will. The politician genuinely wants to lead, but his role is one that no man of genuine excellence could tolerate. Says Mencken, "no educated man, stating plainly the elementary notions that every educated man holds about the matters that principally concern government, could be elected to office in a democratic state, save perhaps by a miracle. His frankness would arouse fears, and those fears would run against him."[13]

The politician is thus one who knows how to evade the truth and who panders to the current fears, superstitions, and needs of the mob. His very sources of power lie "in the gross weaknesses and knaveries of the common people—in their inability to grasp any issues save the simplest and most banal, in their incurable tendency to fly into preposterous alarms, in their petty self-seeking and venality," in short, in their complete incapacity for the duties of civilians in a commonwealth. Sometimes the statesman may succeed in acting on principles, but this is rare. Mostly he must spend his time explaining the weaknesses of the mob and ministering to the needs of the various minorities that prey upon the mob. He must know how to manipulate the series of "interlocking despotisms" that constitute the working sovereignty of the democratic state.

> The art of politics, under democracy, is simply the art of ringing it. Two branches reveal themselves. There is the art of the demagogue, and there is the art of what might be called, by a shot-gun marriage of Latin and Greek, the demaslave. They are complimentary, and both of them are degrading to their practitioners. The demagogue is one who preaches doctrines he knows to be untrue to men he knows to be idiots. The demaslave is one who listens to what these idiots have to say and then pretends that he believes it himself. Every man who seeks elective office under democracy has to be either one thing or the other, and most men have to be both.[14]

This is not hyperbole. Mencken is not describing the democratic politician at "his inordinate worst," but in the "full sunshine of his normalcy." He is not referring just to politicians on the lowest levels, to "some cross-roads idler striving to get into the State Legislature by the grace of the local mortgage-sharks and evangelical clergy," but the whole political spectrum from top to bottom. Even the candidate for the presidency must be tarred with the same brush—if he had not at some time dissembled, compromised his principles, known the taste of boot polish, and "suffered kicks in the tonneau of his pantaloons," he would long since have dropped from the running.

In Mencken's eyes, even intelligent Americans are so thoroughly enamored of politicians, so pathetic in their faith in the democratic process, that they blot the truth from their minds. They take every opportunity to raise national political figures to the level of heroes. American history is largely political history, that is, political chronology, and in the short span of our national life we have created a Valhalla of political figures that outshine achievement in every other realm. For Mencken the romantic delusions of American political history are among our greatest intellectual self-deceptions. Our history is cluttered with dreams that are not very much above the level of Parson Weems's fanciful life of Washington.

There is an idea that seems to corrupt all our thinking about politics, "that politicians are divided into two classes, and that one of those classes is made up of good ones." Our politics has always been based on this assumption, and every political campaign is a concentrated effort to instill the idea that it is necessary to remove from office a set of politicians who are bad and put in another set who are supposed to be better. This nearly universal conception may be due to the tendency of the human mind to compose exclusive categories—the logical either-or fallacy known to philosophers—or perhaps it is one of the inherent weaknesses of the two-party system, where one party must be right and the other wrong (a multi-party system would probably be less conducive to simplistic thinking, although since the people really don't do much of the thinking in modern democracies it is hard to tell whether this would help), or it may be that it is just one of the concomitants of our national faith in the political process. For Mencken, the notion is refuted by experience. "For if experience teaches us anything at all it teaches us this: that a good politician under democracy, is quite as unthinkable as an honest burglar."[15] When we think we have found an honest politician it is almost invariably somebody whose prejudices harmonize with our own, or who has convinced us so—that is to say, a successful politician. Successful politicians we have, effective politicians we have, convincing politicians we have, but honest politicians are not possible.

In Mencken's writings it is hard to find praise for any American president since the time of Jefferson. There is the possible exception of Lincoln and Grover Cleveland, but even these he treated with very guarded praise indeed. None of the presidents of the twentieth century fared well at his hands and most fared very badly indeed. Some of the presidents Mencken attacked most strenuously—Roosevelts I and II and Woodrow Wilson—have been lionized so long and well as great idealists by historians that attacks on them are unintelligible to the average student of American history today.

For Mencken the very fact that presidents of the United States are lionized and raised to heroic stature should be reason enough for suspicion. Washington and Jefferson had intended to keep the presidency limited and recessive. Their hope was to rule out kings and courtiers from the government. As late as the time of John Quincy Adams nothing was felt to be unusual about a president of the United States running for the House of Representatives—today this would be too demeaning for the president, who, after leaving office, must continue to pass himself off as a great statesman—building libraries and monuments to himself. With the coming of Jacksonian democracy, the kings and courtiers that Washington and Jefferson hoped to lock out of government were back to stay. A democracy seems to need gods and heroes, kings, and giants. We're constantly looking for a hero or a father figure in the office of the president; but then, true to the nature of our democratic system, we push some crooked lawyer, some senile army man, some foolish country newspaper editor or third-rate college professor into the office and then proceed to wonder why he doesn't act with the magnanimity of a Washington or the intelligence of a Jefferson.

Mencken's dismal view of American politics is a logical product of his general political philosophy. While the people are indeed sovereign in a democracy, the general level of human intelligence is not high enough to permit true leadership of "the people." It is inevitable that the politician who answers to the sovereign mob will be far from lofty in character and intelligence. Men like Washington and Jefferson could exercise their intelligence and imagination because they were not required to yodel day and night before the public. To be sure, men of breeding and intelligence may occasionally stray into politics—Mencken suggested that a man like Theodore Roosevelt might be a good example—but only the shortest exposure to the political scene is necessary before they too will abandon all the rational habits they may have acquired and begin taking on the habits of the multitude. Mencken does not permit the excuse that the politician need so demean himself only until election day, that thereafter he may abandon his slogans and half-truths and get down to the business of carrying out his duties—in Mencken's mind the slightest tincture of political thought and activity as encountered in America will condemn one to a life of decreased intellectual activity, and will deflect the pursuit of truth. The politican saturates himself so long and so completely in half-truths that for him to recognize, much less enunciate, truths of a stern and difficult sort is a practical impossibility.

Because he held out ideals for politicians that even he himself admitted could not be realized in our time and in our kind of government, Mencken's essays on contemporary American politicians are not widely read and quoted today. They remain among his highest achievements as a writer. Over the years Mencken studied the major political figures of his time, and eventually eviscerated or decapitated nearly all of them. Mencken's characterizations of men like Bryan and Wilson, Harding and Coolidge, and the two Roosevelts are among the most perceptive writings of their kind in American history. In these essays he steadfastly explains and justifies his own convicition that American politicians in our present climate are either demagogues, demaslaves, or both, and that there can be no other possibilities.

Theodore Roosevelt was doubtless a fine example of a demagogue in Mencken's definition, which is to say, he was the sort of man who preached ideas he knew to be untrue to people he knew to be fools. Mencken began his essay on Roosevelt, "Roosevelt: An Autopsy "—which appears in *Prejudices, Second Series*—by pointing out that political biography in America is almost invariably bad and undependable, and that he can think of no work in this area that remotely compares with Morley's life of Gladstone or Trevelyan's life of Macaulay. Invariably American political figures get a treatment not very much different from that accorded George Washington by Parson Weems, which is to say, romantic fancy. Such, for example, are all the lives of Lincoln, a superb practical politician who spent his days enchanting the boobery "on the prairie and sawing off the horns of other politicians," but who in the school history books is rendered as "an austere and pious fellow, constantly taking the name of God in whispers," or as a shining idealist, holding all his vast powers by the magic of an inner and ineffable virtue." In recent times, says Mencken, most of our political biography is written by academic historians. These are much more subtle and learned fellows than Parson Weems, but still, poor souls timidly holding college posts and "ten times more cruelly beset by the ruling . . . social order than ever the Prussian professors were by the Hohenzollerns. Let them diverge in the slightest from what is the current official doctrine, and they are turned out of their chairs with a ceremony suitable for the expulsion of a drunken valet."[16]

It is not surprising to find, then, that all the biographies of Theodore Roosevelt are "feeble, inaccurate, ignorant, and preposterous." Not that all are merely pious or sentimental in the manner of Weems's Washington or Sandburg's Lincoln; there may indeed be a much greater conscious effort at analysis and objectivity; but still writers of history are addled by all the democratic myths, all the passion for heroes and hero worship, and tend to take the mouthings of the heroes themselves at face value. Insofar as they question the ideas and activities of a particular politician, it is from the posture of some other political faction.

The political career of Theodore Roosevelt is a perfect example of the kind of pitfall that awaits the professional biographer or historian. If you follow Roosevelt's public career and the development of his political thought, if you give over your hours to studying the documents, letters, and mementos of his administration and later public life, you will come away with a picture of Roosevelt about as far away from the truthful picture as possible.

Standing before us today is a picture of Roosevelt as a major early leader of the Progressive movement. At the time when

Mencken's essay about him was written a different Roosevelt—the World War I Roosevelt—was the predominant public image, so it is no surprise that Mencken also had a great
deal to say about this image. What of Roosevelt's attitude to
the war? In Mencken's eyes, Roosevelt's instincts and deeper
sentiments were about as far from those of Wilson as possible.
"His instincts were profoundly against a new loosing of
democratic fustian upon the world; he believed in strongly
centralized states, founded upon power and devoted to enterprises far transcending internal government," but he was
forced into combat with Wilson, "a mob-master with a technique infinitely more subtle and effective than his own,"
forced to enunciate philosophies directly counter to those he
knew to be true, and in the end, in his unequal combat with
Wilson, he was forced into "absurdities so immense that only
the democratic anaesthesia to absurdity saved him. To make
any progress at all he was forced into fighting against his own
side. He passed from the scene bawling piteously for a cause
that, at bottom, it is impossible to imagine him believing in,
and in terms of a philosophy that was as foreign to his true
faith as it was to the faith of Wilson."[17]

Roosevelt's whole political career seems to have had a
similar fate. He was always finding his personal convictions
washed away by the winds of political change. He got into
politics not as a Populist or reformer of the Bryan stripe, but
rather as "an amateur reformer of the snobbish type common
in the eighties, by the *Nation* out of the Social Register." His
original motives for reform were all developed on an aristocratic base. As a young man he discovered that his hometown
of New York was being run by hooligans like Michael
O'Shaunnessy and Terence Googan, and it was his belief that
the highbred young fellow of wealth and education ought to
be using his time to clean the scum out of town hall, that
government service should be the ideal career for the privileged young man-about-town. Like his Dutch forebears, he
believed in the concentration of power in the hands of an
aristocracy, hopefully an enlightened aristocracy, and in
strong central government, the gathering of power into the
hands of the few fit to govern. The heroes of his youth were

Federalists like Morris and Hamilton, "and he made his first splash in the world by writing about them and praising them." His daily associations were with the old Union League crowd of high-tariff Republicans, most of whom took Roosevelt's boyish crusades half-humorously, but who were at root not at all disposed to the ideals of the reform movement.

The Republican leaders played Roosevelt for what they could get out of him. They turned him loose as a candidate for mayor of New York, but he took a terrible drubbing. Basically he was a political playboy in the 1890s, with little to suggest that he had any real political future ahead of him. Then there was a shift in the nature of the reform movement. Bryan style reform had come out of the West and was taking on a milder form for Eastern consumption. It displaced the genteel spirit of reform that emanated from the Harvard and Union League clubs. There was nothing, says Mencken, in the Populist movement to suggest that Roosevelt would swallow it—"it was full of principles that outraged all his pruderies"—but somehow it seemed to do magic for his political career and he swallowed it whole.

> His entire political history thereafter, down to the day of his death, was a history of compromises with the new forces—of a gradual yielding, for strategic purposes, to ideas that were intrinsically at odds with his congenital prejudices. When, after a generation of that sort of compromising, the so-called Progressive Party was organized and he seized the leadership of it from the Westerners who had founded it, he performed a feat of wholesale englutination that must forever hold a high place upon the roll of political prodigies. That is to say, he swallowed at one gigantic gulp, and out of the same herculean jug, the most amazing mixture of social, political, and economic perunas ever got down by one hero, however valiant, however athirst—a cocktail made up of all the elixirs hawked among the boobery in his time, from woman suffrage to the direct primary, and from the initiative and referendum to the short ballot, and from prohibition to public ownership, and from trust-busting to the recall of judges.[18]

All these causes ran counter to his own convictions. "He didn't believe in democracy, he simply believed in government." He stood for a paternalism of the Bismarkian pattern, for rigid government control of all phases of life—from coal mining and meat packing to the regulation of spelling and marital rights. Democracy in the sense of dispersion of authority, and popular will—the very things that the Populists stood for—was foreign to his thoughts and habits. "His instincts were always those of the property-owning Tory, not those of the romantic Liberal."

Theodore Roosevelt was neither a populist democrat in the Bryan sense nor a free trade Republican, he was something of a prophet who called for an expansion of the federal government and a meddling in foreign affairs at a time when neither of these causes was popular with either political party. It was he (not Wilson or Roosevelt II) who enunciated the theory "that political heresy should be put down by force." It was he who predicted the growth of imperialism in the twentieth century and sympathized with the idea, and predicted "the inevitability of frequent wars under a new world system of extreme nationalism," the necessity of organizing the backward nations into "groups of vassals, each under the hoof of some first-rate power." Mencken's conclusion was that had Theodore Roosevelt lived beyond his time into the next decade or two he might have been the man of the hour, his ideas might have come to a great second flowering.

As it was, he suffered the fate of any politician in a democracy. His ideas were of little use to him and he could not enunciate them. He had to keep them under wraps and give voice to others for which he had no stomach; he had to shift ground so often that he alternately appeared the fool and the hero. Ultimately his career was schizoid. His strongest and best ideas he could never put into play because he was forced to stoop to the common level. "When he struck out for realms above that level he always came to grief," and lost the respect of the public. Unlike Wilson, he was a man of strong imagination, a bold political thinker, but in the end his talents and political abilities were for naught. "His instinct prompted him to tell the truth," just as it was Wilson's instinct to "'shift and dissimulate." On the other hand, his lust for glory, his lust to survive in a political contest, was always stronger than his lust to tell the truth. "Tempted sufficiently, he would sacrifice anything and everything to get applause. Thus the statesman was debauched by the politician, and the philosopher was elbowed out of sight by the popinjay."[19]

Roosevelt, however, is not really typical of American politicians as Mencken saw them. A demagogue he was of necessity, but there was always a streak of imagination and intelligence struggling to break through. In a demaslave like William Jennings Bryan, there was no higher being struggling to break the bonds. In Bryan there was no divided self, no inner struggle; the man was all of one piece, and this unified self was low, mean, and dispirited. We cannot say of him as we could of Theodore Roosevelt that he was a man of forceful imagination, who compromised his ideas. He had no ideas. This does not mean that he was without a certain kind of primitive elemental force, that he did not stand above the mob. He had the force, but "what animated him from end to end of his grotesque career was simply ambition—the ambition of a common man to get his hands upon the collar of his superiors, or, failing that, to get his thumb into their eyes. His whole career was devoted to raising ... half-wits against their betters, that he himself might shine."[20]

Mencken's essay on Bryan is probably his most brilliant piece of political commentary, although perhaps not his most judicious. Years later, when writing his autobiography, Mencken admitted that he was a bit unfair to Bryan when he composed the latter's obituary shortly after the Scopes trial. In comparing him with other prominent political "breast beaters" of the twentieth century, Mencken was inclined to raise the mark on Bryan and rate him among the best rhetoricians of his kind: "Jennings emitted English that was clear, flowing and sometimes not a little elegant, in the best sense of the word. Every sentence had a beginning, a middle and an end. The argument, three times out of four, was idiotic, but it at least hung together."[21]

When Mencken wrote his obituary of Bryan for the Baltimore *Sun* in 1925, he laid on him every charge he had ever made against the politician in America, and then some. Bryan, he said, had no principles at all, no ideas that he was unwilling to compromise; he played solely on people's superstitions and baser emotions. Sincerity? There was no such thing in the man unless it was his liking for country things—"the tune of cocks crowing on the dunghill . . . the heavy, greasy victuals of the farmhouse kitchen. He liked country lawyers, country pastors, all country people. He liked the country sounds and country smells." In his political actions there was no sincerity whatsoever, and he found himself now on one side of the fence, now on the other—whatever was necessary to heat up his yokels. Was he sincere when he tried to shove the Prohibitionists under the table, or later when he began to lead them with loud whoops? Was he sincere when he bellowed against the war, then became a strong militarist? "Was he sincere when he denounced the late John W. Davis, or when he swallowed Davis? Was he sincere when he pleaded for tolerance in New York or when he bawled for the faggot and the stake in Tennessee?" Sincerity requires some fixity of mood or attitude, some coherent mental outlook. Bryan's only thoughts were on the shibboleths of the moment, his only desire to hit upon some cause that would enflame his rural followers.

If the fellow was sincere, then so was P.T. Barnum. The word is disgraced and degraded by such uses. He was, in fact, a charlatan, a mountebank, a zany without shame or dignity. His career brought him into contact with the first men of his time; he preferred the company of rustic ignoramuses. It was hard to believe, watching him at Dayton, that he had traveled, that he had been received in civilized societies, that he had been a high officer of state. He seemed only a poor clod like those around him, deluded by a childish theology, full of an almost pathological hatred of all learning, all human dignity, all beauty, all fine and noble things. He was a peasant come home to the barnyard. Imagine a gentleman, and you have imagined everything that he was not.[22]

Bryan seems to have been the archetype of the American politician, the animal seen in its purebred form—the sort Mencken himself might have invented had no real-life burlesque been available.

Woodrow Wilson had some of the rudimentary traits of a civilized man, but this made him far more insidious than Bryan. "Bryan lived too long, and descended too deeply into the mud, to be taken seriously . . . by fully literate men, even of the kind who write school books." He passed from the scene at Dayton, Tennessee, a poor mountebank, "a character in a third-rate farce, witless and in bad taste." The country had grown up around him, had become sophisticated, while he remained a bumpkin. The "self-bamboozled Presbyterian," Dr. Woodrow Wilson, late of Princeton University, was a different kettle of fish, and couldn't be dismissed quite so easily. Mencken, who referred to Wilson in a *Smart Set* issue of 1921 as "The Archangel Woodrow," admitted that, unlike Bryan, he was a man of ideals, but these ideals were dangerous, and time has proved that they continue to work their magic on the writers of history books. He continues plausible as a hero whereas Bryan does not. Basically he was a puritan, says Mencken, "of the better sort, perhaps, for he at least toyed with the ambition to appear as a gentleman, but nevertheless a true Puritan." Not one to simply follow whatever cause would enflame the multitudes in their present mood, Wilson was rigid and unbending, but he had the knack of covering over his purposes, obscuring his intentions under a smoke screen of hollow rhetoric. He envisioned his role as president, indeed America's role in history, as being one of high moral purpose, and like all moralists and reformers, he could use his moral principle to justify almost any course of action.

Wilson, like most austere moralists, was lacking in that most important human trait of all—magnanimity. The one thing Wilson couldn't abide was a deviating opinion; he had no patience with the weaknesses of other people. Confronted on his death bed with the case of Eugene Victor Debs who was languishing in jail, Wilson decided that Debs had to finish the

sentence for his heresies. "As a purely logical matter, he saw
clearly that the old fellow ought to be turned loose; certainly
he must have known that Washington would not have hesi-
tated, or Lincoln. But Calvinism triumphed as his intellectual
faculties decayed."[23]

Mencken laid at Wilson's doorstep most of the puritan
hysteria that had infected big government in the twentieth
century—harassment by the government of those who dispute official doctrine, spy hunts, seizure and search of the
mails, suspension of the rights of free speech and assemblage.
It was in the mood of the war years that the American
Protective League and similar patriotic groups arose which
sponsored such activities as splashing yellow paint on the
houses of people "suspected of having doubts about the Wilson idealism," pinning white badges of cowardice on young
men not found in military garb, and so on. The mood of the
war years was a kind of hysteria that had not been seen in
America at any previous time, not even in the Know Nothing
frenzy of the 1850s.

It was in 1916 to 1917 that Mencken suffered disillusionment
with Wilson and began to attack him in the press. Mencken
believed that Wilson's motives concerning the European conflict were hypocritical, that while he cried for peace he was
preparing for war, planning ways to get the United States
involved. Mencken agreed on this matter with the position
taken by the Progressives, pacificists, and socialists in 1917,
and which was reiterated by the Nye Committee in 1934 and
1935, that the United States had become more and more
economically identified with the allies in the years before the
war and had become so deeply committed to the allied cause
that neutrality was no longer a possibility. Indeed, in the very
midst of the period when neutrality was being pledged by the
White House, the United States was taking steps to enforce
the sea rules against Germany and wink at them for England,
so that the ultimate showdown could not have been avoided.

All this resulted in a national mood of pussyfooting and
deceit, and when the war actually came, the Germans had to
be identified as villains. The populace was expected to swallow the idea that a German victory would result in the

downfall of Western civilization, and the death of all liberty and human decency. Whether or not Mencken is right that Wilson acted in bad faith, one thing can hardly be denied, namely that Wilson practiced a very "devious brand of diplomacy" (to borrow the term of Arthur S. Link, the foremost Wilson scholar of recent years), and that his evangelical approach to foreign affairs, beginning with the Mexican interference, has infiltrated American diplomatic thinking since and continues to get us into difficulties around the world.

Politics and the Corruption of Language

Most of Mencken's attacks on Wilson, and on his successor Warren G. Harding, are specifically directed against their language, against their rhetorical methods of manipulating people and of obfuscating and clouding their intentions. Mencken seems to have developed the idea, later so well expressed by George Orwell in "Politics and the English Language," that the use of language to obscure meaning is one of the most widely used techniques of modern states. Orwell had made a careful study of the propaganda techniques used by the fascists and communists during the Spanish Civil War and had shown how totalitarian regimes hid their actions with meaningless phrases and lying euphemisms—the bombarding of defenseless villages being called *pacification*, the robbing of peasants' farms and the sending of the owners trudging along the roads with no more than they can carry being called *transfer of population*, or *rectification of frontiers*, and so on. In short, the language of politics not only obscures, it corrupts by allowing one to distort the truth. Consider, says Orwell, some comfortable English professor defending Russian totalitarianism. He cannot say outright, "I believe in killing off your opponents when you can get good results by doing so." Therefore, he will probably say something like this:

> While freely conceding that the Soviet regime exhibits certain features which the humanitarian may be inclined to deplore, we must, I think, agree that a certain curtail-

ment of the right to political opposition is an unavoidable concomitant of transitional periods, and the rigours which the Russian people have been called upon to undergo have been amply justified in the sphere of concrete achievement.[24]

In this inflated and ridiculous style, observes Orwell, "a mass of Latin words falls upon the facts like soft snow, blurring the outlines and covering up all the details."

We must not assume that this tendency to use obscurantist language is characteristic only of the communist and fascist regimes. Orwell studied its use in the politics of his native England, and seems to have concluded that democracies as we know them in the twentieth century are variant forms of totalitarianism. Mencken, of course, was convinced that American democracy drifts toward totalitarianism, even though the style of it is much different than that found under the Russian or Chinese flag. In the case of a democracy the unyielding agencies of force arise from a number of smaller pressure groups rather than a single party organization or an oligarchical government. In a democracy the various power or pressure groups must be orchestrated, and this is done by politicians who have a gift for obscure and meaningless phrases which allow them to go about their business while giving offense to as few people as possible. Still, the demagoguery of the American politician is so corrupting to thought that the politician becomes enmeshed in it himself in a way that is probably less necessary or likely in a closely ordered dictatorship. In American politics the politician comes to believe his own bosh; he has been obliged to hawk his ideas to the populace so long that he eventually comes to think of them as truth. Thus it was with Woodrow Wilson. We cannot easily say of him whether he was a demagogue or a demaslave; doubtless he was a very delicate combination of the two. Mencken believed it would have been impossible for him to swallow his own rhetoric of the war years had he not fallen into some kind of rapture or trance which in turn obliterated his own logical processes, his own superior educational background. Speaking of Wilson's wartime speeches, Mencken remarked:

Reading his speeches in cold blood offers a curious experience. It is difficult to believe that even idiots ever succumbed to such transparent contradictions, to such gaudy processions of mere counter-words, to so vast and obvious a nonsensicality. . . . When Wilson got upon his legs in those days he seems to have gone into a sort of trance, with all the peculiar illusions and delusions that belong to a pedagogue gone *mashugga*. He heard words giving three cheers; he saw them race across a blackboard like Marxians pursued by the *Polizei*; he felt them rush up and kiss him.[25]

To Mencken, Wilson's literary style was the most certain sign of the man's corruption. The bombast of his speeches, his heavy dependence upon "greasy and meaningless words," his "frequent descents to mere sounds and fury, signifying nothing," were sure signs of his diminished or forsaken rationality. As his political career progressed, Wilson learned the art of reducing all the difficult public issues of the hour to "sonorous and unintelligible phrases, often with theological overtones," and relied on these phrases for all his public communication. He was thus, to be sure, a master politician of a democratic state, for he was able to give the people the kind of words they wanted to hear—words that would give them comfort and security. What they want is "the sough of vague and comforting words—words cast into phrases made familiar to them by the whooping of their customary political and ecclesiastical rabble-rousers, and by the highfalutin style of the newspapers that they read. Woodrow knew how to conjure up such words. He knew how to make them glow and weep."[26]

The speeches of Warren G. Harding, the small-town newspaperman from Marion, Ohio, who took the reins from Wilson in 1921, are perhaps even better examples of the vacuity of political language. Several days after Harding's inauguration, Mencken commented on his inaugural address, coining the term "Gamalielese" to describe the style. Harding's English, said Mencken, "reminds me of a string of wet sponges; it reminds me of tattered washing on the line; it reminds me of stale bean soup, of college yells, of dogs barking idiotically through endless nights. It is so bad that a sort of grandeur creeps into it. It drags itself out of the dark abysm (I was about to write abscess!) of pish, and crawls insanely up the topmost pinnacle of posh. It is rumble and bumble. It is flap and doodle. It is balder and dash."

Upon hearing the address Mencken says that he was inclined to offer a prayer for a return "to the rubber stamps of more familiar design, the gentler, more seemly bosh," of Woodrow Wilson. Of course he could never raise the hatred for Harding that he could for Wilson. Harding was neither a puritan nor a gentleman, a mere cipher, really, lacking therefore the treacherous element that so often pervades political life. He was still a perfect and easy foil for Mencken's wit. The war was over and Harding did not need to be taken with deadly seriousness; during his tenure one could sit back and laugh while the forces he represented carried the burden of steering the government. Harding gave us as good, or better, an example of the inanity and hollowness of political language than Wilson.

Wilson's style, after all, was rather unexciting. "It was simply the style of a somewhat literary and sentimental curate, with borrowings from Moody and Sankey and Dr. Berthold Baer. Its phrases lisped and cooed; there was a velvety and funereal gurgling in them; they were made to be intoned between the second and third lessons by fashionable rectors, But intrinsically they were hollow. No heart's blood was in them; no gobs of raw flesh." For real excitement we had to wait for Harding. Here was a style of oratory to make one puff and pant. "In his style there is pressure, ardency, effortcy, gasping, a high grunting, Cheyne-Stokes breathing. It is a style that rolls and groans, struggles and complains. It is a style of a rhinoceros liberating himself by main strength from a lake of boiling molasses."[27]

A number of contemporary observers held the opinion that Harding's speeches were obscure or unintelligible. Not at all, said Mencken. The Gamalian style is nothing more than an outrageous puffing up of very simple and elementary ideas— it is what the textbooks of rhetoric call "elevated discourse."

It came to birth on the rustic stump, matured among the chautauquas, and received its final polish in a small-town newspaper office; it is directed to the mentality of the yokelry of the hinterland, an audience which has little faith in compact well-knit arguments, but which prefers "to be bombarded, bawled at, overwhelmed by mad gusts of parts of speech." The yokelry wants to hear hard words and trombone phrases. "If a sentence ends with a roar it does not stop to inquire how it began. If a phrase has punch, it does not ask that it also have meaning." Here in the Menckenian style at its best, is the Gamalian style in a nutshell:

> That style is based upon the simplest of principles. For every idea there is what may be called a maximum investiture—a garb of words beyond which it is a sheer impossibility to go in gaudiness. For every plain word there is a word four times as big. The problem is to think the thing out in terms of harmless banality, to arrange a series of obvious and familiar ideas in a logical sequence, and then translate them, one by one, into nouns, verbs, adjectives, adverbs, and pronouns of the highest conceivable horsepower—to lift the whole discourse to the plane of artillery practice—to dignify the sense by all the arts of sorcery. Turn to the two immortal documents. The word *citizen* is plainly banal; even a Congressman can understand it. Very well, then, let us make it *citizenship*—and *citizenship* it becomes every time. But even that is not enough. There comes a high point in the argument; a few more pounds of steam must be found. *Citizen* now undergoes a second proliferation; it becomes *factor in our citizenship*. "We must invite . . . every factor in our citizenship to join in the effort"—to restore normalcy. So with *women*. It is a word in common use, a vulgar word, a word unfit for the occasion of statecraft. Also, it becomes *womanhood*. Again, there is *reference*; it swells up a bit and becomes *referendum*. Yet again, *civil* becomes *civic*—more scholarly, more tasty, more nobby. Yet again, *interference* has a low smack; it suggests plow-horses that interfere. *En avant!* there is *intermediation!* And so with whole phrases.[28]

Mencken's preoccupation with the language of politics is not merely an amusing sidelight to his critique of politics in a democracy. In a democracy a politician becomes corrupted by his own rhetoric, and it is essential to uncover the mechanism of corruption. There is a striking similarity between Wilson and Harding, in spite of the obvious differences in their respective styles and mentalities. In both cases, political rhetoric, and thereby political issues, are reduced to the harmless and the banal. The government goes about its work under the table, so to speak; it answers to the demands of pressure groups when and if necessary, but it makes every effort to render the issues that actually command the attention of the electorate innocuous and inconsequential, while still capable of exciting and stirring the emotions. The trick of the politician in a democracy is to enflame the citizenry with ideas that are diverting and entertaining, but basically harmless and meaningless, so that, *sotto voce*, they can go about making the kinds of deals and decisions that have to be made if the government is to function and prosper. The public will does not get expressed in a democracy, since the public is not fed the issues, but only the issues dressed up in the way that the politicians choose to dress them up.

We must not assume that the American political system functions well in spite of these handicaps. It does function, to be sure, and Mencken believed that democracy as a form of government will always succeed in muddling through. We must not however, draw the conclusion that the politicians feed the people all the intellectual opiates they need before election day, but afterward roll up their sleeves and go to the business of intelligent statecraft. It was Mencken's complaint against men like Wilson and Harding that they became mesmerized by their own mouthings uttered on the hustings. Language corrupts thought, and political language corrupts absolutely. There can be no doubt that the Archangel Woodrow really believed that he was maintaining the peace while preparing for war. A cutaway view of the contents of the brain of Warren G. Harding, if such were possible, would reveal a picture of America built of the very truisms and simplistic slogans that he uttered in his inaugural address.

The biggest charge that can be made against the political system in a democracy is that it is the principal breeding ground of rigid and stereotyped ideas and social habits, the principal factory of error and untruth. Politics is the chief organ and agency of populist puritanism. In America politics is not a harmless sideshow. It is the arena where half-truths and untruths are blown up to frightening proportions, where some people find ways to force their will on others, where freedom and liberty lose their spirit and gusto.

IV

The Psychopathology
of Everyday Life

For Mencken, America was the most exciting, colorful, and amusing society that the world had ever seen. It never failed to provide rich challenges to his comic imagination, and he found its social oddities and eccentricities so profuse and lively that even his own phenomenal physical energy didn't permit him to catch them all on paper. Mencken shared the belief that America is a novel experiment among the nations and societies of the world. In this youthful vigor that is America he also perceived a tincture of madness. Americans have energy, drive, and exuberance, but these convert to frenzy and anxiety more often than to high civility and social stability. If one marvels at life in America, one also cannot help wondering how we manage to keep our sanity.

The causes of our spiritual uneasiness and of our occasional manic passions are not hard to trace. They are rooted in the form of government that we have chosen—populist and egalitarian democracy—a form of government that has the manifest weakness of promising things it cannot possibly deliver. Especially in our era of great material prosperity, the citizenry is led to dream of a kind of pot of gold at the end of every favorite rainbow. But these dreams are dreams which can never be fulfilled. American is indeed the promised land, but it promises too much. Its promises are ultimately too extravagant; and promises without fulfillment are the very things neuroses, personal or social, are built upon.

Consider the affluence and property of America—the qualities which are the fruits of the Industrial Revolution and of America's possession of great natural resources. On paper and in theory, affluence must be accounted a good. It has created the largest middle class of any country in history. It has brought limitless opportunities for leisure which should in turn provide for spiritual enrichment and social betterment. It has freed millions of people from backbreaking labor in a lifetime of toil, a fate which throughout history held people in conditions not very far removed from slavery.

However, we have to ask ourselves what the masses have been freed *to*. They have been freed *from* the heaviest burdens of physical labor, and this should of itself provide them with the leisure and time to use their intelligence and imagination to make a better and more fulfilling spiritual life for themselves. We know from simple observation this is not really true. There is leisure, to be sure, leisure of a kind that has been denied to the masses throughout history. However, in Mencken's thinking, the common man's leisure has done little to elevate him, has not done much to make him happier than he was. While at one time his life was laid out for him in orderly fashion, he is now adrift in the world, free to make a fool of himself or to be duped by politicians, chiropractors, reformers, or anybody with enough cleverness to turn his head or enflame his passion. Most importantly, he has been freed of moral and social responsibility, for in a democracy, as opposed to a republic, the responsibilities of government are largely given over by the people to the government. He has also been left exposed to psychological agitation and annoyance. An egalitarian democracy carries with it the promise of equal affluence and prosperity for all, but this promise is insane and irrational; it can never be completely met and must result in a citizenry that is constantly in agitation over the achievements, prosperity, and life style of other people. One's own contribution to the common weal is scarcely considered; the American becomes an anticitizen, concerned mainly with his rewards vis-à-vis the other people.

Democracy in America is something of a disease with its own striking and widespread manifestations. First of all, the very idea of egalitarian democracy is a contradiction in terms, a logical impossibility. It is predicated on the notion that we should bring everybody up to the average both socially and economically, and this is a logical absurdity. Second, even if egalitarian democracy were possible, common sense observation of our attempts to achieve it show that it is morally debilitating and damaging to society.

In regard to the first of these criticisms of democracy, Mencken relied heavily on the Social Darwinism of William Graham Sumner, the Yale social philosopher whose works he had studied and admired over the years and to whom he frequently referred in his essays and letters. Sumner's social philosophy contained a sharp criticism of egalitarian democracy and of the view that people can and ought to be free to do whatever they want. Sumner was a classical economist in the tradition of Malthus, and he rejected this notion as a false ideal impossible of attainment. Because of the affluence of our society, the patent absurdity of this notion is obscured, but only the smallest amount of digging beneath the surface of economic reality will uncover what is wrong with it. If people, either collectively or as individuals are led to believe that the world owes them whatever they want, they have forgotten the basic economic truth that material goods are in short supply.

Following the classical economic approach, the foundation of Sumner's social philosophy was that social stability is dependent upon the man-land ratio. "It is this ratio of population to land," said Sumner, "which determines what are the possibilities of human development or the limits of what man can attain in civilization and comfort." By land is not meant acreage alone, but available natural resources. The nature and quality of civilized life are dependent on the land and resources available to sustain it. Sumner's ideas are based on the assumption that things are in short supply. Natural resources are not easy of access, although in our highly advanced industrial society, supported by an accumulation of many generations of human effort, we are lulled into the belief that the fruits of this society have always been there. We must never forget that these resources are obtained only by effort, and that they are actually in short supply.

The error in forgetting the basic truths about the scarcity of land and resources and the struggle needed to obtain them is that in our forgetfulness we tend to build air castles; we believe that we have certain natural rights and privileges.

We are born to no right whatever but what has an equivalent and corresponding duty right alongside of it. There is no such thing on this earth as something for nothing. Whatever we inherit of wealth, knowledge or institutions from the past has been paid for by the labor and sacrifice of preceding generations; and the fact that these gains are carried on, that the race lives and that the race can, at least within some cycle, accumulate its gains, is one of the facts on which civilization rests. The law of the conservation of energy is not simply a law of physics; it is a law of the whole moral universe, and the order and truth of all things conceivable by man depends upon it. If there were any such liberty as that of doing as you have a mind to, the human race would be condemned to everlasting anarchy and war as these erratic wills crossed and clashed against each other. True liberty lies in the equilibrium of rights and duties, producing peace, order and harmony.[1]

The trouble is, said Sumner, American history has taught the American people an altogether different and erroneous lesson. It has taught them that they can have liberty without responsibility, freedom without effort. It has taught them that whenever they feel want all they need to do is ask, and the government, or some mysterious agency of the universe, will do something about it. In falling into this habit of mind one forgets that if the government or some other agency gives a certain person or group of persons what they ask for, it does so by taking resources from some other place. This must be true unless resources are limitless.

Under democracy, government instills a psychology of demand. When some power or pressure group demands, the government must promise to act, especially if the power group is loud or forceful enough. Often the promises cannot be made good, and government has to muddle along as best it can to keep people happy. What is more important, even when promises to the people can be made good, the largesse has to be paid for by somebody, and in Sumner's view, the segment of the citizenry which usually has to pay the bill is the segment that can least afford to pay and that least deserves to pay. It is that segment which provides the stability and continuity of civilization, and makes the smallest number of demands on it.

The man who pays the bill is the one Sumner called "the Forgotten Man." The Forgotten Man is not the great industrialist or capitalist—as many of Sumner's critics concluded—but "the clean, quiet, virtuous, domestic citizen, who pays his debts and taxes and is never heard of out of his little circle." It is he who bears the burden of comfortable civilization and keeps it on an even keel. He commands our attention and respect because he puts more into the world than he takes out of it.

This is not a moral doctrine. The Forgotten Man commands our respect not because of some abstract moral quality in his existence. The essential worth of the Forgotten Man is a statistical contribution—that of paying the bills. This is not a moral worth, but a practical necessity. We assume that society is a richly endowed collective. "When you see a drunkard in the gutter you are disgusted but you pity him." You want something to be done. The policeman comes along and picks him up and takes him away. This satisfies you. "You say that 'society' has interfered to save the drunkard from perishing. Society is a fine word, and it saves us the trouble of thinking to say that society acts. The truth is that the policeman is paid by somebody, and when we talk about society we forget who it is that pays. It is the Forgotten Man again."[2]

To the naive, the drunkard and the thief can be salvaged in the name of society because society has the resources to take care of them. For the more perceptive, however, the resources come from redistributing riches obtained elsewhere in the economy. For Sumner, this wealth is overrated, and more apparent than real. What others see as affluence he sees as the result of good husbandry and careful management of opportunities. If capital, land, and resources were in fact boundless, we could make our society according to our dreams—or at least the attempt to do so would make some sense. (However, Sumner, like Mencken, had a Darwinian pessimism about the universal perfectability of the human animal, and would probably be skeptical of the possibilities of universal human progress no matter what the resources.)

What is wrong, then, with trying to use the resources of society to help reform the drunkard, or pay the bills of the man who refuses to work? Nothing, as long as we see that doing so has consequences and that we are willing to accept the consequences. It was Sumner's belief that if you place too heavy a burden on the Forgotten Man, society returns to anarchy or to some lowered state of civilization in which society enjoys fewer of the refinements it has built up for itself over the centuries.

Mencken found himself drawn to Sumner's concept of the Forgotten Man, and to the social philosophy that gave birth to this notion. Mencken's orderly upbringing and the concepts of duty, industry, punctiliousness, thrift, and regularity which were instilled in him would have inclined him to favor this type of responsible citizen to the newer American type, bred since the Civil War, who partakes of the fruits of society while assuming as little responsibility for it as possible, and to whom work, thrift, and an orderly domestic life mean little. Sumner's father had not been a prosperous burgher like the elder Mencken, but an English handicraft worker who emigrated to America from Lancashire when his trade was ruined by the factory system. Still, Sumner must have learned from his own father many of the same precepts that Mencken learned from his father August. In an autobiographical sketch for the history of his college class at Yale, Sumner wrote that his father was one of a disappearing class—those worthy, independent, self-supporting individuals who mind their own business, ask no favors, and though "weighed down with the costs and burden of the schemes for making everybody happy, with the cost of public beneficence, with the support of all the loafers, with the loss of all the economic quackery," make no complaint.[3]

Sumner's alarm over America's tendency to drift away from the virtues cherished by his father were expressed in economic terms. Mencken added a psychological and behavioral dimension to Sumner's socioeconomic analysis. This dimension became the most characteristic ingredient of Mencken's critique of American life.

For Mencken, the shift from the self-reliance of the early American individualist to the irresponsible collectivist who is the typical citizen of today was more than one of economic significance; the shift has affected the psyche and the social behavior of individuals. Mencken believed that the new American climate created by egalitarian democracy is responsible for a vicious circle of desire; it produces a kind of human being who is forever struggling, caught up in a battle for fulfillment that can never be won. It is this individual frustration which accounts for our unhappy lifestyle. Americans are very active and lively people, but activity and liveliness must not be confused with happiness or contentment. Americans are too full of struggle, of envy, of animal aggression to be truly happy and contented.

Psychic frustration did not infect early American man. It did not affect the frugal Yankee, the industrious frontiersman, or any settler who had to struggle to carve a spot for himself out of the wilderness and establish himself and his family in a new world. For these, the struggle to tame the land or to build a settlement was enough for a lifetime; the democrat's suspicion of his neighbor had not yet developed, although it began first in the towns of New England with the greatest pretentions to democracy and the greatest inclination toward theocratic politics. The citizen of the old republic rooted himself in firm economic realities which precluded a neurotic concern with the moral behavior and worldly possessions of his neighbors. He was rooted in his life's work, and also in devotion to his community or to some community of interest. The new American, on the other hand, is rootless; the only thing that tugs at him is inchoate desire; he is a moth drawn to an unknown lamp, condemned to throw himself against it in endless frustration.

Mencken contended that a healthy and stable individual

results from a healthy sense of community, of mutual trust. In a democracy the sources of trust are removed. Material prosperity and the ideas of the sovereignty and equality of the people develop a psychology of noninterdependence, a feeling that there is something out there that other people are depriving me of, something that the world owes to me and me alone. Money is not always what is involved. For some people it is sufficient to injure other people in intangible ways. It may be sufficient merely to force one's theology or political ideology on somebody else. Men in a democratic state are not motivated by brotherhood and charity. Each is there to struggle against the others, to wrest something from the hands of his neighbor.

The American Pageant of Desire

Modern America generates a colorful pageant of desire, and the root of Mencken's attempt to understand life in America is his critique of this pageant. The objects of desire are spun out of the common life, but they have no moral significance since the common life has been cut away from the only sorts of activities in which values may be found. America is a kaleidoscopic progression of tantalizing lights toward which the multitudes are drawn, but which mean little on attainment.

This vision of the American experience as unsatiable desire drew Mencken to the novels of Theodore Dreiser, and is the reason why Mencken, found him the most moving and perceptive American novelist of the twentieth century. Dreiser was not a thinker whose ideas would be harmonious with Mencken's; indeed his superstitions, naiveté, and flights to quacks and ouiji boards would ordinarily have made Mencken his adversary. But if the intellectual framework of Dreiser's books was repugnant, Mencken was never able to find a writer who more nearly captured in imaginative form the America he was trying to render in the discursive essay. Dreiser was the novelist of desire, who saw the American tragedy in which one is condemned to reach out, while the grasp closes on nothing. Dreiser can seem to find no ultimate purpose to life in America, said Mencken. "He can get out of it only a sense of profound and inexplicable *disorder*, of a seeking without a finding. There is not only no neat programme of rewards and punishments; there is not even an understandable balance of causes and effects." Living in America is like sailing cockelshell boats upon an angry sea. "The waves which batter the cockleshells change their direction at every instant. Their navigation is a vast adventure, but intolerably fortuitous and inept—a voyage without chart, compass, sun or stars."[4]

Dreiser's major characters all are caught up in a voyage of ambition and desire; their tragedy is not, however, one of not attaining the object of their desire, although this may happen; more often their tragedy is that the object once attained is not fulfilling. Consider two of Dreiser's heroines—*Sister Carrie* and *Jennie Gerhardt*. Both in the typically American pattern struggle to escape poverty, ignorance, and physical miseries; both escape the fate which appeared to be their lot. Both succeed through seduction, but in neither case is this what interests Dreiser. Dreiser's tales are not "maudlin fables of virtue's fall,"—promiscuity is not at the root of the tragedy of either Carrie or Jennie. The tragedy of Carrie and Jennie, observed Mencken, "is not that they are degraded, but that they are lifted up, not that they go to the gutter, but that they escape the gutter." In America the problem is not so much that one loses the race, but that winning means so little.

The same is true of Dreiser's heroes, who endure tortures that are remarkably similar. Frank Cowperwood and Eugene Witla achieve worldly advancement, but this "widens their aspirations beyond their inherent capacities," and so results in final frustration. In early reviews of Dreiser's books, the humanists and moralists could see in the tragedies of Witla and Cowperwood only some defect of personality; they attributed the fall of these protagonists to their sexual excesses—they assumed Dreiser's lesson to be that licentiousness leads to personal tragedy and social disintegration. The fact about Witla and Cowperwood, said Mencken, "is that they are *not* mere Don Juans—that they are men in whom the highest idealism strives against the bonds of the flesh. Witla, passion-torn, goes down to disaster and despair. It is what remains of the wreck of his old ideals that floats him into peace at last. As for Cowperwood, we have yet to see his actual end—but how plainly his shadows are cast before! Life is beating him, and through his own weakness."[5] This is the typically American pattern of tragedy—defeating of oneself through one's own strengths.

In a recent study of two of Dreiser's major novels, *Sister Carrie* and *An American Tragedy*, Ellen Moers finds some recurring themes which reveal the state of mind which Dreiser shares with Mencken. In several chapters dealing with the prevailing imagery of *Sister Carrie*, Moers finds the recurrent use of a language of lights—of theater lights and all the city lights of attraction. Carrie's Chicago becomes, in Dreiser's hands, a brilliantly illuminated theater of desire. Carrie makes no distinction between the arc lights of the streets, the display lights of the stores, the garish gas lights of the theater marquee, or the thousands of lights overhead in the office windows.

> The gleam of a thousand lights is often as effective as the persuasive light in a wooing and fascinating eye.[6]

Another theme in *Sister Carrie* is the theme of insect life, of a cycle of birth and death composed of meaningless flutterings and attractions. There is no better imagery for Mencken's view of American life. Americans are moths, beautiful moving creatures doomed to dash themselves against the thousands of lights which attract them. They lack powers of discretion; the lights are too many, and for those who reach them there is no fulfillment, no cessation, no rest; one can be fascinated by the activity and the color, but must be struck by the futility of it all.

For Mencken, this is not the necessary fate of humanity. Mencken is neither fatalist nor nihilist. The ordinary man throughout most of human history has not been free to flutter aimlessly from light to light; he has been anchored to a life pattern, a habit of work that is firmly fixed. For the man of ordinary resources and normal intellectual capacity this is still the best of possibilities. Like Sumner's Forgotten Man, one may lay down a life's pattern of regularity and responsibility; in doing so one contributes both to one's own stability of mind and to the stability and permanence of society. However, larger and larger numbers of citizens in industrial America are not satisfied with regularity, and the joys of work; they would rather be aflutter, seeking some reward paid to them out of the richness and property of the commonwealth, or perhaps simply the reward of being heard, being allowed to make noise or to throw up some sparks.

It is not the activity of Americans that gets them into trouble; activity is one of their virtues and accounts for whatever charm and fascination there may be in their social life. It is the superabundance of irrational activity that is the root of their trouble. Under ideal conditions, activity should be harnessed through some meaningful pattern of work to the common good of humanity. When it is not so harnessed there is a breakdown in social stability, a crisis of nerve in interpersonal life.

Mencken is not simply an apologist for one or two life styles; he does not find productive and meaningful activity only in city intellectuals, writers, musicians, or other members of an intellectual elite. Mencken never believed that there is anything intrinsically corrupting or demeaning about being a farmer as opposed to being the editor of a smart magazine; his objection was not to the vocation of farming as such, or, indeed to any vocation, but to the peripheral activities of farmers and most other citizens under a democracy. It was never the husbandry of farmers that annoyed him, but their bad citizenship, their tendency to be distracted from the business of farming and making a decent living for their families, and their penchant for making bad laws, embracing stupid religions, and falling victims to worthless intellectual notions and idiotic reforming schemes. What is wrong with the farmer is that he has too much freedom to flutter around, to embroil himself in ideas which he has neither the capacity nor the moral force to evaluate in a rational manner. Under the hardship conditions of early American life (or of most historical civilizations) the farmer's world would have been tightly organized, individualistic, independent; he would enjoy neither the leisure nor the license to stick pins in the social order that supported him. With the greater affluence of post-Civil War America, and with egalitarianism as the official philosophy of the land, the farmer is rewarded for being a bad farmer and a bad citizen—with unfortunate consequences for society, and for the farmer himself, since he condemns himself to a life of frustration.

For Mencken, one need not be an intellectual or a wit to be respectable, one need only be devoted to a life of healthy activity, orderliness, and regularity, and to the principle that one ought to put as much or more into the world as one takes out of it. Sophistication and alertness to the present intellectual currents of the world, and to the state of scientific knowledge was always prized by Mencken, but he maintained friendships with people whose culture he considered feeble or misguided. According to his biographer, Carl Bode, Mencken maintained a long friendship with the well-known Johns Hopkins surgeon and gynecologist Howard A. Kelly, nearly all of whose ideas outside the sphere of medicine he regarded as naive, foolish, philistine, or nonsensical. Mencken always harbored an exaggerted respect for medical men which may account for his friendship with Kelly, but most of the evidence suggests that Mencken could accept any man on his own terms, if he had some solid achievement to his credit—and this achievement need not be in the intellectual domain.

Mencken held work in high esteem as a wide-ranging moral ideal. Work is productive of social harmony and individual mental health, and mass leisure always carries with it the danger of intellectual aberrations and social and psychological disintegration. In attempting to relieve democratic man of responsibility as citizen and worker, society only opens to him a Pandora's box of unseemly possibilities.

Except for its lack of cosmic or religious underpinnings, Mencken's critique of the unrooted democratic man closely resembles that of the great Victorian prophets of democratic doom, especially Carlyle, who also believed that democratic

man worships false notions of liberty. For Carlyle, democracy
has spawned the notion that the end of man is a life of ease.
Democracy teaches that there are endless delights from which
to choose, many deviant paths along which we may stray, but,
in Carlyle's thinking, all such notions are deceptive; there is
but one path a man can follow and that is the path which
enables him to realize and fulfill himself. If a man has a
purpose, a life work, he has need of no other paths. If he has no
work or purpose, he lives in a chaos of distracting ideas and
corrupting blandishments. Lack of work, of true vocation,
gives rise "to new very wondrous life-philosophies, new very
wondrous life-practices! Dilettantism, Pococurantism, Beau
Brummelism, with perhaps an occasional half-mad protesting
burst of Byronism." To the masses this world of "ward-motes,
open vestries, pollbooths, tremendous cheers," with liberty to
give the vote at the "election-hustings, saying 'Behold, now I
too have my twenty-thousandth part of a Talker in our National Palaver," to purchase "social isolation," each man
"standing separate from the other, having no business with
him but a cash account" appears to be ceaseless good fun. For
Carlyle, all the wondrous gains of democracy lead to slavery
rather than freedom, chaos rather than stability.

Mencken's critique of American culture, like Carlyle's critique of Victorian England, consisted of an encyclopedia of the
aberrations of democracy. His work was an attempt to delve
into the habits of man cut loose from purposive activity. What
happens to man when he is no longer rooted in some system of
work? We have already seen that leisure and affluence expose
democratic man to the pitfalls of politics and the blandishments of politicians; that politics becomes for him one of the
gaudiest, richest and most expensive forms of entertainment.

Politics is not the only profitable racket in a democracy. A
careful reading of Mencken's writings shows that he studied
the American's weakness for fads, quackeries, and intellectual aberrations in a wide variety of fields. Indeed, his collection and labeling of them became not only his all-consuming
passion but his professional trademark. He appears to have
reached the conclusion that Americans have both the leisure
and the prosperity to be taken in or duped by schemers and

tricksters in every corner of life, and that dupery or quackery of one sort or another has become a national pastime to an extent unknown in any other culture or at any other time in history. Mencken seldom saw in any of these popular fads any possibility for the advance of human knowledge or human welfare; invariably he saw in them little more than ways of making an easy dollar at the expense of the ignorant and the foolish. Mencken wrote very early in the *Smart Set* that America seems to be prey to various and sundry modifications of a "New Thought" most of which were frauds.

> The New Thought, taking it by and large, is probably the most prosperous lunacy ever invented by mortal man. Every one of its multitudinous sublunacies, from psychical research to anti-vaccination, from vegetarianism to the Emmanuel Movement, and from zoophilism to Neo Buddhism, is gaining converts daily and making excellent profits for a horde of male, female and neuter missionaries. Why work at gravel roofing or dishwashing in the heat of the day when you can open a table tapping studio in any convenient furnished room house and rake in the willing dollars of the feeble-minded, the while you make their eyes bulge and the xanthous freckles on their necks go lemon pale?[7]

One of the characteristics of the quackery that flourishes in our time is its tendency to be cut to the scale of the masses—quackery must not only be for the people, but by and of the people. There must be a place for everybody to get in on the action; every line of work must have about it something that can be developed into a fraud or racket. Fields as lofty and demanding as religion, which require a certain amount of verbal skill and legerdemain, can hardly be expected to answer all the demands. There is a brisk demand for fields that require almost no cerebral endowment at all.

Consider chiropractic, for example, a quackery which flourishes "in the backreaches of the Republic and begins to conquer the less civilized folks in the big cities." Chiropractic is fitted perfectly not only to the mentality of its patients, but also to the skills of its practitioners. The basic principle of chiropractic is so simple that it can be understood and appreciated by even the densest country bumpkin. It is so simple that it can be taught to "ambitious farm-hands and out-at-elbow Baptist preachers in a few easy lessons." The backwoods, deprived of respectable medical care, is a paradise for chiropractors, who might otherwise have to wile away their hours in ignoble honest toil. "Any lout with strong hands and arms is perfectly equipped to become a chiropractor. No education beyond the elements is necessary. The whole art and mystery may be imparted in a few months, and the graduate is then free to practice on God's images. The takings are often high, and so the profession has attracted thousands of recruits—retired baseball players, plumbers, truck-drivers, longshoremen, bogus dentists, dubious preachers, village school superintendents."[8]

Quackeries and fads do not exist only to cozen the poor and the stupid. In America there are enough of them to go around for all—there are quackeries to catch well-to-do suburban matrons, college professors, anyone in fact with money in his pocket and a soft spot in his brain. When psychoanalysis came on the scene in America shortly before World War I, Mencken immediately perceived in it all the enchanting possibilities for urban doctors, and the concomitant fascination for idle and affluent housewives. Quackery on a very high level, to be sure, but, like all quackeries, immensely entertaining for the victim, immensely profitable to the practitioner.

> Hard upon the heels of the initiative and referendum, the Gary system, paper-bag cookery, the Montessori method, *vers libre* and the music of Igor Feodorovitch Stravinski, psychoanalysis now comes to intrigue and harass the sedentary multipara who seeks refuge in the women's clubs from the horrible joys of home life. The thing is much more dangerous to toy with than its forerunners in Advanced Thought, and at the same time much more fascinating—dangerous because it turns the uplift inward and may lead to sudden embarrassments, and fascinating because those sudden embarrassments have to

do with the forbidden subject of sex, the one permanent interest of all who go in skirts. Already it becomes impossible for a fashionable doctor to hold his trade without setting up a psychoanalytic laboratory behind his tile-and-nickle surgery, with a rose-tinted bunch-light to tone down his bald head, and zinc etchings of Pasteur, Metchnikoff and the Mona Lisa on the walls. Appendectomy and tonsillectomy go out of vogue, along with Bulgarian bacilli and Rabindranath Tagore.[9]

Mencken is offering here not an attack on psychoanalytic theory—he often spoke favorably of Freudian ideas in his writing—but a view of psychoanalysis within the larger setting of the human comedy. Most of us tend to look upon psychoanalysis, Montessori, the latest system of dieting, or Zen Buddhism as connected with the perennial search for truth. Psychoanalysis may be true or untrue; it may be partially true and untrue; it may be functional for one age and useless for another. Mencken the writer is not concerned with ideas in intellectual isolation. His main interest in the various fads, quackeries and experiments that chase each other through twentieth-century American history is not in their truth or falsity but in their popular meaning and function. His theory about fads like psychoanalysis is that they succeed in coming to prominence in American life not because of any truth that may inhere in them, but because they have the power to charm and because they can yield rich rewards to their supporters—fattening either their wallets or their reputations.

Such is the search for truth in America. Americans are not a people moved by strong and powerful ideas; they choose to bob up and down on a constantly changing stream of weak but thrilling ideas. In America the tempo of this kind of activity is speeded up, and before we have digested one kind of nonsense we are forced to swallow another.

American culture, as seen through Mencken's eyes, is best represented by the pageant presented to the world in the women's magazine. It is a kaleidoscopic world of fads and attractions, a passing fantasy in which diets are up and diets are down, sex is in and sex is out; in which children should be listened to or not listened to, toilet training is at three months or at three years. All of these causes have their advocates ready to hawk their wares as soon as the opportunity arises. America is the market-oriented society *par excellence,* and what is behind the extravagant marketplace of ideas is leisure and material prosperity. More people have the time and money to make fools of themselves than at any other time in history.

The pace of life is souped up, but it is not rendered more meaningful—only more exciting. Americans live in a fast-paced world of enchanting, stimulating, but not fully coherent ideas. There are too many ideas on the market, and too many ideas are dangerous since they war with one another, resulting in spiritual and intellectual disequilibrium.

There is another side to the coin. The marketplace in shoddy and titillating ideas can be traced not only to the existence of affluent buyers, but to the multitude of eager sellers. Americans are a people on the lookout for exciting new vocations, and there is no shortage of people willing to peddle Zen Buddhism or the latest fashion in psychotherapy. The impetus begins at the very lowest level of society. Even the most humble worker is anxious to be delivered from the sufferings and indignities of honest toil, and seeks to make out that his work is more ennobling than it seems. Given the principle that all people are equally important, it follows quite naturally that one of the most notable characteristics of life in America is the tendency for all people to seek ways to shuffle off dull, routine, and unexciting employment in favor of stimulating, prestigious, and ego-inflating employment.

There is an intimate connection between proliferating forms of entertainment and forms of work. Just as American cultural life tends to produce a multitude of bogus fads and ideas, so it seeks to lift all forms of work out of the dull and the mundane and endow them with an exaggerated importance. This effort, says Mencken, is readily understandable. The vast majority of men in any society are slaves, that is, men who suffer work only as a necessary evil. Only a few humans in any place or any age are what Beethoven called "free artists," that is, men who would gladly do what they do even if all economic pressures were removed. The vast majority of men will pay any price to mitigate the yoke of labor, or, if possible, throw it off entirely. The latter is not always possible, and throughout most of history it was not possible at all. However, in the more prosperous and impressionable American world, it is frequently easy to give a false appearance of dignity and ease to almost any kind of work. Familiar to us all, said Mencken, are "the many absurd devices to pump up lowly trades by giving them new and high-sounding names."

Consider, for example, the activities of the real estate agent and the undertaker. Both jobs in an unembellished form offer little to challenge the imagination. Hence the attempt is made to dignify them by hocus-pocus. The real estate agent "lets it be known grandly that he is an important semi-public functionary," devoted to service and high purpose, "and begins to call himself a realtor, a word as idiotic as flu, pep or gent." So it is with "the ambitious washer of the dead—until lately a sort of pariah in all civilized societies." He becomes a mortician, or, perhaps, following the gruesome imagination of an Evelyn Waugh, something even more magnificant. "At regular intervals," said Mencken, "I received impressive literature from a trade-union of undertakers calling themselves the Selected Morticians. By this literature it appears that the members thereof are professional men of a rank and dignity comparable to judges or archbishops, and they are hot for the sublest and most onerous kind of Service, and even eager to offer their advice to the national government."[10]

This American tendency to prod the individual ego to heights of vulgar achievement was dealt with at length in The American Language. There Mencken points out that our language has copiously produced euphemisms, and used titles and honorifics which allow the ordinary citizen to escape mundane names for his daily work.

> The American, probably more than any other man, is prone to be apologetic about the trade he follows. He seldom believes that it is quite worthy of his virutes and talents; almost always he thinks that he would have adorned something far gaudier. Unfortunately, it is not

always possible for him to escape, or even for him to dream plausibly of escaping, so he soothes himself by assuring himself that he belongs to a superior section of his craft, and very often he invents a sonorous name to set himself off from the herd. Here e.g. *mortician* for *undertaker, realtor* for *real-estate agent, electragist* for *electrical contractor, aisle manager* for *floor-walker, beautician* for *hair-dresser, exterminating engineer* for *rat-catcher*, and so on.[11]

So also with honorific titles. In America today, in spite of an early history of suspicion of all titles of honor or rank, titles are a glut on the market. It is true, of course, that the Germans, the Italians, and even the English diligently bestow titles upon their men of rank, "but on the other hand, they are very careful to withhold such titles from men who do not legally bear them. In England, for example, it would be unheard of to have nearly every practitioner of every healing art known as *doctor*; indeed in England a good many surgeons do not have or do not use the title." In America every chiropodist or chiropractor is *ipso facto* a doctor, and in *The American Language*, Mencken pointed out that the New York district attorney in 1926 issued a public warning that a multitude of healers had appropriated the title of *doctor*. Among these were doctors of: aerotherapy, astral healing, antothermy, bio-dynamo-chromatic-therapy, chromo-therapy, diet-therapy, electro-homeopathy, electro-napro-therapy, geo-therapy, irido-therapy, mechano-therapy, neuro-therapy, naprapathy, photo-therapy, physic-therapy, quartz-therapy, sanitratorism, spondylotherapy, spectro-chrome-therapy, spectra-therapy, tropo-therapy, theomonism, telatherapy, vitopathy, zodiac-therapy, zonet-therapy and Zoroastrianism.[12]

Similarly overworked is the title *professor*. "In all save a few of our larger cities every male pedagogue is a professor, and so is every band leader, dancing master and medical consultant. Two or three generations ago the title was given to horse-trainers, barbers, bartenders, phrenologists, caterers, patent-medicine vendors, acrobats, ventriloquists, and pedagogues and champions of all sorts."[13]

The excessive use of euphemisms for positions of employment or honorifics, titles, and other marks of achievement has always been self-defeating. The impetus is only truly productive when status is firmly imbedded in social reality. Where egalitarianism prevails, extravagant titles are small comfort. The barber or the pest control man have developed techniques to make people believe that they are as important and productive as a symphony orchestra conductor, but they know that they are not.

The American's love of prestige and status conceals a genuine doubt of his own significance. Mencken believed that the only healthy and tolerable condition is to have a true vocation, a kind of work that is fulfilling in and of itself. If a man wants to be something other than what he actually is, and needs a gaudy title to soothe his feelings of superiority, he is nothing more than a slave—and slaves are universally unhappy. America is a nation of slaves. We are a nation of unhappy souls who lack fulfillment in what we do, and therefore are ceaselessly struggling to find something to fill the void in our lives.

Mencken offers a wide latitude for the free man, the man of liberal vocation. He hardly expects every man to be a Beethoven or a Henry L. Mencken. There is nothing wrong in being a clerk or a farmer. Under the conditions of American life the farmer and the clerk are constantly being tempted away from a life style where they might fulfill and satisfy themselves; they are whipped into a frenzy by politicians and evangelists; they are taught by the government that more attention must be paid to them. Still, this does not mean that the farmer or the clerk has to be a slave, one who spends his waking hours desiring to be something else. A farmer might be a happy man and a free man, even if he were not an aristocrat of the spirit like Beethoven or Shakespeare.

In Mencken's museum of human types, the ordinary man of limited intellectual resources can fare none too badly if he lives in the right kind of social order. If conditions are such that he can realize his potential, engage in work which involves him in a spiritual way, even if on a low level, he can live a life of happiness and satisfaction. If, on the other hand, he is subjected to a social system which tantalizes him by promising him more than it can deliver, then his lot will invariably be one of envy, frustration, and annoyance. He will be forever reaching out for some bauble just beyond his grasp, and if one bauble is caught, a dozen more will present themselves just up ahead.

The tragedy of America, then, is that its social life is not conducive to happiness, fulfillment of the human spirit, innocent joy, or spontaneous emotion, but rather to a deadening of manners and morals, an anaesthesia to any pleasures save the purely mechanical and artificial. In America, said Mencken, "there is a vast and complex machinery for taking the slave's mind off the desolateness of spirit." There are

> moving pictures to transport him into a land of romance, where men (whom he always identifies with himself) are brave, rich and handsome, and women (whom he identifies with his wife—or perchance with her younger sister) are clean, well-dressed and beautiful; newspapers to delight and instruct him with their sports pages, their comic strips and their eloquent appeals to his liberality, public spirit and patriotism; public bands and the radio to play the latest jazz for him; circuses and parades; baseball, races, gambling, harlotry and games in arenas; a thousand devices to make him forget his woes.[14]

Of course they are all devices; they do not make him forget his woes and in fact only tend to intensify them by giving him a fuller realization of where he is lacking. A consumer or spectator culture is a surrogate for a genuine creative one.

There are signs that our culture is vicarious, that it is depressing and unnerving rather than nourishing and liberating. We have mentioned a number already—the preoccupation with idle amusements, the overabundance of fads and distracting pastimes. A feverish overconcern for money is another. Writing at the very height of the Coolidge prosperity, Mencken was quick to point out that Americans, more than any other people in history, are inclined to see virtue entirely in terms of money—money, after all, is a vicarious, a symbolic, thing, and it is the one above all the others of which we have made a national totem. Money, said Mencken, is perhaps the only thing with the power to stimulate the imagination of man in our democratic state. "He can not only imagine hundreds of ways of getting happiness out of money; he devotes almost the whole of his intellectual activity, such as it is, to imagining them, and he seldom if ever imagines anything else." Dreams of money generate the whole life style of the American man. "Even his sexual fancies translate themselves instantly into concepts of dollars and cents; the thing that confines him so miserably to one wife, and to one, alas, so unappetizing and depressing, is simply his lack of money; if he only had the wealth of Diamond Jim Brady he too would be the glittering Don Giovanni that Jim was."[15]

Mencken did believe that civic responsibility and virtue were most likely to be found among people of finer breeding, that is, those raised in a patrician environment. In the crude, money-grasping business society and its captains of industry, he could see little possibility for the advancement of society. In the Rockefellers and Schwabs he saw little more than lowly "traders and usurers," in Judge Elbert H. Gary, Chairman of the Board of the United States Steel Corporation, "an emperor and pope of all the Babbitts." The American capitalist provides no genuine leadership because money—and more money—completely circumscribes his interests and his culture. The United States, said Mencken, is "the first great empire in history to ground its whole national philosophy on business." There have been other "trading nations" in the past, but none were so completely dominated by the trafficker. "Even in Carthage there was a Junker hierarchy." England, that nation of shopkeepers, has always had an aristocracy that "has held its own against the men of trade," even if this aristocracy has been "made up mainly of military freebooters, enterprising adulterers, the issue of the latter, and, in modern times, shyster lawyers, vaudeville magnates, and the proprietors of yellow newspapers."[16] Only in America are the trader and the usurer king and hero.

Mencken believed, along with Carlyle, that in an industrial society the captain of industry ought to be an aristocrat. "The

Leaders of Industry," said Carlyle, "if Industry is ever to be led, are virtually the Captains of the World! if there be no nobleness in them, there will never be an Aristocracy more." Mencken regretted, with Carlyle, that the captains of industry we actually have are unsuited to lead. The culture of the captain of industry is nothing but business; he venerates nothing but money. "He respects money in each and every one of its beautiful forms—pennies, nickles, dimes, dollars, five-dollar bills, and so on *ad infinitum.* He venerates those who have it. He believes that they have wisdom."[17] A true leader of mankind cannot be grounded in pennies, nickles, and dimes, and wisdom is not the mouthings of those who possess the most of them. Until the Rockefellers and Garys see this there is no hope that a natural aristocracy can arise from their midst.

At the same time, we must beware of the assumption that the "reformers" of business are free of the crass materialism of the businessman. One of the defects of our money-oriented society is that the dynamism of money catches nearly everybody up in it. What of the Muckrakers, the Progressive reformers who stamp up and down the countryside preaching the abuses of big business and the corrupting power of mammon?

Mencken did not believe the money disease was limited to the businessman. The reformers and uplifters suffer from the very same disease. "Even the Socialists, who profess to scorn money, really worship it. Socialism, indeed, is simply the degenerate capitalism of bankrupt capitalists. Its one genuine object is to get more money for its professors; all its other grandiloquent objects are afterthoughts, and most of them are bogus." Most self-styled reformers and do-gooders in the democratic milieu appear to be out to banish injustice and inequality, but closer inspection shows their motives usually involve some scheme to take money from the pocket of A to put it in the pocket of B. All the reform and do-good schemes afloat in the world ultimately involve redistribution of money, taking from one person's pocket to put it in another's. The average American's political ideals, too, are nearly always for sale. "His fundamental political ideas nearly all contemplate raids upon capital, even when they appear superficially to be quite free from economic flavor, and most of the political banshees and bugaboos that alternately freeze and boil his blood have dollar marks written all over them."[18]

Here we return to Mencken's characterization of democratic man as a creature of envy. The envy which is the end product of egalitarianism is also the mother of the American's veneration of money. We crave money because we are envious of others who have more of it, just as the puritan loves his moral indictments because he is disturbed by people enjoying more of life than he does. The capitalist is ever finding himself outdone by others up above, or being bitten by fleas from below. These fleas below, who are they? Socialists, do-gooders, reformers who cannot rest until they have sucked some blood from the man who is better endowed, or at least made his life somewhat uncomfortable. Here again is a tragedy of the democratic state—it pits man against man in envy so that they cannot find for themselves a harmonious existence or a stable culture.

The Shoddy Quality of Human Life in a Democracy

The American people are unable to attain a refined standard of living in spite of material prosperity. Affluence is by no means a guarantee of a high standard of living. Americans may have more money to spend than any other people in history, and they make every effort to turn their cash into the good life, but more often than not they fail.

Mencken felt that one of the reasons for this is that Americans are a mobile people who have failed to grasp the necessity and importance of establishing a permanent home. Especially in cities, Americans find themselves repeatedly torn up and replanted. This offends the human instinct to take root and flourish in one place. In New York, for example, even the rich find it impossible to make a permanent home for themselves. "The very richest man, in New York, is never quite sure that the house he lives in now will be his next year—that he will be able to resist the constant pressure of business expansion and rising land values. I have known actual millionaires to be chased out of their homes in this way, and forced into apartments."[19] Apartment house living was especially repugnant to Mencken; the apartment, even the a-partment of a wealthy man, is not a place for permanent personal possessions. Even if there is sufficient space to keep them, an apartment dweller comes to think of personal pos-sessions as being transient and fleeting things. He develops the mentality of an insect caught in a dark jar. Apartment house living may have a certain amount of gaudy glamor to it, but underneath it offers no spiritual *Lebensraum*.

> Such a habitation, it must be plain, cannot be called a home. A home is not a mere transient shelter: its essence lies in its permanence, in its capacity for accretion and solidification, in its quality of representing, in all its details, the personalities of the people who live in it. In the course of years it becomes a sort of museum of these people; they give it its indefinable air, separating it from all other homes, as one human face is separated from all others. It is at once a refuge from the world, a treasure-house, a castle, and a shrine of a whole hierarchy of peculiarly private and potent gods. This concept of the home cannot survive the mode of life that prevails in New York.[20]

Mencken often defended his native Baltimore, as dis-tinguished from other northern and eastern cities, on the ground that it was a more leisurely, commodious city, with a certain air of gentility and refinement. He seems to have approved of city life, and to have shared the feeling of Socr-ates who refused to leave the city gates of Athens because within the walls of the city were to be found the best in conversation, the best in civilized life. Cities are only tolera-ble as long as they provide a feeling of permanence—if one can enjoy lasting friendships, personal possessions, solid ties. New York in the 1920s offered no such permanence. The New Yorker was a vagabond. "His notions of the agreeable become those of a vaudeville actor. He takes on the shallowness and unpleasantness of any other homeless man. He is highly sophisticated and inordinately trashy."[21] He mistakes sophistication for culture, and Mencken believed that culture cannot thrive and prosper under the hyperkinetic conditions that prevail in the average American metropolis.

In more recent years, Vance Packard, in *A Nation of Strangers*, found that the same thing could be said about the suburbs. Even if the suburbs offer a spaciousness that is lacking in the city, they are spiritually an extension of the urban style of living—they offer few opportunities for permanent friendships and alliances, and the kind of culture that prospers there is cold, impersonal, and shallow.

For the poor who live in urban industrial America the situation is even more bleak, not because the poor are poor, but because urban poverty becomes a way of life that is cultivated for its own sake. In his travels through the industrial heartland of America, Mencken observed that the poor often seem to have no desire to alleviate their poverty, make no effort to brighten up their homes or towns. Also, they are not as poor as their environment suggests; they could afford to beautify their homes and communities, but refuse to do so. Riding through the steel towns of Pennsylvania east of Pittsburgh in the comfortable setting of a Pullman, Mencken noted that the towns were not only dirty, as one would reasonably expect them to be, but ugly as well. From East Liberty to Greensburg, a distance of twenty-five miles, there was not a building in sight "that did not insult and lacerate the eye. Some were so bad, and they were among the most pretentious—churches, stores, warehouses, and the like—that they were downright startling: one blinked before them as one blinks before a man with his face shot away."[22]

The countryside itself, said Mencken was not lacking in beauty, and he believed that with only the smallest of efforts these people could have created decent surroundings. After all, the poor of America are far more affluent than the poor of many other countries, who seem to know how to live more aesthetically. People here seem to go out of their way to surround themselves with ugliness. "There seems to be a positive libido for the ugly," a passion to make the world unbeautiful. "It is impossible to put down the wallpaper that

defaces the average American home of the lower middle class
to mere inadvertence, or to the obscene humor of the manufac-
turers. Such ghastly designs, it must be obvious, give a
genuine delight to a certain type of mind." That the lower
classes are consigned to a life of squalor and ugliness because
of poverty is rejected by Mencken; to a large extent they
choose these circumstances. The houses in the coal region are
ugly, but for the very same amount of money the people could
have gotten much better ones; they could have even built
better ones themselves. Obviously they prefer what they
have. "Here is something that psychologists have so far neglected: the love of ugliness for its own sake, the lust to make
the world intolerable. Its habitat is the United States."[23]

America's industrial might has not guaranteed the establishment of refinement and civility either in the lives of the
poor or in the lives of the rich. The poor, whether urban or
rural, seem locked in a condition of despair—a despair characterized by a stubborn unwillingness to brighten up the
world. Whether it is the coal towns of Pennsylvania with their
grime and unseemly architecture or the lonely farmhouse, the
outlook and culture of workday America is very bleak indeed.
The affluent world of the great cities, on the other hand, is one
of gaudy spectacle, pseudo-sophistication, and constant but
uninspiring motion and activity. For Mencken, these are the
fruits of a civilization based on money and the promise of
money; moral and aesthetic values, learning and imagination,
all must go into hiding to thrive in some dark place, cultivated
only by a few.

Mencken believed that the business ethos has brought
about a demasculinized society where male virtues and characteristics play a secondary role, except in the sphere of
business. America is a society where the function of sustaining culture and civility becomes a female responsibility—or a
responsibility of the feminized male. Such is the position
which emerges from Mencken's ironically titled book, *In
Defense of Women*. The American woman has had to bear the
burden of sustaining American culture, since men are shut off
in the uninspiring realm of business.

This view was not new with Mencken; it had been part of

the zeitgeist of the American intellectual for some time, and was long a belief of Europeans. Van Wyck Brooks gave expression to it in 1908 in *The Wine of the Puritans*, in which he called attention to a schism in American life between the "transcendental and the commercial," and insisted that women seem to be the custodians of the former. Brooks, who grew to manhood in one of the New Jersey bedroom suburbs, was obsessed with the relative weakness and lack of effectiveness of the male spirit in American life. In *The Opinions of Oliver Allston*, a thinly disguised collection of autobiographical sketches and literary opinions, Brooks declared this problem to be a frequently recurring theme in the American novel. Commenting on Thomas Wolfe's *Of Time and the River*, Oliver Allston writes:

> In this American novel, like so many others, the father is a broken reed, the mother in her way, strong and even heroic. This is the Sherwood Anderson pattern also; indeed one might call it the all-American pattern. It is typical of this country on all social levels. "The American man is a failure," and how often one has to repeat it in so many connections. The mother, in our typical novel, is usually stable, the father unstable at best. This seems to indicate by general agreement, whether conscious or not, that our scheme of life is more propitious for women than for men.[24]

Mencken's "defense" of women is based on his belief that a business and commercial society invariably brings out the worst traits in the male animal, that the American man avails himself of every opportunity to make a fool of himself. Outwardly and publicly there has always been a tendency to denigrate the role of the female. However, excluding the first-rate men—always rare in any society—in American life women have always been a special blessing, have provided much of the native intelligence and force of character without which no civilization can endure.

Mencken held that "the average American woman, whatever her deficiencies, is greatly superior to the average Amer-

ican man." The male in our society regards his lowly "collection of cerebral rubber-stamps" as a sure sign of superior
intelligence and sagacity.

> A man thinks that he is more intelligent than his wife
> because he can add up a column of figures more ac-
> curately, and because he understands the imbecile jargon
> of baseball and the stock market, and because he is able to
> distinguish between the rival ideas of rival politicians,
> and because he is privy to the minutiae of some sordid
> and degrading business or profession, say soap-selling or
> the law. But these empty talents, of course, are not really
> signs of a profound intelligence; they are, in fact, merely
> superficial accomplishments, and their acquirement puts
> little more strain on the mental powers than a chimpanzee
> suffers in learning how to catch a penny or scratch a
> match. The whole bag of tricks of the average business
> man, or even of the average professional man, is inor-
> dinately childish. It takes no more actual sagacity to
> carry on the everyday hawking and haggling of the world,
> or to ladle out its normal doses of bad medicine and worse
> law, than it takes to operate a taxi-cab or fry a pan of
> fish.[25]

The usual business and professional men in America, said
Mencken, are so many blank cartridges. He quoted Charles
Francis Adams, a man who enjoyed—or endured—a life-long
association with men of affairs and leaders of state and who
insisted that he had never heard a single one of them say
anything worth hearing. If these men of affairs were genuinely intelligent they would never be able to succeed at their
gross and drivelling concerns. "One could not think of Aristotle or Beethoven multiplying 3,472,701 by 99,999 without
making a mistake, nor could one think of them remembering
the range of this or that stock for two years, or the number of
ten-penny nails in a hundredweight, or the freight rate on
carpet sweepers from Akron, O., to Newport News." Nor
could one imagine them remembering baseball averages or
being proficient at golf, billiards, bridge or "any of the other of

the idiotic games at which what are called successful men commonly divert themselves."[26]

Men urge the inferiority of women on the grounds that women never succeed at the occupations which fascinate men in our society—"tuning pianos, repairing clocks, practicing law (i.e., matching petty tricks with some other lawyer), painting portraits, keeping books, managing factories." All of these occupations are within the physical powers of the average woman, and within her intellectual range. That women do not take them up is due to their more cultivated minds and to their rugged, no-nonsense ability to penetrate the buncombe that surrounds the average male occupation.

However, Mencken held the suffragette in low esteem. He saw her as an unbright member of the female sex, a woman hankering after the pastimes and so-called prerogatives of the average unimaginative male. Most intelligent women are above the man-made fallacies and sentimentalities that fire up the suffragette. Where the suffragette goes wrong in her thinking is easy to see:

> She is a woman who has carried her envy of certain of the superficial privileges of men to such a point that it takes on the character of an obsession, and makes her blind to their valueless and often chiefly imaginary character. In particular, she centers this frenzy of hers upon one definite privilege, to wit, the alleged privilege of promiscuity in amour, the modern *droit du seigneur*. Read the books of the chief suffragette wild women, and you will find running through them an historical denunciation of what is called the double standard of morality. . . . The existence of this double standard seems to drive the poor girls half frantic. They bellow raucously for its abrogation, and demand that the frivolous male be visited with even more idiotic penalties than those which now visit the aberrant female. . . . What these virtuous beldames actually desire is . . . that the franchise of dalliance be extended to themselves.[27]

Furthermore, she pants for male vocations and a male style

of life. She believes that she can improve her position in the world by aspiring to these things. Only the more foolish women fall victim to this mode of thinking. The average woman is far too clever to be fooled by the tinsel with which the third-rate man bedecks himself; she is content with her own kind of superiority and is more successful than the male in detaching herself from the blustering and blundering world of striving and gain. Quite sensibly she perceives and prefers the quiet superiority of the traditional female role in American culture.

For all his ironic praise of the female role in our society, the main point Mencken makes in his book, In Defense of Women, is that for the preservation of culture we rely too heavily on women and on female virtues. Our country is not lacking in intelligent and awesome women; what it lacks is first-class men, men of high character and imagination. Mencken himself was openly an apologist for male virtues, and his praise or defense of women is written in the melancholy vein of a man who is chagrined that women have to play such an overwhelmingly dominant role in our society. The female virtues of commonsense, realism, orderliness, decorum, solidity of character, and linear intelligence are both praiseworthy and necessary. What America needs more of, however, are the male virtues celebrated by Mark Twain in Huckleberry Finn and Tom Sawyer: high imagination, forthrightness, exuberance, and boyish innocence, perhaps judiciously mixed with a little mischievousness and impracticality. We need what we had more of in the old America, men driven by wild impractical fancies, bursts of industry and imagination. From the virtues of the average shopkeeping or bookkeeping male we can expect far less than we can of the woman of mediocre intelligence. Above all, no respectable culture can grow from a social order where the first-rate man is squelched and the third-rate man is boosted to the top rung of the commercial ladder and venerated for his meager, monetary achievement.

Are there, then, no first-rate men in America? Is there no redeeming higher culture? Mencken was ambivalent in his answer. We know, for example, that he championed American writers both old and new, that he respected American scientists and intellectuals. However, he believed that our best creative minds live in isolation and that society does not sufficiently reward them for their efforts. Too, he felt that there is no point where the higher culture can transfuse into the blood of the people. While our society has had many moments of consummate creative activity and achievement— as in the nineteenth-century Renaissance—these moments are nothing but moments; our better minds, our greatest artists, are constantly getting lost or misplaced, their circles of influence breaking up and disappearing. America was fortunate in having produced an Emerson, a Hawthorne, or Melville—and so early in its history. How little these figures contribute to the American life style should give us pause. Perhaps there is something about industrial and urban America that erases higher achievements before they can be engraved on our national consciousness; perhaps we move so fast that we cannot intellectually assimilate all the changes going on around us.

Mencken believed that our higher culture is anemic and lacks the power to sustain itself. He believed that the higher culture we do have has largely been insular—cut off from the mainstream of American life. While we have not been entirely without philosophers, artists, poets, and intellectuals, the best of them have lived a lonely existence, and have not changed the common life. Whitman, we are often told, glutted himself upon the common life, but the common life was never stirred very much by Whitman.

Unfortunately, the institutions for the preservation of culture have not always been strong in America; more often they do their work poorly and inadequately. Nowhere have educational institutions thrived so well as in America, but Mencken was skeptical of their ultimate value. Outwardly they prosper; they have the appearance of glowing good health and remarkable achievement. However, they reinforce all the habitual American weaknesses and deficiencies.

V

The Anemia
of the Higher Culture

Americans are known throughout the world as a people of
hustle and bustle, of industrial might, of practical energy, and
of drive and ambition. The question has been raised whether
America has a real civilization to match its achievements in
the practical realm. Is there a higher culture in America? Do
we Americans enjoy a harmonious unity of learning and
practice, intellect and will? Or have we built a fractured and
splintered civilization in which the separate compartments of
life exist side by side in mutual distrust? Above all, have we
given a good account of ourselves in the arts, in philosophy,
and in the world of learning?

In answering questions like these, Mencken was guided by
his Nietzschean perspective on the quality of life in democratic states. America is a great material civilization that has
found employment for more poets, oboe players, artisans, and
thinkers of all kinds than any earlier civilization in history.
But is America really fertile ground for the development of the
best that is thought and said?

Mencken's view, like Nietzsche's, is that democratic states
develop large and complex institutions of learning and sufficient opportunities for cultural development, but that these
are not conducive to the greatest freedom of expression; that
culture is widely spread to the general public, but that this

tends to become gaudy and pretentious rather than substantial; that the arts will flourish but mostly by turning out more standardized, prepackaged products for mass consumption. The truly unfettered thinker or artist will be no more common in a democracy than he has been in any earlier period of history. A prosperous economy will give artists and intellectuals more leisure to produce, but at the same time there will be less free air, more distractions, and more compulsion to conform to standardized patterns and to turn out products that will entertain minds that are simple and lazy.

Mencken devoted a good deal of his energies in the 1920s to questions of education. Americans, he thought, have an overzealous and unsubstantiated faith in the usefulness of universal education. They believe that culture can be spread to large segments of the population. When we establish the right of every citizen to basic literacy, we move on to the belief that every citizen ought to have a high school diploma, then perhaps a college diploma, or even a Ph.D. Mencken's view was that the mass of men are uneducable because they are lazy and prefer simple formulaic ideas to complex and demanding ones. The average citizen will make a show of learning; he will try hard to please a teacher, even though what he wants is to be let alone. In ideas, he wants safety and security rather than challenge and effort. In the end, therefore, the highly prolific and widespread institutions of learning must devote themselves to safety, conformity, and uniformity.

Mencken believed that a democratic state is not propitious for the development of the best and freest art, for the most creative thinking. The artist must often pander to popular taste or perish; the thinker must attach himself to stale institutional modes of thought from which he can deviate only at his peril. The higher culture in America is widespread, outwardly prosperous, idolized, but inwardly it is weak and anemic. It is no more central to the workings of everyday life than the higher culture of any previous civilizations. The lot of the true artist or intellectual is no easier than it has ever been.

Before exploring these ideas further, it would be good to contrast Mencken's views on the higher culture in America with another view, in some ways similar and in other ways different, which became influential in the first decades of the twentieth century. In a now famous address, "The Genteel Tradition in American Philosophy," delivered before the Philosophical Union of the University of California in 1911, George Santayana developed a view of the higher culture that subtly blends and contrasts with the one Mencken started to develop around the same time.

Like Mencken, Santayana believed that the higher culture in America was weak and anemic. He had different reasons for believing this. Santayana believed that the higher culture was pure enough where it existed, but that it was somehow cut off, estranged, from the rest of American life. In his address on "the genteel tradition" Santayana pointed out that one of the most curious characteristics of the American people is that they are not at all lacking in culture, as one might expect in a young country where material preoccupations have tended to absorb people's attention. America has seen a great deal of cultural activity. "Not only have you already had time to philosophize in California," Santayana told his listeners, "but the Eastern colonists from the very beginning were a sophisticated race." Still, American culture seems remote, unattached, estranged. The trouble is, "America is a young country with an old mentality." The wise old head doesn't go together with the fresh young body.

> The truth is that one-half of the American mind, that not occupied intensely with practical affairs, has remained, I will not say high-and-dry, but slightly becalmed; it has floated gently in the backwater, while alongside, in invention and industry and social organization, the other half of the mind was leaping down a sort of Niagara Rapids. This division may be symbolized in American architecture: a neat reproduction of the colonial mansion—with some modern comforts introduced surreptitiously—stands beside the sky-scraper. The American Will inhabits the sky-scraper; the American Intellect inhabits the colonial mansion. The one is the sphere of the American man; the other, at least predominantly, of the American woman. The one is all aggressive enterprise, the other is all genteel tradition.[1]

Santayana's lecture dealt mainly with American philosophy, showing how the Calvinism of early New England fed on religious beliefs and cultural traditions borrowed from the Old World, and how this became totally unsuited to the American life style. Calvinism continued in a stale and wasted condition, or was converted into newer but similarly anemic forms—to transcendental idealism, for example, or to the kind of Hegelian idealism that flourished at the Harvard Graduate School during Santayana's tenure there. His point had wider implications. The genteel tradition ran not only through professional philosophy, but through all of American life; even the arts were born old, or inherited the thin blood of the Calvinist tradition. This does not imply that American art has been second-rate, but that each artist has had to develop independently. "If anybody arose with a special sensibility or a technical genius, he was in great straits; not being fed sufficiently on the world he was driven in upon his own resources."

Such geniuses did arise, and in good number. Consider, for example, Poe, Hawthorne, and Emerson, the three American writers whose personal endowment Santayana considered to be the richest. They could not simply retail the genteel tradition as they encountered it. "Life offered them little digestible material; . . . they were fastidious, and, under the circumstances, they were starved." Emerson fed on books, but "he read transcendentally not historically," that is, he read to discover and develop himself, not to discover the world around him. "To feed on books, for a philosopher or a poet, is still to starve." Or, stated another way, the culture that must depend on these genteel writers and philosophers must starve. Little in our best literature speaks directly to the conditions of American life. The genius of Poe, Hawthorne, or Emerson was employed on some kind of "inner play or digestion of vacancy."

It was a refined labour, but it was in danger of being morbid, or tinkling, or self-indulgent. It was like a play of intra-mental rhymes. Their mind was like an old music-box, full of tender echoes and quaint fancies. These fancies expressed their personal genius sincerely, as dreams may; but they were arbitrary fancies in comparison with what a real observer would have said in the premises. Their manner, in a word, was subjective. In their persons they escaped the mediocrity of the genteel tradition, but they supplied nothing to supplant it in other minds.[2]

Much of Santayana's address devoted itself to the few attempts of later Americans to break the spell of the genteel tradition, to develop some kind of genuinely indigenous culture. He saw Walt Whitman, for example, as representing a very definite and incisive break with the genteel tradition. Whitman's Bohemianism, his earthy materialism, his concern for the inarticulate principles that animate the community, separated him from the pale and anemic native literary tradition. But he paid the price for this revolt in that he has not been assimilated into the culture. He has done little as a harbinger of new standards; he has mostly functioned as a destroyer of the old.

William and Henry James, on the other hand, were more serious threats to the tradition, because from the start they were a part of it. Both were "as tightly swaddled in the genteel tradition as any infant geniuses could be, for they were born before 1850, and in a Swedenborgian household." Yet both burst their bands completely. Henry did it "by turning the genteel tradition, as he turned everything else, into a subject matter for analysis," that is to say, he overcame it by understanding it. Ultimately, however, this meant removing himself from the mainstream, so that in Santayana's eyes it was William, more than Henry, who confronted the American tradition on its own ground. By championing dissident philosophies, by acknowledging the newer sciences, by opening his mind to "all that might seem, to polite minds, odd, personal or visionary in religion and philosophy," by accepting the normal practical masculine America, William had "broken the spell of the genteel tradition."

In this address, delivered the year before his departure from America, Santayana mentioned a few other spots where "chinks might be found in the armour of the genteel tradition."

He mentioned, without naming any particular examples, the American humorists. The humorists "only half escape the genteel tradition; their humor would lose its savor if they had wholly escaped it." Nevertheless, this rich American heritage cannot be discounted, and its prevalence "in and out of season, may be taken as one more evidence that the genteel tradition is present pervasively, but everywhere weak."

Santayana's ideas are worth noting because they are characteristic of the views of the American intelligensia at the end of the nineteenth century and the beginning of the twentieth. A very similar vision can be found in Whitman's *Democratic Vistas*. Here, too, we find the idea of two American cultures, one the work of "genteel little creatures whose perpetual pistareen paste pot work" was the best that we could hope for at the upper levels, the other the work of practical men who have developed no culture at all. A similar duality is suggested by Henry Adams's symbolism of the Virgin and the Dynamo. In *America's Coming of Age*, published in 1915, Van Wyck Brooks gave a statement of the American dilemma not much different from Santayana's:

> So it is that from the beginning we find two main currents in the American mind running side by side but rarely mingling—a current of overtones and a current of undertones—and both equally unsocial: on the one hand the transcendental current, originating in the piety of the Puritans, becoming a philosophy in Jonathan Edwards, passing through Emerson, producing the fastidious refinement and aloofness of the chief American writers, and resulting in the final unreality of most contemporary culture; and on the other hand the current of catchpenny opportunism, originating in the practical shifts of Puritan life, becoming a philosophy in Franklin, passing through the American humorists, and resulting in the atmosphere of our contemporary business life.[3]

One of Brooks's aims in writing *America's Coming of Age* was to begin a search for a unifying thread, an organic principle, which would allow the writer to bridge the chasm

between the weak highbrow culture and the vigorous
lowbrow one. Brooks found the precursor of such a "middle
tradition" in Whitman, and it was on the basis of this "middle
tradition" that Brooks offered a manifesto to a new generation
of American writers.

When Mencken started elaborating his critique of American culture in the 1920s, he was not drawn to the formulation
that two traditions existed side by side but in material isolation. He did not accept Santayana's idea that there was
something zestful and refreshing about American industry
and practical achievement. At the same time, he did not accept
the idea that what was wrong with the genteel tradition is
that it was detached from the fabric of American life. He
agreed that there was something weak and anemic about the
higher culture, but believed that this was because it was
enmeshed in all of the disturbances that characterize a democracy. What is wrong with so many earlier visions of America,
including Santayana's, is that they were conceived without
close contact with the historical nitty-gritty of American life.
The dualism of the high and low, the genteel and the practical,
were, as theory, easy to accept, but they were incapable of
penetrating very deeply.

Mencken was inclined to accept the existence of something
very much like Santayana's genteel tradition. On the other
hand, he perceived some signs of force in the older New
England writers that Santayana missed. Consider Emerson,
for example. Mencken agreed with Santayana that Emerson
had a timid and cautious side, that his ideas tended to be
borrowings from one respectable tradition or another, and
that while in his own day he was thought to be something of a
revolutionary he was, in fact, "imitative and cautious—an
importer of stale German elixirs sometimes direct and sometimes through the Carlylean branch house, who took good
care to dilute them with buttermilk before merchanting
them."[4]

There is another side to Emerson that is sometimes forgotten by the kind of person who takes Emerson as his mentor
and spiritual leader. There is Emerson the free thinker, the
rebel who asked his fellow countrymen to start out on their

own, to rip up all the old paths to knowledge and virtue, to "defer never to the popular cry." When we hear from "the professors" that they are taking Emerson as their guide we can assure ourselves that it is not this Emerson that they are talking about. It is "precisely within the circle of Emersonian adulation that one finds the strongest tendency to test all ideas by their respectability, to combat free thought as something intrinsically vicious, and to yield placidly to 'some great decorum, some fetish of government, some ephemeral trade, or war, or man.'" No country is more implacable in its rejection of Emersonian individualism than Emerson's own. "It is surely not unworthy of notice," said Mencken, "that the country of this prophet of man thinking is preceisely the country in which every sort of dissent from the current pishposh is combatted most ferociously, and in which there is the most vigorous existing tendency to suppress free speech altogether."[5] The Emerson that is followed by his countrymen today is not worth following. It is the Emerson who said "thou shalt not follow" who alone should be followed.

For Mencken, there is a tradition of revolt in American life and literature, and this is our strongest, perhaps our only, valuable tradition. This tradition of rejecting tradition is the most important of all American traditions. All of our first-rate writers owe their distinction to a revolt against their time. To try to turn them into spokesmen for American purity and conformity is to strike from them their most distinguishing characteristic.

> Can it be that even pedagogues are unaware that Emerson came to fame by advocating a general deliverance from the stupid and flabby tradition his name is now evoked to support, that his whole system of ideas was an unqualified protest against hampering traditions of every sort, that if he were alive today he would not be with the professors but unalterably against them? And Emerson was surely not alone. Go through the list of genuinely first-rate men: Poe, Hawthorne, Whitman, Mark Twain. One and all they stood outside the so-called tradition of their time; one and all, they remained outside the tradi-

tion that pedants try so vainly to impose upon a literature in active being today. Poe's poems and tales not only seemed strange to the respectable dolts of his time; they seemed downright horrible. His criticism, which tells us even more about him, was still worse: it impinged upon such dull fellows as Griswold exactly as *Jennie Gerhardt* impinged upon the appalled tutors in the alfalfa colleges. And what of Hawthorne? Hawthrone's onslaught upon the Puritan ethic was the most formidable and effective ever delivered, save only Emerson's.[6]

So it was with Whitman. The professors of the 1870s failed to mention him just as they failed to mention Dreiser or Cabell in 1920. Much the same may be said of Mark Twain. As late as 1910 the professors "were still teaching that Washington Irving was a great humorist and Mark a mere clown." If we hold with Santayana that America has not developed a "tradition," it is because we are looking for something that the higher American culture has always rebelled against—some kind of lineage of savants and sages. For Mencken, it is just this tendency to hunt for a cultural royalty that has obscured our best heritage, and it is just this tendency that our best writers have sought to extinguish. Our national genius, insofar as it can be found, is one of individualism and revolt.

Santayana leveled against the genteel tradition the charge that its ideas were borrowed; he believed that what America needed was its own set of ideas. Mencken was troubled not so much by the tendency of the Americans to borrow ideas from their Anglo-Saxon forbears as by the hostility of American society to excellence and achievement in the intellectual world. In his "Diagnosis of our Cultural Malaise," in the *Smart Set* for February 1919, Mencken attributed our lack of an intellectual and cultural awakening to two factors: first, our inability to develop a native aristocracy, either political or intellectual, with the consequence that "the banal ideas and cautious, stupid habits of mind of the great masses of inferior men prevail among us as nowhere else on earth," and second, our inability to shake loose the colonial mentality of timidity and restraint. We remain as much a spiritual and intellectual colony as we were on July 3, 1776. "The things we lack are precisely the things that all other groups of colonists, however rich and potent, lack, to wit, self-confidence, the indomitable will to self-expression, intellectual courage, pride amounting to disdain, and, above all, a thorough organization of society in all its ranks. The upper rank is always missing; it remains anchored to the motherland."[7]

The motherland we are anchored to has itself become a land of timid, overcautious, and even cowardly minds. The English culture we now venerate is not worth venerating. It may have given the world great individuals—a Shakespeare or a Milton, an Arnold or Macaulay—but when Americans look to England for moral and intellectual guidance they look to the pharisee class, to the high priests of pretentiousness. To Mencken, the Anglo-Saxon is, in the main, a third-rate intellect. He lacks courage, "the ease and tolerance, the fine adventurousness and love of hazard which goes with a fine sense of firm security." The Anglo-Saxon lacks a genuine sense of superiority, the conviction that what he does is genuinely worth doing. His civilization is thus inferior to that of France or Germany—civilizations built on romance, daring, and gusto.

> The Anglo-Saxon of the great herd is, in many important respects, the least civilized of men and the least capable of true civilization. His political ideas are crude and shallow. He is almost wholly devoid of aesthetic feeling; he does not even make folk-lore or walk in the woods. The most elementary facts about the universe alarm him, and incite him to put them down. Educate him, make a professor of him, teach him how to express his soul, and he still remains palpably third-rate. He fears ideas almost more cravenly than he fears men.[8]

Admittedly the Anglo-Saxons have given a good account of themselves. Their enterprise is unquestioned, their culture is safe, well-protected, and innocuous. Mencken believed that the success of the Anglo-Saxons has been "not so much to their merits but to their defects—and especially to their high capacity for being alarmed and their aversion to what might be called romance—in other words, to their harshly practical minds, their disdain of intellectual enterprise, their dull common sense."[9] For Mencken the world of business and the world of intellect are alike in the Anglo-Saxon countries; the businessman goes on safely hoarding his pennies; the intellectual goes on with his own cultural hoarding—reducing art and all genuine passion to the safe, the inert, the lifeless, the socially acceptable.

As Mencken viewed the cultural world at the beginning of the 1920s—we may discount, if we wish, his Teutonic prejudices during the war years—all the facts before him suggested "that American thinking, when it concerns itself with beautiful letters as when it concerns itself with religious drama or political theory, is extraordinarily timid and superficial— that it evades the genuinely serious problems of life and art as if they were stringently taboo—that the outward virtues it undoubtedly shows are always the virtues, not of profundity, not of courage, not of originality, but merely those of an emasculated and often very trashy dilettantism."[10] In 1920, Mencken believed that we have been a people who recognize our literary figures only after they have been rendered respectable, after the preservers and conservers of *Kultur* have put their imprimitur on them and they are guaranteed to be harmless. The greatest tragedy in the world of letters is that it is controlled by wearers of badges, weepers at chatauquas, one hundred percent patriots, admirers of Richard Harding Davis, readers of the *Saturday Evening Post*, devotees of Hamilton Wright Mabie's "white list" of books, or, at the very best, by "the solemn highly judicial coroner's inquest criticism of More, Brownell, Babbitt and their imitators."

The Feud with the New Humanists

Mencken's running feud with the New Humanists between 1915 and 1930—especially with Paul Elmer More, Irving Babbitt, and Stuart Pratt Sherman—gives us the core of his complaint against the prevailing higher culture in America.

More and Babbitt were far removed from the mentality of the Y.M.C.A. literary guild and represented a distinctly advanced level of achievement when compared with American scholars of preceding generations. Mencken once remarked that More was "the closest thing we have to a scholar in America—God save us all." At the same time there was a certain common ground between Mencken and the Humanists, since both shared a skepticism about the fruits of democracy: both agreed that our civilization tended to produce the shoddy and the vulgar; both agreed that in a democratic society there is much to hinder the growth of a genuine aristocracy of the spirit.

Beyond this point Mencken and the New Humanists parted company. On the surface the battle was waged over questions of aesthetics and literary criticism. During his *Smart Set* years Mencken devoted himself to promoting writers and literary trends that were anathema to the Humanists. The real reason for Mencken's constant goading of the Humanists was deeper. His disagreement with their literary tastes was only an outward manifestation of his dislike of their intellectual style. In Mencken's opinion, the Humanists were only conservers of bygone standards; they had no ideas of their own. They scorned the low estate of American letters, but they offered nothing of their own to improve this estate, indeed were also contributors to it. Read what they write, says Mencken, and you will find that "it is correctly done, it is never crude or gross. It has about it the faint perfume of college-town society. But when this highly refined and attenuated manner is allowed for what remains is next to nothing." They are simply followers who seek protection in each other's society; intellectuals, but of a standardized, institutionalized kind.

This is the reason Mencken felt them to be untrustworthy guides to literature. They do not themselves share the inspiration of the creative writer and therefore only champion things cut to their own size. The same objection to the literary theories of the Humanists was made by the liberal critics of the 1930s, but it was never stated more deftly and precisely than it was by Mencken, during the great feud of the previous decade. What ails the literary ideas of the Humanists is "a dearth of intellectual audacity and aesthetic passion."

> Running through it, and characterizing the work of almost every man and woman producing it, there is an unescapable suggestion of the old Puritan suspicion of the fine arts as such—of the doctrine that they offer fit asylum for good citizens only when some ulterior and superior purpose is carried into them. This purpose, naturally enough, most commonly shows a moral tinge. The aim of poetry, it appears, is to fill the mind of lofty thoughts—not to give it joy, but to give it a grand and gaudy sense of virtue. The essay is a weapon against the degenerate tendencies of the age. The novel, properly conceived, is a means of uplifting the spirit; its aim is to inspire, not merely to satisfy the low curiosity of man in man. The Puritan, of course, is not entirely devoid of aesthetic feeling. He has a taste for good form; he responds to style; he is even capable of something approaching a purely aesthetic emotion. But he fears this aesthetic emotion as an insinuating distraction from his chief business in life: the sober consideration of the all-important problem of conduct. Art is a temptation, a seduction, a Lorelei, and the Good Man may safely have traffic with it only when it is broken to moral uses—in other words, when its innocence is pumped out of it, and it is purged of gusto.[11]

The Humanists do not love literature *qua* literature; they only use it, and then only after warping it to their own moral and intellectual ends. Mencken's view of the function of literary criticism, on the other hand, is that if it is to have any hope of adding to our culture it must itself be responsive to art, must indeed *be* a kind of art, or, at least partake of the spirit of art. We should never try to get scientific or philosophical truth from criticism because art is that which has not yet been cast in a firm conceptual mold like a syllogism or a scientific model. The best that criticism can do is to try to get inside the gut of literature as it touches our lives, "to pronounce verdicts that are valid here and now, in the light of living knowledge and prejucide." No criticism can expect to reach a principle of universal applicability, and no critic can have anything worth while to say about literature by judging it wholly by the standards of the past. The best critic is the "fellow who submits himself frankly to the flow of his time, and rejoices in its aliveness." We must hold Sainte-Beuve a good critic "because he saw everything as a Frenchman of the Second Empire." If we fault many of his judgments today, it still remains true that they were honest and intelligent when he formulated them. The same may be said of Macaulay, another historical and social critic. He fell into many errors, but his work holds up as criticism because it retains the charm and peculiar truth of art. Professor Balderdash at the average American freshwater university "is a bad critic, for he judges what is done in the American Empire of 1926 in the light of what was held to be gospel in the pastoral Republic of a century ago."[12]

The critic who has something truly worthwhile to say about literature is a man who himself is in the swim, who involves himself with the world as it is presently being lived and enjoyed. Mencken's feud with professors of literature—including the Humanists—was rooted in his belief that professors are only interested in literature after it has been mummified. The professors of literature would have nothing to do with Whitman or Twain when they were alive—they thought them to be naughty, unseemly, or downright nasty. By 1915 or 1920 the professors began to discover Whitman and Twain, but by then they were behind in discovering writers like Dreiser or Cabell. They can accept as established writers only those who have already been made into museum pieces, who have been consigned to the dark, genteel, and none-too-troublesome past.

Mencken believed that the reigning literary critics had tried to keep literature alive, but that they had done a poor job of it because they themselves were not interested in the forces of literature. They had other axes to grind, most of which were peripheral to literature. Mencken believed that the practicing literary critic should himself be a writer, a man responsive to

aesthetic values. During the years he was composing his
Prejudices he found very few such responsive critics on the
American scene. In the light of the history of literary criticism
in the last forty years it is possible to confuse Mencken's ideal
of criticism with what has been called "aesthetic" criticism. It
was not a particular aesthetic doctrine Mencken was preaching, but the indispensability in the critic of a responsiveness
to art. This ideal pertained not only to literary criticism but to
all kinds of intellectual activity.

A recent student of the history of American literary criticism says of the long-standing dispute between Mencken and
the New Humanists that for all Mencken's trumpeting of the
virtues of "aesthetic criticism," he himself didn't practice it.
"No critic," says this writer," ever beat the drum more loudly
for an aesthetic criticism of literature than H. L. Mencken.
Whenever he discussed contemporary critics and builders of
American traditions, his scorn for their non-literary yard-
sticks filled page after page of the *Prejudices*. Yet his own
standards were nothing if not non-literary. Though he noisily
rejected anything but an aesthetic judgment on an aesthetic
question . . . his own interest in the nature of man and society
led to a criticism based exclusively on extraliterary consid-
erations."[13] Mencken's war cry was not a call for aesthetic
criticism but for an artistic approach to life. Mencken's quar-
rel with More and Sherman was not that they dispensed
moral judgments rather than literary judgments. While he did
scold them on this point, his main objection was to their lack
of imagination and creative drive. The literary critics of his
day served as a convenient example of what was wrong with
intellectual life in America.

Mencken's call for aesthetic criticism was made from the
stance of the general critic. Mencken had never been exclusively a literary critic, although in his *Smart Set* years, and
to a lesser extent throughout his life, he did function as a
literary critic in the more restricted sense as well. He was a
critic of ideas, of culture, so that the objection that he was not
uniformly an aesthetic critic is a mistaken judgment of his
career as a writer. Mencken's central concern was with what
literary critics ought to be doing if they are literary critics and
what intellectuals ought to be doing if they are intellectuals.

Even when we consider the problems of literary criticism in isolation we have to distinguish what Mencken meant by "aesthetic criticism." As a working literary critic Mencken did follow his own credo that aesthetic works require an aesthetic judgment, although it is necessary to understand that for Mencken the notion of "aesthetic criticism" needs to be defined somewhat broadly. When Mencken used the term aesthetic criticism he seems to have meant the opposite of pedagogical criticism; the former was a department of literature, the later a department of conceptualized learning. Literature itself, like every art, is an intensification of experience, a rendering of the ordinary in some powerful expressive form. The man who would explain or criticize literature must possess some of its strength and gusto; if he is not, the only thing he can do is reconvert literature, step it down, so to speak, to some more inert and phlegmatic form of experience.

It is said in defense of the more scholarly branches of criticism that they perform a function which the artist himself does not perform and should not be expected to perform; they provide intellectual analysis, give us some kind of framework by which works of art can be judged or evaluated. Mencken's opinion, the kind of intellectual activity necessary to do justice to literature is not found in any of the academic approaches to criticism. Mencken presupposes that the critic

is a civilized and tolerant man, hospitable to all intelligible ideas and capable of reading them as he runs. This is a demand that at once rules out nine-tenths of the grown-up sophomores who carry on the business of criticism in America. Their trouble is simply that they lack the intellectual resilience necessary for taking in ideas, and particularly new ideas. The only way they can ingest one is by transforming it into the nearest related formula—usually a harsh and devastating operation. This fact accounts for their chronic inability to understand all that is most personal and original and hence most forceful and significant in the emerging literature of the country. They can get down what has been digested and redigested, and so brought into forms that they know, and carefully

> labeled by predecessors of their own sort—but they ex-
> hibit alarm immediately when they come into the pre-
> sence of the extraordinary.[14]

The critic must be a man of flexible intelligence, of wide information (specialized information alone is not sufficient), of genuine hospitality to ideas, which means ideas not already part of his mental baggage. He must be willing to strike out in any direction. "The really competent critic must be an empiricist. He must conduct his exploration with whatever means lie within the bounds of his personal limitation. He must produce his effects with whatever tools will work. If pills fail he gets out his saw. If the saw won't cut, he seizes a club."[15]

Another important characteristic of the critic is related to the function of art itself. The critic, like the writer, must be able to communicate; he must be able to render the difficult and the ineffable with clarity and simplicty. Just as the writer takes hold of the chaotic flux of experience and by dramatic and selective alchemy makes it clearer, more vivid, more intelligible, so the critic, who is a link between the artist and the public, must have the means and the talent to further elucidate the aims, purposes, and meanings of the work of art. "What is recondite must be made plainer; the transcendental, to some extent at least, must be done into common modes of thinking," which is to say thinking that can be understood by the general run of humanity. The critic, like the writer, should speak in a universal idiom; he must seek to address mankind, not just a few other birds of his own feather. Critics who speak in a language that has meaning only to other critics have adopted a very limited vocation for themselves. They seal themselves off from the general reading public, but at the same time they aren't useful to their co-specialists, either. The co-specialists, with the same or similar rubber stamps at their disposal, ought to be able to reach the same pedestrian conclusions on their own initiative.

Mencken's feud with the New Humanists was motivated by two separate but related concerns. On the one hand, he was striking out at them on aesthetic and literary grounds because they wouldn't move over for the younger writers he was encouraging as editor and literary critic. More importantly, he took out after the Humanists because they represented examples of the kind of standardization and mummification that goes on in American intellectual life. The trouble with the intellectuals, the *ordentliche Professoren,* is that they shy away from the challenge of creativity. The anemia of Humanist literary criticism was but a representative case of the anemia of our higher intellectual life; an example of the tendency of the cultural leaders in our society to stifle the best that is done in all areas of learning.

The Deceptive Dream of Education

We have been moving closer to the subject of institutionalized learning, and this brings us to another of Mencken's favorite objects of study—the world of education. Next to politics and puritanism, Mencken had more to say about the shortcomings of education than about any other realm of American life. His critique of the various specialized fields, of which literary criticism is one, cannot be fully understood unless we grasp how these special fields are affected by the educational process, how education acts to create cultural lethargy. Mencken's suspicion of both the means and ends of education grew out of his Darwinian and Nietzschean prejudices against the static and inert. Education as we know it in our society is the cultivation of rigid and uncreative patterns of thought. Education is devoted, not to the making of man as a thinking animal, but to the preservation of things that have already been thought. Alfred North Whitehead, another philosopher of process with roots in the Darwinian tradition, believed that the whole of Western thought got off to a bad start—probably somewhere among the ancient Greeks— when it began speaking of a man's education as analogous to a trap or a box in which things are stored, so that the man who has managed to trap the most information is the most learned, the most advanced, and therefore the most filled with potential and promise. To the questions "Why do we teach quadratic equations?" or "Why do we teach foreign languages?" we are given an answer something like this:

The mind is an instrument, you first sharpen it and then you use it; the acquisition of the power of solving a quadratic equation is part of the process of sharpening the mind. Now there is just enough truth in this answer to have made it live through the ages. But for all its half-truth, it embodies a radical error which bids fair to stifle the genius of the modern world. I do not know who was first responsible for this analogy of the mind to a dead instrument. For aught I know, it may have been one of the wise men of Greece, or a committee of the whole lot of them. Whoever was the originator, there can be no doubt of the authority which it has acquired by the continuous approval bestowed upon it by eminent persons. But whatever its weight of authority . . . I have no hestitation in denouncing it as one of the most fatal, erroneous and dangerous conceptions ever introduced into the theory of education. The mind is never passive; it is perpetual activity, delicate, receptive, responsive to stimulus. You cannot postpone its life until you have sharpened it. Whatever interest attaches to your subject matter must be evoked here and now. That is the golden rule of education, and a very difficult rule to follow.[16]

Unfortunately, as Whitehead himself insists, the tool or storehouse concept of education is the one that most educators maintain, so that there can be no escaping the conclusion that educational institutions as we know them "bid fair to stifle the imagination of the modern world." This is Mencken's positon. In America, especially, cultural and intellectual fortunes decline as the power and scope of formal education rise. No nation in the history of the world has expanded its educational system as widely as we; no people have had the degree of faith in education that we have; yet, in Mencken's mind, this faith in education has never been justified. Our gargantuan educational system is responsible for a decline in thinking, genuine creative intellectual activity. Our belief in education is not only unjustified but misleading and dangerous.

It is dangerous for the reason cited by Whitehead. It assumes that the passive, repository mind can be productive. If we accept the notion that every intellectual advance in human culture is the product of activity, of struggle against settled and motionless ideas, then we can see that the attempt to foster institutions of learning must be counterproductive. The lack of creativity in education is not revealed only in unreceptivity to new ideas. The function of education itself is also open to question, especially as faith in it rises to outlandish heights. The average professor of literary criticism is not only unable to entertain the latest work of literature, he never questions his own profession of teaching or the relationship of his special "discipline" to the entire range of human culture. He merely assumes that such a relationship exists.

The only real knowledge comes from active thinking, whereas education is usually residual—what is left behind after thought has taken place. It may be, as Whitehead suggests when he says that the storehouse or "instrument" theory of education is a half-truth, that a certain number of inert ideas are the necessary supports of active ideas. One cannot become a writer without a familiarity with writing, a philosopher without familiarity with the works of other philosophers. However, the history of education demonstrates a preponderant emphasis on learning in its inert rather than in its active form. Education in America perpetuates the belief that the greatest and most valuable man of learning is the one who has shoveled away the most intellectual raw material. Like all philosophers of process, Mencken rejects this idea.

Even if the storage theory of knowledge were entirely true, there would be another objection to our exaggerated respect for education. With his Darwinian pessimism about the perfectability of the human race in the aggregate, Mencken was skeptical of the effectiveness of even the most rudimentary educational processes. He believed that basic education could affect only a very small fragment of the population. He found two great follies corrupting our educational thinking: "One is the folly of overestimating the receptivity of the pupil; the other is the folly of overestimating the possible efficiency of the teacher."[17]

One of the great fallacies of democratic states is the belief that universal education will confer some great blessing on society. This fallacy is based on the belief that those who are subjected to education will be moved or transformed by it.

> What is always forgotten is that the capacity for knowledge of the great masses of human blanks is very low— that, no matter how adroitly pedagogy tackles them with its technical sorceries, it remains a practical impossibility to teach them anything beyond reading and writing, and the most elementary arithmetic. Worse, it is impossible to make any appreciable improvement in their congenitally ignoble tastes, and so they devote even the paltry learning that they acquire to degrading uses. If the average American read only the newspapers, as is frequently alleged, it would be bad enough, but the truth is that he reads only the most imbecile *parts* of the newspapers. Nine-tenths of the matter in a daily paper of the better sort is almost as unintelligible to him as the theory of least squares. The words lie outside his vocabulary; the ideas are beyond the farthest leap of his intellect.[18]

Mencken believed that the human primate has at his command a great skill at mimicry, so that under pressure from teachers he can make sounds which suggest that he has digested what has been taught him. Teachers and the society which stands behind them have been good at forcing these sounds. In the old days the birch and the strap were the instruments; today, fear of social failure and occupational oblivion are the instruments which force the multitudes down the path of education. Mencken could perceive no evidence that the multitudes were any better off for this forced march. What happens is that education is adjusted so that all can pass. The whole process becomes perfunctory, students being allowed to show the outward signs of learning by repeating what they are told (American students become especially proficient, even ingenious, at this), while giving every evidence of inaptitude for any kind of higher thought.

Mencken insisted, in his usual stubborn and impolite way, that the masses are not really being educated, but simply thrown into the educational machinery; that they are being stuffed with ideas that they are incapable of rationally analyzing. In such a system the gifted and intelligent students must suffer along with the mediocre and dull students. The educational system should be geared to the advancement of the best minds, but our system of universal education neglects the gifted in favor of the average; the underlying philosophy being that the average can be something more than average.

Mencken had no faith in the increasing efficacy of education. The evidence of his own experience showed him that most of what is called education is habit-learning, the performance of perfunctory tricks. He believed that most of this habit-learning could be absorbed, outside classroom walls, in only a fraction of the time it takes to acquire it inside. "The truth is, that all the education rammed into the average pupil in the average public school could be acquired by the larva of any reasonably intelligent man in no more than six weeks of ordinary application, and that where schools are unknown it actually *is* so acquired. A bright child, in fact, can learn to read and write without any save the most casual aid a great deal better than he can learn to read or write in a classroom, where the difficulties of the stupid retard it enormously and it is further burdened by the crazy formulae invented by pedagogues."[19]

Mencken's philosophy of education is that the only real education is that which a man acquires for himself by becoming involved creatively and imaginatively in some vital life function. Learning as a pack of raw materials on one's back is of little significance; the bearer of such a pack will not be able to carry it long, and in no case will he have any affection for the pack. Education that is not integrated somehow with an individual's life functions, with his own deepest calling, will invariably be nothing more than dead weight.

Education, especially when it is magnified and intensified as it is in our society, tends to be one of the restraining forces that negate the vital urges of life. It keeps people from functioning on their own and involves them too long in tedious chores, rote learning, rituals of various kinds from the ABCs to the Ph.D. Stephen Leacock, the Canadian economist turned humorist, made the point better than anyone else when he remarked in his essay, "Education Eating Up Life" that as education grows longer, life grows shorter. We encourage people to prepare for life, but do little to encourage them to live it.

> Fifty years ago people learned to read out of a spelling-book at six years old, went to high school at twelve, and taught school (for money) on a third-class certificate at sixteen. After that, two years in a sawmill and two at a medical school made them doctors, or one year in a sawmill and one in divinity fitted them for the church. For law they needed no college at all, just three summers on a farm and three winters in an office. All our great men in North America got this education. Pragmatically it work-ed. They began their real life still young. . . .
>
> Now it is all changed. Children at school at six years old cut up paper dolls and make patterns. They are still in high school till eighteen, learning civics and social statistics—studies for old men. They enter college at about nineteen or twenty, take prerequisites and post-requisites in various faculties for ten years, then become demonstrators, invigilators, researchers, or cling to a graduate scholarship like a man on a raft.[20]

In expanding our educational system so that it cuts too deeply into life we have also produced an overly large class of teachers, educators, theorists, and administrators who are promoters of the tendency of education to eat up life. A great deal of the blame for the sluggishness and lethargy of our educational system must be placed on the educators. Once again Mencken reverses the usual platitudes. Where it is customary to believe that the teacher is a vital guardian and sustainer of the culture, Mencken insists that nine times out of ten the pedagogue is not preserving anything that is worth preserving. He is a person who has found in the world of education a safe shelter from reality, a place where he can perform the same acts over and over again. Mencken's charge against the pedagogue is that he seeks to reenact something from life rather than to live; he puts his faith in what has already found approval, not in his own personal drive.

The teacher is an enforcer of habits, and in the process he comes to have faith only in habits. Nothing worthwhile has ever come from the enforcement of habitual activity—no science, no art, no philosophy, nothing of significance in any department of human experience. All the good of the world comes from the creative force, the élan vital, to use Bergson's phraseology. Some teachers are people who can think creatively and individually, but in Mencken's opinion education is nearly always a habit-enforcing activity, and when we see that more and more people are taking it up as a profession we can only conclude that a larger and larger segment of the population is devoting itself to lifeless and uninspiring pursuits. We cannot avoid this pessimistic conclusion by using the excuse that teaching is an auxiliary activity for people who are practicing specialized disciplines—that they are really psychologists, art historians, or literary scholars. These specializations are, ninety percent of the time, carried on within a pedagogical framework, with a pedagogical habit of mind, and the pedagogical mind rarely rises above the mundane and the habitual.

We are victims of delusion when we think of the average educator as a person of exceptional talent or intellect. "He is simply one who has been stuffed with formal ideas and taught to do a few conventional tricks. Contact with him far from being inspiring to any youth of alert mentality, is really depressing; his point of view is commonplace and timorous; his best thought is no better than that of any other fourth-rate professional man, say a dentist or advertisement writer." In a few rare instances he may be a first-rate man, but generally the most that we can expect is that he be worthy and industrious in an unimaginative way. It is absurd "to ask him to struggle out of his puddle of safe platitudes and plunge into the whirlpool of surmise and speculation that carries on the fragile shallop of human progress."[21]

This is the educator in the aggregate. Mencken's barbs directed at schoolmarms or the birch-wielding schoolmaster cut even more deeply. Not only are the pedagogues at this level mediocre and uninspiring, they have a negative influence. Not only do they fail to challenge the young to anything that is above the level of mechanical habit-learning, but their very presence is stultifying and detrimental. "School days are the unhappist in the whole span of human existence. They are full of dull unintelligible tasks, new and unpleasant ordinances, brutal violations of common sense and common decency." The source of this unhappiness is invariably found in the person of the teacher, who any healthy-minded child must look upon either as a disagreeable policeman or as an unpleasant fool. The tragedy of youth in our society, which leads to a stunting of their spiritual development, is that they are forced to have as their constant companions these male and female schoolmarms, "persons of trivial and unromantic achievement, and no more capable of inspiring emulation in a healthy boy than so many midwives or dogcatchers."[22]

Mencken believed that this condition was worsening. The invention of the science of pedagogy—educational theory—he regarded as a long step in the wrong direction; it simply reinforced the rigid and unimaginative thinking that has always incapacitated the teacher. In the old days the birchman had simple methods to match his simple mind. Today he has to master a complex subject matter that is likely to make an even bigger fool of him than if left in a state of natural innocence. The new pedagogy Mencken believed to be "largely the confection of imbeciles. . . . In the whole realm of human learning there is no faculty more fantastically incompetent than pedagogy." Read the pedagogical journals, read the Ph.D. theses in the field. "Nothing worse is to be found in the literature of astrology, scientific salesmanship, or Christian Science. But the poor schoolma'ams, in order to get on in their trade, must make shift to study it, and even to master it."[23] It is small wonder that those who can escape to lawful domestic love do so, and that those who remain are so burdened with addlepated theories and techniques that they cannot impart any learning that is not sterile and unimaginative.

It was the lofty professors who were the most interesting

game for Mencken, since their claims were so much more extravagant. Mencken did find some professors of genuine intellectual distinction, but he believed that the general run of professors display elaborate pretensions ot learning without offering any firm evidence of it. The professors would like to draw a sharp line between their activity and that of the schoolmarms, for they claim to be possessed of much more highly specialized learning. They have convinced the public that they stand at the forefront of our intellectual and cultural life, and that the advancement of our civilization depends on the good work of the universities.

Mencken had no faith in the high quality of the so-called higher education. He held that on the whole it is uninspired, dull, and routine. If it is indeed "higher" education it is so only quantitatively, not qualitatively. Higher education performs the same function as the primary and secondary schools do, the production of standardized thought. "The thing it combats most ardently is not ignorance, but free inquiry; it is devoted to forcing the whole youth of the land into one rigid mold. Its ideal product is a young man who is absolutely correct in all his ideas—a perfect reader for the *Literary Digest,* the *American Magazine,* and the editorial page of the *New York Times.*"[24]

Students are not trained to free inquiry because the professors themselves are not used to it. College teaching, Mencken believed, was becoming more and more a routine chore, performed by standardized schoolmasters "with no clear tradition behind them," men who are not gentlemen, and who have not "learned to think clearly and decently." Like the schoolmarm, the college professor has little in his equipment to insprire the young or to challenge their imagination. The youth of more civilized background finds little in his college experience to cause him to want to stay on as a teacher. "The air is too thick for him; the rewards are trivial; the intrigues are too old-maidish and degrading." The chairs, even in the larger universities, tend to be filled by yokels, "peasants in frock coats—oafs from the farms . . . horribly stuffed with some standardized learning," men with little in the way of solid background and genuine culture behind them. They are

not our best and most forceful minds. They "have got themselves what is called an education only by dint of herculean
effort. Exhausted by the cruel process, they are old men at 26
or 28, and so, hugging their Ph.D.'s, they sink into convenient
instructorships, and end at 60 as ordentliche Professoren."[25]

Mencken believed that when the universities were fewer in
number and more elitist in nature they had an easier time
attracting first-rate men and spawning further first-rate men.
As the trend to bring more and more people into the profession
of college teaching continues, quality will suffer, both among
students and teachers, for the teachers are onetime students
who have been lassoed into the profession. Democratizing the
universities has pulled professors down the path to mediocrity.

> A glance at Who's Who in America offers a good deal of
> support for all this theorizing. There was a time when the
> typical American professor came from a small area in
> New England—for generations the seat of high literacy,
> and even of a certain austere civilization. But today he
> comes from the region of silos, revivals and saleratus.
> Behind him there is absolutely no tradition or aristocratic
> aloofness and urbanity, or even of mere civilized decency.
> He is a hind by birth, and he carries the smell of the
> dunghill into the academic grove—and not only the smell,
> but also some of the dung itself. What one looks for in
> such men is dullness, superficiality, a great credulity, an
> incapacity for learning anything but the fly-blown rudi-
> ments, a passionate yielding to all popular crazes, a
> malignant distrust of genuine superiority, a huge mega-
> lomania.[26]

Mencken's criticism of the professor is that he prefers the
standard, the settled, the safe, the mundane kinds of knowledge to the adventuresome, the disruptive, and the inventive.
The professor looks for a comfortable perch of easy authority
and sets his psychic life in low gear so that he will attract no
attention; his ideas are all tame and fireproof; they will
enflame no passions and awaken no controversies. If one

hears of an academic involved in some controversy, nine times out of ten it is one that has been sanctioned some-where—perhaps by some professional coterie or peer group.

The scholar tends to become a coward. This is how American society likes him. As Mencken saw it in the 1920s, this cowardice often took the form of truckling under to the mon-eyed interests or to the authority and intellectual style of the Babbitts. In a review of Upton Sinclair's The Goose Step for the American Mercury in 1923, Mencken lamented that the dominance of American universities by industrialists and capitalists has tended to force a definite cowardice and small-ness of character on the academic. He now lives in prosperous times, said Mencken, and the university has all kinds of money flooding into it that it did not have a few generations ago. "But in order to get that ocean of money, and to pay for the piles of pseudo-Gothic that now arise over the land, scholar-ship in America has had to sacrifice free-inquiry to the preju-dices and private interests of its masters—the search for truth has had to be subordinated to the safeguarding of railway bonds and electric light stocks."[27]

The force of this authority has a depressing effect not only on the independence of the professor but on his personal character. He is no longer free because he knows that some stockbroker, bank director, or railway looter, "if the spirit moved him would be perfectly free to hound a Huxley, a Karl Ludwig, or a Jowett from the faculty, and even to prevent him from getting a seemly berth elsewhere," and that such out-rages have been perpetrated not once but hundreds of times. Fear keeps the professor docile. It also keeps his thinking dull and stereotyped, especially in those areas which threaten the capitalist employer. "What is taught in astronomy or paleon-tology or Greek cannot nail the manufacturer to the board, and so he does not issue any orders about it, nor does his agent, the university president." He keeps his eyes on fields like history, economics, education, sociology, or even litera-ture, any in fact which deal with ideas likely to hit him where he lives, "and at the slightest show of heresy takes measures to protect himself." The fields dealing with ideas call for the highest professional character and responsibility, but in the modern university they are least free, and their professors most mediocre and timid. It is in these regions

> that conformity is most comfortable, and that the professional character is in most decay. Even here, to be sure, a few stouthearted survivors of an earlier day hold out, but they are surely not many, and they will have no successors. The professor of tomorrow, in all departments that have to do with life as men are now living it in the world, will either be a goose-stepper or he will be out of a job.[28]

If Mencken were alive today he would probably have to devote more of his attention to the phenomenon of the self-institutionalizing of the professor than to his cowardice in the face of forces outside the university or professional guild. In the last several decades the professor has been institutionalized by specialty. The public has told him that his specialty is important, that he might be called to Washington for some consulting work—even if he is a professor of classical philology. In aggrandizing his profession he trades one form of limitation on his freedom for another. If he has lost the collar supplied him by the stockbroker or the industrialist, he tends more and more to wear the collar of his peer group. In a recent study, *Anti-Intellectualism in American Life,* Richard Hofstadter noted that in many ways intellectuals had it better when they stood away from the centers of power, when they had to function as an isolated caste of society. The windfall that has come to them since the Second World War has not been all for the good. While the professor has won for himself a greater respect as a public figure, he has bartered away his authority as a free man of thought. "One hears more and more," says Hofstadter

> that the intellectual who has won a measure of freedom and opportunity, and a new access to influence, is thereby subtly corrupted; that, having won recognition, he has lost his independence, even his identity as an individual. . . . He becomes comfortable, perhaps even moderately

prosperous, as he takes a position in a university or in government, or working for the mass media, but he then tailors himself to the requirements of those institutions. He loses that precious tincture of rage so necessary to first-rate creativity in a writer, that capacity for negation and rebellion that is necessary to the candid social critic, that initiative and independence of aim required for distinguished work in science. . . . We live in an age in which the avant-garde itself has been institutionalized and deprived of its old stimulus of a stubborn and insensate oposition.[29]

The agency which institutionalizes the professor is his profession. The professor gives up his role as a man of independent learning and becomes a specialist in child psychology, in social engineering, or in the poetry of the Romantic era. On this tendency Mencken had a great deal to say, long before it had been carried to its present lengths. For example, his complaint against the New Humanists was that they insisted on forming themselves into a "school"—huddling together for self-protection and self-advancement. Irving Babbitt was said to have had a map in his Harvard office with pins indicating the placement of Humanists in English Departments around the country. Mencken would have had nothing but contempt for the holders of those pin-spots, however prestigious the chairs involved, for this game was to him a manifestation of the professor's desire to use his profession as a protective network and as a means of forcing his ideas on others.

The tendency to professionalize and standardize the intellect is not limited to literary scholars, although the defect sits more sorrowfully on their shoulders since they concern themselves with language and literature, the broadest and deepest expressions of the human spirit. Similar examples might be found in any other department of learning. The reader of an economics journal will find that most economists are given to highly stereotyped group thinking. They may appear to have great clashes of ideology, but these are within narrow confines; all must use the same jargon, all must display the signs and symbols that lead to guild approval. So it goes with philosophers, psychologists, penologists, and all the rest. It may be permissible to bump up against the other sheep occasionally, but only after one has been duly certified as a sheep, dressed in the same clothing, and adorned by the same badges.

The most debilitating disease of professionalism is the inability to break out of one's cage. One can speak seriously and deeply only to other professionals. One never questions the authority and importance of one's specialized field. No light of humor ever falls on the cherished subject matter. One may be a philosopher and ask any question, provided that the question is not whether philosophy itself is worth doing. The specialist never reaches out to any general human culture; he never wishes to speak in a common human idiom. Only in the argot of one's special field is there safety and guaranteed authority.

Mencken's critique of the moral and intellectual tone of the higher learning would not have to be altered in its basic substance if it were written in the 1970s—only its particulars would need to be changed. Mencken believed America had not developed enough strong individual talent, not enough brave and forthright men with ideas of their own. Individual talent is especially difficult to produce in a society which puts a premium on conformity, which pays people well for ideas that are safe and predictable. Most intellectuals believe themselves to be men of independent mind, always ready to strike out at some social injustice or shopworn idea. Mencken believed that the "intellectual" is usually one who can be counted on to develop and sanction his own shopworn ideas and stereotypes. A sign of this is that the latest warcry of the intellectual invariably takes some form of right-thinking, of ultimate truth discovered. It is nearly always accompanied by the belief that those in the know have as one of their responsibilities the enforcement of the latest "right idea" upon the poor benighted souls outside the walls of the academy.

Mencken's final judgment on the higher culture in America is that it is too rigidly institutionalized, too dependent on collective and totalitarian patterns of thought. History shows us that all great achievements in literature, science, the arts, or in any department of intelligent learning have been produced by individuals working on the periphery of habitual thought and action; individuals often despised by society and nearly always struggling against the mainstream. America has had such individuals, too—more than her share perhaps. Mencken was convinced that under the pressure of totalitarian democracy and a complex technological civilization the opportunities for the man of independent thought would become more and more sharply curtailed, that the man who wants to survive in a conformist state would increasingly have to choose the safe and easy path, to limit himself to thinking as others do.

We are a people with great material wealth, and this wealth ought to be able to support a great spiritual civilization. However, our social institutions are ponderous, inert and sickly; they suffer from the ills of populist democracy, and thus they have persistently worked against the rise of this great civilization.

Notes

All references to the works of Henry L. Mencken are to the editions of Mencken's works cited in the list on page 238.

Introduction

1. Edmund Wilson, *The Shores of Light: A Literary Chronicle of the Twenties and Thirties* (New York: Farrar, Straus and Giroux, 1952), p. 294.
2. Alistair Cooke, "An Introduction to H. L. Mencken," in *The Vintage Mencken* (New York: Vintage Books, 1955), p. v.

Chapter I

1. *Happy Days, 1880-1892*, p. 252.
2. *Ibid.*
3. *The Smart Set,* November 1908, reprinted in *H. L. Mencken's Smart Set Criticism,* ed. W. H. Nolte (Ithaca: Cornell University Press, 1968), pp. 31-32.
4. *Newspaper Days, 1899-1906*, p. 3.
5. *Happy Days*, p. 175.
6. *Newspaper Days*, pp. 73-74.
7. *Ibid.*, p. 69.
8. There is some dispute as to who recommended Mencken. In later years Theodore Dreiser claimed the credit. For a discussion of this

question see Carl Bode, *Mencken* (Carbondale: Southern Illinois University Press, 1969), pp. 60-61.

9. Mencken to Sara Haardt, 10 July 1923, the Princeton University Library collection of Mencken's correspondence.

10. The story behind the rejection of "Blue Review," and the final selection of *The American Mercury* is told in M. K. Singleton, *H. L. Mencken and the American Mercury Adventure* (Durham: Duke University Press, 1962), pp. 33-34.

11. Quoted in Singleton, p. 35.

12. *Criterion* 6 (December 1927): 572-73, quoted in Singleton, pp. 190-91.

13. Walter Lippmann, "H.L. Mencken," in *Men of Destiny* (Seattle: University of Washington Press, 1969), p. 63. This book was originally published by Macmillan in 1927.

14. Ibid., p. 70.

15. Ibid., pp. 64-65.

16. *Prejudices: Fifth Series,* pp. 190-91.

17. Ibid., p. 194.

18. *Prejudices: Third Series,* p. 176.

19. Ibid., pp. 177-78.

20. Ibid., p. 178.

21. Ibid., p. 26.

22. Ibid., p. 16.

23. Ibid., pp. 17-18.

24. Ibid., pp. 32-33.

25. "The Free Lance," *Baltimore Sun,* 29 September 1914.

26. *Prejudices: Third Series,* pp. 35-36.

27. Ibid., p. 43.

28. Ibid., pp. 60-61.

29. *The American Language,* 4th ed., 1970, p. 91.

30. George Orwell, *The English People* (London: Collins, 1947), p. 36. Orwell disagrees with Mencken to some extent. Adoption of the American language, he thinks, would result in a loss of vocabulary in a number of areas. "For though American produces witty and vivid turns of speech, it is terribly poor in names for natural objects and localities. . . . If we really intended to model our language on American we should have, for instance, to lump the lady-bird, the daddy-long-legs, the saw-fly, the water-boatman, the cockchafer, the cricket, the death-watch beetle and scores of other insects altogether under the inexpressive name of *bug.* We should lose the poetic names of our wildflowers, and also, probably, our habit of giving individual names to every street, pub, field, lane, and hillock." (p. 38).

31. *The American Language,* p. 95.

32. Ibid., pp. 94-95. Quoted from Basil de Selincourt, "Pomona or the Future of English," London, 1929.

33. Ibid., p. 92.

34. *Prejudices: Fourth Series,* pp. 55-56.

Chapter II

1. *Notes on Democracy,* p. 9.
2. Ibid., p. 45.
3. *Essays of William Graham Summer,* ed. A. G. Keller and M. B. Davie (New Haven: Yale University Press, 1934), 2:198-99.
4. *Notes on Democracy,* p. 7.
5. Ibid., pp. 20-21.
6. Ibid., pp. 21-22.
7. Ibid., p. 30.
8. *Prejudices: Fourth Series,* pp. 45-46.
9. Ibid., p. 47.
10. Ibid., p. 56.
11. Ibid., p. 57.
12. *Notes on Democracy,* pp. 152-53.
13. *Smart Set,* 45 (January 1915): 435.
14. *The Nation* 114 (3 May, 1922): 517-19.
15. Sinclair Lewis, *Babbit* (New York: Harcourt Brace & Co., 1922), p. 151.
16. *Notes on Democracy,* p. 61.
17. Ibid., p. 157.
18. Ibid., p. 155.
19. Ibid., p. 49.
20. Ibid., pp. 172-73.
21. Ibid., pp. 174-75.
22. Carl Bode, *Mencken* (Carbondale and Edwardsville: Southern Illinois University Press. 1969), p. 84.
23. *The Philosophy of Friedrich Nietzsche,* pp. 72-73.
24. Ibid., pp. 163-64. This is a quote or paraphrase from Nietzsche's *Der Antichrist.*
25. *Notes on Democracy,* pp. 10-11.
26. Ibid., pp. 12-13.
27. Ibid., pp. 14-15.
28. Ibid., p. 16.
29. Bode, *Mencken,* p. 306.
30. David Riesman, *The Lonely Crowd* (New Haven: Yale University Press, 1950), p. 22.
31. Cf. Erich Fromm, *Man For Himself;* C. Wright Mills, "The Competitive Personality," *Partisan Review* 13 (1946); Arnold Green, "The Middle Class Male Child and Neurosis," *American Sociological Review* 11 (1946).
32. *The Lonely Crowd,* p. 198.
33. *Notes on Democracy,* pp. 22, 23.
34. Richard Hofstadter, *The Paranoid Style in American Politics* (New York: Alfred A. Knopf, 1966), pp. 3, 4.
35. C. Wright Mills, *White Collar* (New York: Oxford University Press, 1956), p. xx.

Chapter III

1. *Prejudices: Fourth Series*, p. 234.
2. Ibid., pp. 227-28.
3. Ibid., pp. 223-24.
4. Ibid., pp. 233-34.
6. Ibid., p. 232.
7. Ibid., pp. 224-25.
8. *Letters of H. L. Mencken*, ed. Guy J. Forgue, p. 281.
9. *Notes on Democracy*, p. 74.
10. Ibid., pp. 75-76.
11. Ibid., pp. 97-98.
12. Ibid., p. 99.
13. Ibid., p. 103.
14. Ibid., pp. 102-103.
15. *Prejudices: Fourth Series*, pp. 129-30.
16. *Prejudices: Second Series*, pp. 104-105.
17. Ibid., pp. 108-109.
18. Ibid., pp. 121-22.
19. Ibid., p. 132.
20. *Prejudices: Fifth Series*, p. 68.
21. *Heathen Days, 1890-1936*, p. 287.
22. *Prejudices: Fifth Series*, pp. 67-68.
23. "The Archangel Woodrow," originally appeared in *The Smart Set*, January 1921, pp. 142-43. It was not included in the *Prejudices*, but can be found in *The Vintage Mencken*, ed. Alistair Cooke (New York: Vintage Books, 1955), pp. 116-20.
24. George Orwell, "Politics and the English Language," in *The Collected Essays, Journalism and Letters of George Orwell*, (New York: Harcourt, Brace & World, Inc., 1968), 4:136.
25. "The Archangel Woodrow," in *The Smart Set*, January, 1921, pp. 142-43.
26. Ibid.
27. *Baltimore Evening Sun*, 7 March 1921.
28. Ibid.

Chapter IV

1. *Essays of William Graham Sumner*, ed. A. G. Keller and M. R. Davie (New Haven: Yale University Press, 1924), 1:473-74.
2. Ibid., pp. 480-81.
3. Harris E. Starr, *William Graham Sumner* (New York: Henry Holt & Co., 1925), pp. 17-18.
4. *H. L. Mencken's Smart Set Criticism*, ed. William H. Nolte

(Ithaca: Cornell University Press, 1968), p. 249. The original review of Dreiser's *A Hoosier Holiday* appeared in *The Smart Set* in October 1916.

5. Ibid., p. 252.

6. Theodore Dreiser, *Sister Carrie* (New York: Dell, The Laurel Dreiser, 1963), p. 24.

7. *The Smart Set*, September 1911. Reprinted in Nolte, p. 133.

8. *Prejudices: Sixth Series*, p. 219.

9. *The Smart Set*, September 1918. Reprinted in Nolte, p. 147.

10. *Prejudices: Fourth Series*, pp. 263-64.

11. *The American Language: Supplement I*, p. 284.

12. Ibid., p. 271n.

13. Ibid., p. 272.

14. *Prejudices: Fourth Series*, p. 265.

15. *Prejudices: Third Series*, p. 109.

16. *Prejudices: Fifth Series*, p. 272.

17. Ibid., p. 275.

18. *Prejudices: Third Series*, p. 110

19. *Prejudices: Fifth Series*, p. 239.

20. Ibid., p. 240.

21. Ibid., p. 242.

22. *Prejudices: Sixth Series*, p. 188.

23. Ibid., pp. 191-93.

24. Van Wyck Brooks, *The Opinions of Oliver Allston* (New York: E. P. Dutton, 1941), p. 120.

25. *In Defense of Women*, pp. 13-14.

26. Ibid., pp. 15-16.

27. Ibid., pp. 143-44.

Chapter V

1. George Santayana, *Winds of Doctrine* (New York: Harper & Bros. [Torchbook ed.], 1957), p. 188.

2. Ibid., pp. 192-93.

3. Van Wyck Brooks, *America's Coming of Age*, (Garden City, New York: Doubleday & Co. Inc., 1958), p. 4.

4. *Prejudices: First Series*, p. 191.

5. Ibid., pp. 192-93.

6. *Prejudices: Fourth Series*, p. 17.

7. *The Smart Set*, February 1919, reprinted in *H. L. Mencken's Smart Set Criticism*, ed. W. H. Nolte (Ithaca: Cornell University Press, 1968), pp. 3-4.

8. *Prejudices: Fourth Series*, p. 40.

9. Ibid., p. 41.

10. *Prejudices: Second Series*, p. 18.

11. Ibid., pp. 19-20.

12. *Prejudices: Fifth Series*, p. 207.

13. Richard Ruland, *The Rediscovery of American Literature* (Cambridge: Harvard University Press, 1957), p. 120.

14. *Prejudices: First Series*, pp. 13-14.

15. Ibid., pp. 19-20.

16. Alfred North Whitehead, *The Aims of Education* (New York: The Free Press, 1967), p. 6.

17. *Prejudices: Third Series*, p. 249.

18. Ibid., p. 257.

19. Ibid., pp. 259-60.

20. Stephen Leacock, *The Leacock Roundabout* (New York: Dodd, Mead & Co., 1945), pp. 285-86.

21. *Prejudices: Third Series*, p. 252.

22. *Baltimore Evening Sun*, 8 October 1928.

23. Ibid.

24. *Prejudices: Fifth Series*, pp. 136-37.

25. *Prejudices: Third Series*, pp. 253, 254.

26. Ibid., pp. 254-55.

27. *Prejudices: Fifth Series*, p. 137. This review first appeared in *The Smart Set*, May 1923.

28. Ibid., p. 139.

29. Richard Hofstadter, *Anti-Intellectualism in America* (New York: Vintage Books, 1962), pp. 416-18.

Bibliographical Essay

Mencken is well provided for, bibliographically speaking, by the very excellent and thorough *H.L.M., The Mencken Bibliography*, compiled by Betty Adler (with the assistance of Jane Wilhelm), published by the Johns Hopkins Press in 1961. Miss Adler continued her bibliographical work on Mencken until her death in 1973, and the results appeared regularly in the serial *Menckeniana*. The Enoch Pratt Free Library published a supplement in 1971, *H.L.M., The Mencken Bibliography, A Ten-Year Supplement, 1962-1971*, also compiled and edited by Miss Adler.

There is a recent and partially annotated bibliography in *H. L. Mencken: L'Homee, L'Oeuvre, L'Influence*, by Guy J. Forgue (Publications de la Faculte des Lettres et Sciences Humaines de Nice) which can also be useful to students of Mencken.

Biographies

Nearly all the books devoted to Mencken are set in a biographical framework. Even Douglas C. Stenerson's *H.L. Mencken: Iconoclast from Baltimore* (The University of Chicago Press, 1971), which concentrates on Mencken's ideas, is organized biographically, the ideas being tied by a chronological thread. One interesting exception to this is the early *H.L. Mencken*, by Ernest A. Boyd (New York: McBride, 1925), which is arranged topically and to quite good effect.

It is natural to think that the later biographies of Mencken are better and fuller than those written in the twenties. While this is undoubtedly true, no student of Mencken should neglect contemporary reactions such as those found in Boyd's early study and in Isaac Goldberg's *The Man Mencken: A Biographical and Critical Survey* (New York: Simon, 1925).

While much was written about Mencken in the years between 1925 and 1950, no further full-scale biographies appeared during these years. Since 1950, however, Mencken has been the subject of a number of good, readable biographies and memoirs. The year 1950 saw the appearance of Edgar Kemler's *The Irreverent Mr. Mencken* (New York: Little Brown & Co.) and William Manchester's *Disturber of the Peace: The Life of H.L. Mencken* (New York: Harper & Bros.). Both Kemler and Manchester had the advantage of knowing Mencken and interviewing him at length. Manchester began his work on Mencken while a graduate student in the School of Journalism at the University of Missouri, where he did a master's thesis on Mencken's *Smart Set* criticism. Kemler's work is not extensively documented and Manchester's not at all; nevertheless, they are both lively, readable, and urbane— good introductions to Mencken's life and major activities. In 1952, Manchester's book was published in England with the title *The Sage of Baltimore: The Life and Times of H. L. Mencken* (London: Andrew Melrose).

An interesting but hostile memoir of Mencken appeared in 1956. It is *H.L. Mencken: A Portrait from Memory*, by Charles Angoff (New York: Yoseloff), Mencken's young editorial assistant on the *Mercury*. While this book is unsympathetic and often bitter, it is nonetheless useful for its information about Mencken as an editor and for the issues it raises about the decline of the *Mercury*. Another memoir is *The Constant Circle: H.L. Mencken*, by Sara Mayfield, a close friend of both Mencken and his wife (New York: Dell Publishing Co.,

1968)—a warm and genial book, not highly critical or analytical of Mencken as a thinker. Of more recent appearance is a short but charming sketch of Mencken in Alistair Cooke's *Six Men* (New York: Alfred A. Knopf, 1977).

The late sixties saw the appearance of two solid scholarly biographical works: *H.L. Mencken: L'Homme, L'Oeuvre, L'Influence*, by Guy J. Forgue, (Publications de la Faculte des Lettres et Sciences Humaines de Nice), in 1967, and *Mencken*, by Carl Bode (Carbondale and Edwardsville: Southern Illinois University Press) in 1969. The former is an encyclopedic work with, alas, many of the scholarly indiscretions and excesses associated with the doctoral dissertation. The Bode volume must presently be considered the standard scholarly biography of Mencken and is the result of much original research. It does not neglect Mencken's ideas, although of necessity they are treated sporadically rather than systematically.

Douglas C. Stenerson's *H.L. Mencken: Iconoclast from Baltimore* (Chicago: The University of Chicago Press, 1971) must be listed under the biographies, even though biography does not seem to be the author's main concern. Of all the books to appear in recent years, it is the most consistently analytical and intellectual in its approach, with Mencken's central ideas presented in a compact and easily accessible format. It is debatable whether Stenerson has made Mencken a coherent unity either as a man or as a thinker, but nonetheless the book is a valuable intellectual biography.

Mencken's Writings

Mencken was one of the most prolific American authors, and his career as a professional writer is itself a fascinating study. During his prime Mencken was often able to spend twelve or more hours a day writing, with time out only for meals and a brief nap. The vast quantity of articles, reviews, letters, and literary publications of every type that passed through his typewriter is startling. During the twenties, while he was editing the *Mercury*, he had sufficient time and energy to make regular contributions to the *Sunpapers*, to submit hundreds of articles, of very diverse character, to magazines and newspapers, and to write or assemble a good number of his own books. A complete listing of Mencken's writings is not possible in this space, but a few comments about Mencken's publishing history may be helpful to the average reader. (A more or less complete bibliography is found in *H.L.M.: The Mencken Bibliography*, by Betty Adler; a short list of Mencken's major works follows this essay.)

Mencken generally had good relations with his publishers and never experienced difficulties in finding a publisher for his books, even in the early days when he was relatively unknown. The suggestion for his first full-length book, *George Bernard Shaw: His Plays*, was turned down by Brentano, Shaw's New York publisher, but immediately thereafter accepted by John W. Luce and Co. in Boston. It was published in 1905. The relationship between the Luce firm and Mencken is recounted in a letter written in 1925 by Harrison Schaff, a Luce editor, and reprinted in Goldberg's *The Man Mencken* (pp. 371-77). The Luce firm also published Mencken's second book, *The Philosophy of Friedrich Nietzsche*, in 1908.

Mencken was identified with two other publishing firms before establishing his long relationship with Alfred A. Knopf. One of these was the British publishing house of John Lane, which published *A Book of Burlesques* and *A Little Book in C Major*, both in 1916. Philip Goodman, a New York advertising man and publisher, became a good friend of Mencken's immediately thereafter and published *Damn! A Book of Calumny* and *In Defense of Women* in 1918. The friendship with Goodman lasted a number of years, although the publishing relationship was short-lived. Mencken had already met the young Alfred A. Knopf, who published his *Book of Prefaces* in 1917. After Alfred Knopf reissued *In Defense of Women*, making a best-seller of it, Mencken must have decided that Goodman's talents as a publisher were limited; after 1919 all his books went to Knopf.

The story of Mencken's relations with Knopf both as author and as friend is an interesting one and would be an apt subject for a long study. Carl Bode's *Mencken* has the fullest account of it and is based not only on discussions with Alfred Knopf but on the Knopf files and correspondence. Mencken admired Knopf's skills as a publisher and seller of books, as well as high standards of book production, while Knopf admired Mencken's abilities as writer and editor. Mencken was responsible for the addition of numerous books and authors to Knopf's list (see Bode, pp. 224-27), and was elected to the board of directors of the firm in 1932. Information about the relationship between Mencken and Knopf where the Mercury is concerned may be found in M. K. Singleton, *H.L. Mencken and The American Mercury Adventure* (Durham, N.C.: Duke University Press, 1962).

I have not found in any published source figures to indicate the income Mencken derived from his books while with Knopf. Not even in the twenties did Mencken earn the kind of money Sinclair Lewis earned from his novels; nevertheless, Knopf made strenuous efforts to sell Mencken's works and Mencken's royalties were nothing to sneeze at. Carl Bode calculated that Mencken's income during the dark years of the depression averaged seventeen thousand dollars per year, and although only a small part of this was derived from royalties on his books, even the large revision of *The American Language* sold more than ninety thousand copies as a Book-of-the-Month selection.

In the forties Mencken continued to make money with the three *Days* books, which had already been profitable in serial form in the *New Yorker*. Knopf could not keep all seven volumes of the *Prejudices* in print, but the best essays were anthologized in *A Mencken Chrestomathy* in 1949. *In Defense of Women* and *Notes on Democracy* are no longer on the Knopf list, but as a publisher of Menckeniana, Knopf remains beyond reproach. In 1974 a number of hardback editions, including all the *Days* books, *The American Language*, *Minority Report*, *Treatise on the Gods*, G. J. Forgue's edition of the *Letters*, Louis Cheslock's anthology *H.L. Mencken on Music*, and still another general anthology, Huntington Cairn's *American Scene* remained in print at Knopf. While Knopf has let Mencken's book slip out of print, in 1977 new reprint editions of many of them are being projected by Octagon.

In the last two decades the briskest sales of Mencken's
work have undoubtedly been in two paperback anthologies,
edited by Alistair Cooke and James T. Farrell (see under
anthologies).

Only a small part of Mencken's total output was ever
published in book form, so a few words must also be said
about his career as a writer for magazines and newspapers.
The Adler bibliography yields the most extensive information on this subject, which is not covered in detail here.

Until he began his regular book reviewing for the *Smart Set*
in 1908, most of Mencken's magazine pieces were stories and
poems. The magazines which most frequently published his
work in the early days were *Bookman*, *Criterion*, *Red Book*,
and *Bohemian*.

The magazines with which Mencken's name is most closely
associated are, of course the *Smart Set* and the *American
Mercury*. For a more detailed history of Mencken's relations
with these magazines, see Carl R. Dolmetsch, *The Smart Set,
A History and Anthology* (New York: The Dial Press, 1966),
and M. K. Singleton, *H.L. Mencken and The American Mercury Adventure,* (Durham, N.C.: Duke University Press, 1962).
The latter is excellent in every way. The Adler bibliography
gives a fairly complete listing of the articles and reviews
published in the *Smart Set* and the *Mercury* and provides a
list of pseudonyms used by Mencken.

During his prime Mencken contributed to a good number of
other magazines, and the pattern of his contributions is sometimes surprising. During the twenties he contributed to the
Nation more frequently than to any other magazine outside
the *Smart Set* and the *Mercury*, a strange situation when one
considers that this is where most of the anti-Mencken material was being published during the same years. In 1921 he
became a contributing editor: "This is a joke, the significance
of which escapes me," he wrote to Louise Pound. Other magazines to which he contributed a great deal were *Dial*, *New
Republic*, *Life* (the "old" *Life*), *Vanity Fair*, *Atlantic Monthly*
(with whose editor, Ellery Sedgwick, Mencken was on good
terms), and, during its brief but highly respectable run, *Seven
Arts*. Mencken even tried to lodge some of the early chapters

of *Newspaper Days* with the *Saturday Evening Post*—unsuccessfully. In the thirties Mencken's magazine opportunities were greatly reduced, but he continued to write for the *Mercury* after leaving the editor's chair, and no small part of his income in the late thirties was derived from a deal with Harold Ross of the *New Yorker* to deliver his *Days* sketches for serial publication.

Some of Mencken's best writing appeared in newspapers and not nearly enough of it has been reprinted. For example, until Carl Bode's recent anthology *The Young Mencken* (New York: The Dial Press, 1973), most of "The Free Lance" columns were inaccessible except to those who enjoy the discomforts of the microfilm machine.

The major, signed articles by Mencken in the various Baltimore papers with which he was associated are listed in the Adler bibliography. Mencken's association with the *Sunpapers* lasted from 1906 until the time of his stroke in 1948, and, except during the sensitive World War I years, was always cordial. For information about the origin and history of "The Free Lance," see Adler (pp. 48-49), and Manchester (chap. 3).

Mencken's relation with the *New York Mail* produced some of his best writing, even though it occurred during the stormy period of 1917 and 1918 when Mencken was in eclipse because of his pro-German attitude. William Manchester writes: "Curiously, much of his most enduring prose was written for the *Mail*. . . . In the Twenties, turning with his scissors and paste pot in search of *Prejudices* articles, he repeatedly came back to the *Mail* material, and when, thirty years later, he essayed to select his best out-of-print writing, the *Mail* was represented far out of proportion to the number of pieces printed." (*Disturber of the Peace*, p. 105).

Although he was never fond of Hearst, Mencken made contributions to the *New York American* in 1934 and 1935, and from 1924 to 1928 he contributed to the *Chicago Sunday Tribune* and its syndicate, although the brand of conservatism represented by the papers which bought the *Tribune* syndicate was not harmonious with Mencken's own, so that the relationship was never highly successful. Mencken wrote occasionally for other papers and for the Associated Press.

Letters

Mencken was a prodigious letter writer. Carl Bode estimates that Mencken wrote one hundred thousand letters during his lifetime. Libraries and private collections hold more than fifteen thousand letters, and this prompted G.J. Forgue, editor of the first published collection of Mencken's letters, *Letters of H.L. Mencken* (Knopf, 1961) to suggest that no full listing, much less publication, would ever be possible. Carl Bode, with greater access to the various collections than Forgue, has produced a second, and better, anthology, *The New Mencken Letters* (Dial, 1977). Still other assemblages are possible.

The bulk of Mencken's letters were bequeathed to the New York Public Library, but other large collections are at the Enoch Pratt Free Library, Princeton University, Yale University, and the University of Pennsylvania, the latter containing the complete correspondence to and from Theodore Dreiser, perhaps eight hundred letters.

Anthologies

All the early compilations and collections of Mencken's writings are, naturally, out of print. Of the volumes readily available today, one must mention first the two good hardback anthologies published by Knopf, *A Mencken Chrestomathy* (Mencken's selections), which appeared in 1949, and *H.L. Mencken: The American Scene*, by Huntington Cairns, which appeared in 1965. See also *A Carnival of Buncombe*, edited by Malcolm Moos (Baltimore: Johns Hopkins Press, 1956), mostly political articles from the *Baltimore Sun*.

Two excellent paperback anthologies are available and are also valuable for the editors' introductions: *The Vintage Mencken*, edited by Alistair Cooke (New York: Vintage Books, 1955), and *Prejudices, A Selection* edited by James T. Farrell (New York: Vintage Books, 1958).

A number of specialized anthologies can be highly recommended. Among them are: *H.L. Mencken's Smart Set Criti-*

cism, edited by William H. Nolte (Ithaca: Cornell University Press, 1968), *The Young Mencken*, edited by Carl Bode (New York: Dial Press, 1973), *H.L. Mencken on Music*, edited by Louis Cheslock (New York: Knopf, 1961), and *The Bathtub Hoax, and Other Blasts from the Chicago Tribune*, edited by Robert McHugh (New York: Knopf, 1968), *A Gang of Pecksniffs*, edited by Theo Lippman, Jr., (New Rochelle, N.Y.: Arlington House, 1975).

There are still numerous opportunities for anthologizing Mencken and doubtless more of them will be realized as his works emerge from copyright in the 1970s and 1980s.

Books Edited By Mencken

Mencken edited or wrote introductions to a number of books. Among these were a number of anthologies of his own works which are mentioned or cited elsewhere. He also edited a number of books which were closely related to his own literary activities. For example, he collected or arranged selections from the *Smart Set* and the *American Mercury* during his tenure as editor of those magazines. From the former there was *Pistols for Two*, by Owen Arthur James Hatteras, published by Knopf in 1917. Material from the *Mercury* was assiduously collected by Mencken, cf. *Americana, 1925* and *The American Mercury, Three Years 1924 to 1927*, both published by Knopf. Mencken edited a collection by Sara Powell Haardt, *Menckeniana: A Schimpflexikon* (Knopf, 1928), a juicy sampling of anti-Mencken invective. He also contributed heavily to *The Sunpapers of Baltimore 1837-1937* and wrote most of *The Baltimore Sun Stylebook* (Baltimore: A.S. Abell Co., 1944).

Mencken happily involved himself in family projects. In addition to the *Schimpflexikon* mentioned above, he also edited his wife's *Southern Album* (Garden City: Doubleday, 1936). He wrote a forward to *By The Neck: A Book of Hangings*, edited by his brother August Mencken (New York: Hastings House, 1942). Perhaps the most important work in this category is *The Charlatanry of the Learned*, by his ancestor Johann Burkhard Mencke (New York: Knopf, 1937), which curiously (if not causally) ties Mencken's intellectual traits to those of his forbears.

Of greater importance are the books on major literary or intellectual figures to which Mencken contributed either significant introductions or editorial treatments. Early in his career there was a newly edited *A Doll's House,* by Henrik Ibsen (Boston: Luce, 1909). *The Gist of Nietzsche* (Boston: Luce, 1910), was a series of weak translations. Mencken was to do more work as a booster of Nietzsche at a time when the latter was a mystery to the general public and a bugaboo to philosophers with his translation of *The Antichrist* (New York: Knopf, 1920) and his introduction to *The Nietzsche-Wagner Correspondence,* edited by Elizabeth Foerster-Nietzsche (New York: Boni, 1921).

After 1920, Mencken became increasingly an Americanist, and his introductions to American books are worthy of note. See: *The Line of Love; Dizain des Mariages,* by James Branch Cabell (New York: McBride, 1921); *Major Conflicts,* by Stephen Crane (New York: Knopf, 1926); *Essays,* by James Gibbon Huneker, (New York: Scribner, 1929); *The American Democrat,* by James Fenimore Cooper (New York: Knopf, 1931); *You Know These Lines: A Bibliography of the Most Quoted Verses in American Poetry,* by Merle Johnson, with forward by Mencken (New York: Baker, 1935); *An American Tragedy,* by Theodore Dreiser (Cleveland: World Publishing Co., 1946).

Outside of the above categories, is *A New Dictionary of Quotations on Historical Principles from Ancient and Modern Sources,* selected and edited by Mencken (New York: Knopf, 1942).

Critical Literature on Mencken

Much of the important critical writing on Mencken appears in the major biographical works which have already been mentioned. On the other hand, when one wishes to study the impact of Mencken on the intellectuals of his own time and ours, one must delve into the numerous short treatments that have appeared over the years. A good place to begin the study of Mencken's sympathetic readers is Ernst Boyd's *H.L. Mencken* (New York: McBride, 1925). Boyd was one of the most constant champions of Mencken during the decade, and his book deals directly and solidly with Mencken's ideas. Boyd's shorter treatments should not be neglected. See, for example, his treatment of Mencken in *Portraits: Real and Imaginary, Being Memories and Impressions of Friends and Contemporaries* (New York: Doran, 1924). Also in *Atheneaum,* no. 4698 14 May 1920): 637, "A Modern Reactionary" and "Readers and Writers" in *Independent,* (117: 505), 30 October 1926.

A young Britisher who wrote brilliantly and perceptively on Mencken in the twenties and whose comments on the uniqueness of the *Mercury* appeared in T. S. Eliot's *Criterion* (June 1927, p. 373, and December 1927, pp. 572-73), was Herbert Read.

Among young Americans at this time, three critics stand out as having made important contributions to an understanding of Mencken: Carl Van Doren, Edmund Wilson, and Walter Lippmann. None of these could be expected to be intellectually sympathetic to Mencken, yet all three were generous in their praise of his talents as a writer and acknowledged him as a major figure in twentieth-century literature. (For further comment on these critics, cf. George H. Douglas "Mencken's Critics in The Twenties," *Menckeniana,* Spring 1975, pp. 1-5.)

Of Van Doren, see especially "Smartness and Light, H.L. Mencken, a Gadfly for Democracy," *Century,* March 1923, pp. 791-96, which views Mencken as part of the American mainstream and compares him with Poe, Whitman, and Twain. See also Van Doren's books on American literature during the twenties and thirties: *Many Minds* (New York: Knopf, 1924); *American and British Literature since 1890* (with Mark Van Doren), (New York: Century, 1925); *What is American Literature* (London: Routledge, 1935). In Van Doren's *Three Worlds* (New York: Harper, 1936) Mencken seems to have faded into a literary "personality" but Van Doren had not turned scoffer in the manner of the literary rebels of the thirties.

Edmund Wilson's writings are an excellent source of Mencken criticism, and students of Mencken should check all the references to Mencken in Wilson's *The Shores of Light: A Literary Chronicle of the Twenties and Thirties* (New York: Farrar, Straus and Giroux, 1952). Shortly after he began his association with the *New Republic,* Wilson published "H.L. Mencken" (1 June 1921, pp. 10-13), which found in Mencken "a mind of extraordinary vigor." Later in "The All-Star Literary Vaudeville," (*New Republic,* 30 June 1926, pp, 159-60, he remarks that "although it is true that Mencken's style lends itself to excesses and vulgarities, especially in the hands of his imitators, who have taken over the Master's jargon without possessing his admirable literary sense, I believe that his prose is more successful in its way than that of these devotees of beauty usually is in theirs." This is due not so much to the intrinsic quality of Mencken's ideas as it is to "some strain of the musician or poet" which "has made it possible for Mencken to turn these ideas into literature; it is precisely through the color and rhythm of a highly personal prose that Mencken's opinions have become so infectious." A discussion by Wilson of Mencken's political ideas is found in his review of *Notes on Democracy:* "Mencken's Democratic Man" (*New Republic,* 15 December 1926, pp. 110-11). Wilson continued to write sympathetically on Mencken throughout his career—see "Mencken through the Wrong End of the Telescope," a review of Edgar Kemler's *The Irreverent Mr. Mencken,* in *New Yorker,* 6 May 1950.

Walter Lippmann's "H.L. Mencken" (*Saturday Review of Literature,* 11 December 1926, pp, 413-14), has been discussed in Chapter 1. See also his "New Machiavelli" (*New Republic,* 31 May 1922, pp. 12-14). Unfortunately Lippmann did not offer a reconsideration of Mencken in later years.

Of other writers and critics (mostly American) from the early years, the following should provide a smattering of contemporary opinion: Randolph Bourne, "H.L. Mencken" (*New Republic,* 24 November 1917, pp. 102-103); Burton Rascoe, "Fanfare" (*Chicago Sunday Tribune,* 11 November 1917, p. 7); James Weldon Johnson, "American Genius and its Locale" (*New York Age,* 20 July 1918, editorial page); Louis Unter-

meyer, "A Preface to _____" (*Liberator*, May 1918, pp. 43-45);
Percy Boynton, "American Literature and the Tart Set" (*Free-man*, 7 April 1920, pp. 88-89); Aldous Huxley, "American
Criticism" (*Athenaeum*, 2 January 1920, p. 10; F. Scott
Fitzgerald, "Baltimore Anti-Christ" (*Bookman*, March 1921,
pp. 79-81; Frank Harris, *Contemporary Portraits* (New York:
Brentano, 1923), pp. 143-54; also "H.L. Mencken: Critic,"
(*Pearson's*, May 1921, pp. 405-408), in which Harris maintains
that criticism is the true art of the twentieth century and
Mencken its best practitioner; Joseph Wood Krutch, "Anti-
Christ and the Five Apostles" (*Nation*, 21 December 1921, pp.
733-34); Newton Arvin, "The Role of Mr. Mencken" (*Freeman*,
27 December 1922, pp. 381-82); Burton Rascoe, "A Cantrip of
Critics" (*Shadowland*, February 1923, p. 1); George Genzmer,
"Mr. Mencken Triumphant" (*Nation*, 9 December 1925, pp.
664-65); H. M. Parshley, "H.L. Mencken: An Appreciation"
(*American Review*, January-February 1923, pp. 72-84); Har-
riet Monroe, "Mephistopheles and the Poet" (*Poetry*, July
1926, pp. 210-15); Everhardt Armstrong, "Mencken and Amer-
ica" (*Nineteenth Century*, January 1927, pp. 117-25); R. K.
Gooch, "H.L. Mencken: Notes on Democracy" (*Political and
Social Science Quarterly*, March 1927, pp. 442-44); Elizabeth
Sergeant, "H.L. Mencken" (*Nation*, 16 February 1927, pp.
174-76); Howard Mumford Jones, "Professor Babbitt Cross-
Examined" (*New Republic*, 21 March 1928, pp. 158-60); James
Branch Cabell, *Some of Us, An Essay in Epitaphs* (New York:
McBride, 1930); Frederick Lewis Allen, *Only Yesterday, An
Informal History of the Nineteen Twenties* (New York:
Harper, 1931); Russell Blankenship, *American Literature as
an Expression of the National Mind* (New York: Holt, 1930).

Mencken received a much cooler reception from the younger critics after 1930, but before saying something about the
literature of this period, it is important to mention the Menck-
en-Humanist controversy and the various exchanges that
grew out of it. The best long discussion of the controversy that
I have seen is in Richard Ruland's *The Rediscovery of American Literature* (Cambridge: Harvard University Press, 1967).
An older, but also useful, account may be found in "The Battle
of the Books" section of Robert E. Spiller's *Literary History of*

the United States (New York: Macmillan, 1948). Students will want to go directly to the primary sources, especially the writings of the three major protagonists: More, Babbitt, and Sherman.

Both More and Babbitt refrained from entering combat with Mencken and seldom bothered to mention him. But there are references in More's *New Shelburne Essays* (Princeton: Princeton University Press, 1928), and Babbitt's *On Being Creative and Other Essays* (Boston: Houghton, 1932). Sherman was not above locking horns with Mencken, as he did in 1917 in his article "Beautifying American Literature" (*Nation*, 29 November 1917, pp. 593-94). Subsequent books of Sherman's press the attack with vigor: *Americans* (New York: Scribner, 1922) and *Critical Woodcuts* (New York: Scribner, 1926). A number of other critics in the genteel tradition found themselves both attracted to and repelled by Mencken. Fred Lewis Pattee is a good example. Cf. *Sidelights on American Literature* (New York: Century, 1922); "The Muck-Rake School of Literature" (*Christian Advocate*, 28 April 1917, pp. 523-24); and *The New American Literature 1890-1930* (New York: Century, 1930).

The leftist criticism of Mencken was not slow to develop, although for a few years after the establishment of the *Mercury* such leftist leaders as Mencken's fellow Baltimorian Victor F. Calverton found it imprudent to attack Mencken; occasionally they would even cautiously praise him. After the founding of the *New Masses* by Michael Gold and Joseph Freeman in 1926, the mood shifted abruptly and the leftists had a go at Mencken. In his book *Money Writes*, Upton Sinclair charged that the *Mercury* was closely tied to Wall Street interests. In "Mr. Mencken Calls on Me" (*Bookman*, November 1927, pp. 254-65), Sinclair charged that of "democratic control of industry, . . ." Mencken was "as ignorant as any Babbitt-boob."

By the late twenties nearly all the major leftists had turned against Mencken. By the time of the depression, when their own banner was in the ascendancy, they became extremely bitter in their denunciations. CF. Michael Gold, "Letter to H.L. Mencken" (*The New Masses*, September 1931, p. 3). The mood among the leftists in the early thirties was "Mencken is dead," and numerous reevaluations or devaluations were the order of the day. Cf. V. F. Calverton, "H.L. Mencken: A Devaluation" (*Modern Monthly*, November 1936, pp. 7-10). The best sources of leftist critical opinion of the time are in the longer works devoted to American writing or American criticism. See Granville Hicks, *The Great Tradition* (New York: Macmillan, 1933); Bernard Smith, *Forces in American Criticism* (New York: Harcourt, 1939); Michael Gold, *The Hollow Men* (New York: International Publishers, 1941).

The serious critics of American literature never really abandoned Mencken. Edmund Wilson, in spite of his liberal bent, wrote favorably about Mencken in the forties and fifties. Alfred Kazin thought of himself as part of the literary left of the thirties, but broke with Gold, Hicks, Smith, and the like to deal somewhat sympathetically with Mencken in his *On Native Grounds* (New York: Harcourt Brace & Co., 1942). Even in the thirties, writers who were primarily interested in literature treated Mencken as a major writer. There were the writngs of Carl Van Doren already mentioned, and those of Van Wyck Brooks, whose mammoth historical survey of American letters was planned in the thirties and executed over the next two decades. For Brooks, see: *Sketches in Criticism* (New York: Dutton, 1932). In later years, Brooks wrote what is surely one of the best essays on Mencken in his *The Confident Years, 1885-1915* (New York: Dutton, 1952).

After the Second World War, and especially after Mencken's death in 1956, it became unfashionable to add to the "Mencken is dead" literature and, with few exceptions, like the book and articles of Charles Angoff, most of the writers of the period tried to seek out Mencken's lasting values. Among the more appreciative articles on Mencken since the Second World War, one thinks of the large number written by his old friend Gerald W. Johnson, for example: "Mencken, Scholar, Wit, One Man Tornado," (*New York Herald Tribune Books*, 26 June 1949); "H.L. Mencken, 1880-1956" (*New Republic*, 6 February 1956, p. 18); "Oh, For Mencken Now" (*New Republic*, 30 September 1957). Other articles of substance since World War II are: James T. Farrell, "Dr. Mencken: Criticus Americanus"

(*New World Writing* 6 [Fall 1954]: 64-76); J. Donald Adams, "Speaking of Books" (*New York Times Book Review*, 11, September 1955, p. 2); Alistair Cooke, "The Baltimore Fox" (*Saturday Review*, 10 September 1955, p. 13); also "Last Happy Days of H.L. Mencken" (*Atlantic*, May 1956, pp. 33-38); D. W. Brogan, "H.L. Mencken" (*Spectator*, 17 February 1956, p. 212); Joseph Wood Krutch "This Was Mencken, An Appreciation" (*Nation*, 11 February 1956), which declares that Mencken's prose must be considered among the best of the twentieth century; William Manchester, "H.L. Mencken at Seventy-Five: America's Sam Johnson" (*Saturday Review*, 10 September 1955, p. 11); Alfred A. Knopf, "For Henry, with Love: My Friendship with Mencken" (*Atlantic*, May 1959, pp. 50-54); Stephen E. Fitzgerald, "The Mencken Myth" (*Saturday Review*, 17 December 1960, p. 13); Guy J. Forgue, "Myths about Mencken" (*Nation*, 16 September 1961, pp. 163-65); Douglas Stenerson, "Mencken's Early Newspaper Experience: The Genesis of a Style" (*American Literature*, May 1965, pp. 153-66). Not all of the above are strictly critical but they give an idea of the various directions of the Mencken literature in the last few decades.

Most of the full-length books devoted to Mencken, because of their nature, have been discussed in the biography section.

Mencken Collections

The starting place for doing research on Mencken is the Enoch Pratt Library in Baltimore. In the Mencken collection, which is housed in a room on the third floor of the main library building, there are nearly all of Mencken's typed manuscripts, all the editions and translations of his public works, a large part of his personal library, his clipping books, family documents, portraits, and memorabilia. Under the terms of Mencken's will, this collection is open only to scholars and authors doing research, although it is open to the general public annually on Mencken's birthday.

The bulk of Mencken's correspondence was bequeathed to the New York Public Library, making it the second most important repository of Menckeniana. (The Pratt Library retains Mencken's letters to Marylanders and a small number of others.) The New York Public Library also has a good general collection of Mencken's works and a number of manuscripts. Other major Mencken collections in the United States are at Princeton University, Harvard University, the Library of Congress, and Yale University. For a more complete listing see *A Descriptive List of H.L. Mencken Collections in the U.S.*, compiled by Betty Adler (Baltimore: Enoch Pratt Free Library, 1967).

Mencken's Major Works

George Bernard Shaw: His Plays. Boston: Luce, 1905.
The Philosophy of Friedrich Nietzsche. Boston: Luce, 1908.
A Book of Burlesques. New York: Lane, 1916.
A Little Book in C Major. New York: Lane, 1916.
A Book of Prefaces. New York: Knopf, 1917.
Damn! A Book of Calumny. New York: Philip Goodman, 1918.
In Defense of Women. New York: Philip Goodman, 1918.
Prejudices: First Series. New York: Knopf, 1919.
Prejudices: Second Series. New York: Knopf, 1920.
Prejudices: Third Series. New York: Knopf, 1922.
Prejudices: Fourth Series. New York: Knopf, 1924.
Prejudices: Fifth Series. New York: Knopf, 1926.
Prejudices: Sixth Series. New York: Knopf, 1927.
Selected Prejudices. New York: Knopf, 1927.
The American Language. New York: Knopf, 1919. Revised 1936.
The American Language: Supplement I. New York: Knopf, 1945.
The American Language: Supplement II. New York: Knopf, 1948.
The American Language: The Fourth Edition and the Two Supplements, Abridged with Annotations and New Material, by Raven I. McDavid, Jr. New York: Knopf, 1963.

Notes on Democracy. New York: Knopf, 1926.
Menckeniana: A Schimpflexikon. New York: Knopf, 1928.
Treatise on the Gods. New York: Knopf, 1946.
Making a President. New York: Knopf, 1932.
Treatise on Right and Wrong. New York: Knopf, 1934.
Happy Days, 1880-1892. New York: Knopf, 1940.
Newspaper Days, 1899-1906. New York: Knopf, 1941.
Heathen Days, 1890-1936. New York: Knopf, 1943. The above
        three, taken together, constitute:
The Days of H.L. Mencken. New York: Knopf, 1947.
A Mencken Chrestomathy. New York: Knopf, 1949.
Minority Report: H.L. Mencken's Notebooks. New York:
        Knopf, 1956.

Index